dictionary
of
modern
chess

BYRNE J. HORTON

dictionary of modern chess

The Citadel Press   Secaucus, New Jersey

SECOND PAPERBOUND PRINTING, 1972
PUBLISHED BY CITADEL PRESS, INC.
A SUBSIDIARY OF LYLE STUART, INC.
120 ENTERPRISE AVE., SECAUCUS, N.J. 07094
COPYRIGHT © 1959 BY PHILOSOPHICAL LIBRARY, INC.
MANUFACTURED IN THE UNITED STATES OF AMERICA
ISBN 0-8065-0173-1

FOREWORD

IN ALL THE GREAT LITERATURE of chess there is no other book that accomplishes what Dr. Horton and his colleagues offer here: a concise dictionary of chess in English. It is more than a glossary of terms, a biographical compendium, or a description of the openings, for it combines all of these in one volume. I am happy to endorse this scholarly contribution to the understanding and enjoyment of chess and to recommend it to players everywhere.

JERRY G. SPANN
President of
United States Chess Federation

PREFACE

The Royal Game of Chess, once the intellectual sport of aristocrats, is now universally enjoyed by men, women and children in all social and economic classes. The immortal Emmanuel Lasker expressed the idea that everyone should know chess because the mentality and individuality of the races have found expression in the modern development of the game. Recent evidence seems to indicate that the number of people desirous of learning the game of chess is constantly on the increase.

When a game, like chess, has held world attention for so many centuries, we may take it for granted that the game has solid merits which can not be disregarded and hence is worthy of definitive attention. The time has come that some effort be made to assemble and to coordinate reasonably lucid definitions of those terms which are in common usage among chessplayers as well as those colloquialisms and foreign expressions which are frequently encountered in chess literature.

Not so many years ago, a dictionary was considered to be the tool of a lazy man. It was assumed that a person engaged in intellectual calisthenics of one sort or another, would be grounded in Greek and Latin so as to be able to determine for himself the roots and meanings of most words. Today, the modern emphasis has shifted away from the classical disciplines to the more practical and utilitarian aspects of social living. In this age of specialization, specialized dictionaries are in increasing demand.

A modern specialized dictionary embraces not only classical terminology but also those terms coined and utilized by modern writers. By extension, this Dictionary of Modern Chess has incorporated biographical sketches of chessplayers whose names have become part of our chess heritage. The influences and contributions of these chess notables have been identified and defined within these biographical sketches.

The definitions presented in this Dictionary have several facets. Etymological definitions are concerned with giving the origin or derivations of the words or terms which are being defined. This has been done throughout this Dictionary whenever it was deemed necessary to give a more precise idea of the meaning of the terms. Logical definitions are given whenever possible to indicate the generic terms with their specific differences. Functional definitions are developed to show the purposes, powers and actions of what is being defined. Historical definitions are developed whenever the item defined can be understood better when their historical evolution would be indicated. Whenever possible, these different types of definitions are fused into one composite definition so as to give as complete a definition as possible within the limited undertaking of this Dictionary.

Without being a slave to an established order of procedure, the authors have endeavored to incorporate into the various definitions the following significant and pertinent items.

1. In defining chessmen:
   1) Identification of chessmen: major or minor.
   2) Their symbols in chess notation.
   3) Number of these men on the board at the beginning of the game.
   4) Where they are placed at the opening of the game.
   5) How they move.
   6) Their advantages or peculiar features.
   7) Their disadvantages, handicaps or limitations.
   8) Their value.
   9) Their historic evolution.
   10) Pertinent statements from master chessplayers.

2. In biographical sketches:
   Only those who have made some significant contribution to chess have been included. It is impossible, useless and cumbersome to include everyone who has developed a variation or problem of some sort or another. In these biographical sketches, the authors have, depending upon available data, touched on:
   1) Name, identification, date and place of birth.
   2) Early background; briefly: family, education, and professional activities and interests.
   3) Chess career: when began to play chess, successes achieved: when and where.
   4) Chess contributions: techniques, writings and organizational activities and affiliations.
   5) Statements from well-known critics or chessmasters as to the individual's chessplaying ability and writings.

3. Chess Openings:
   Chess openings are named after either the individual who invented or popularized the opening procedure, or, after the name of the place where the opening was first used in official chessplay. Frequently it is impossible to state when a certain opening play originated even though it can be shown that it is much older than the player whose name is attached to it.

   A presentation of the opening moves constitutes *per se* the definition. For a fuller understanding, this identification of moves is generally followed with some historical reference as to its origin; a brief explanation; a diagram; and, an expert opinion concerning its possibilities.

4. Chess Organizations and Publications:
   These are defined in terms of their functional purposes. For convenient references and completeness, their addresses and other data are given.

This work, being the first Dictionary in the broad field of chess, indubitably has definite limitations. The reader is forewarned that although meticulous and painstaking care has been exercised in years of intense study and research in the preparation of this book, nevertheless, it is readily admitted that there is always room for improvement. Constructive criticism is always welcomed.

The authors have endeavored to be as factual as possible. In order to avoid being dogmatic, and, in order to give greater validity to a definition, the authors have made use of direct statements from experienced chessplayers.

To minimize ambiguities, uncertainties and equivocations, the etymological meaning of a term has been given whenever possible without, however, becoming involved in semantic implications. (Dr. Horton, in addition to English, has been a student of Greek and Latin, French and German, and classical Hebrew.)

The references cited are not necessarily always the best or the most important writings on the particular subject involved. They are given merely as advisory or suggestive as to where the reader can find further information concerning the topic defined.

This *Dictionary of Modern Chess* is offered primarily to all those who are seeking information which will help them to obtain a greater enjoyment and satisfaction in understanding and appreciating the language of chessplayers. If perchance, this Dictionary should be of some use to advanced chessplayers and experts in the field of chess, that will, of course, be very gratifying to the authors.

ACKNOWLEDGMENTS

The authors are deeply appreciative of the time and effort so many chess-masters and others interested in the game of chess have devoted to the development of the science and art of this royal game. We pay tribute to them and gratefully acknowledg their contributions. Their greatness can only be evaluated in terms of their enduring memory and the availability of the fruits of their labors.

It is fitting and proper that we acknowledge in particular the generous assistance of the following individuals who have taken an active interest in helping to a greater or lesser extent to make this Dictionary of Modern Chess as accurate as possible.

Arthur B. Bisguier, United States Chess Champion, 1954-1957.

Larry Evans, United States Champion, 1951-1954.

Bernard Freedman, Past-President of the Chess Federation of Canada, and, Vice-President of the Fédération Internationale des Echecs.

Kenneth Harkness, Business Manager of United States Chess Federation and chess writer.

I. A. Horowitz, Publisher and Editor of *Chess Review*—the picture chess magazine.

Hans Kmoch, Manager and Secretary of the Manhattan Chess Club and an authoritative chess writer.

Edward Lasker, Champion Chessplayer, chess writer and President of the Marshall Chess Club.

Montgomery Major, Editor (1946-57) of *Chess Life* — America's Chess Newspaper.

Harold M. Phillips, Past-President of the United States Chess Federation, and, Vice-President of the Fédération Internationale des Echecs.

Dr. Felix Pollak of Northwestern University, a passionate chess enthusiast from Vienna.

Cecil J. S. Purdy, World Correspondence Chess Champion, Champion Chessplayer of Australia, and, Founder and Editor of *Chess World* magazine.

Anthony E. Santasiere, United States Open Chess Champion of 1945, chess author, critic and analyst.

Ephraim Solkoff, originator of a tournament tie-breaking method.

We also wish to express our thanks and appreciation to the following publishers who graciously permitted us to draw upon their publications which contained the statements and opinions of our authoritative references.

A. S. Barnes & Company
David McKay Company
Pitman Publishing Corporation
Sterling Publishing Company
Simon and Schuster, Inc.
The United States Chess Federation

dictionary of modern chess

A

ABEN-EZRA

A chess-loving Jewish rabbi whose real name was Abraham, son of Mayerben-Ezra. He was born at Toledo about 1119 and died on the Island of Rhodes in 1174. Among his many biblical writings appeared *Charusim al sechok Shahmath* (Verses on the Game of Chess). Willard Fiske, an early American chess writer, paid this tribute to his memory: "May some chess pilgrim, traveling in Palestine, whither his bones were carried, find out the tomb of the erudite old biblical, medicinal, poetical, grammatical, astronomical and chess-loving Aben-Ezra and over it breathe the hope that, after the final checkmate had put an end to his travels and learned labors, he found a lasting rest in the paradise of Abraham."

ACCUMULATION OF ADVANTAGE, PRINCIPLE OF

A concept developed by Steinitz which emphasizes the importance of accumulating small advantages that develop rapidly into more significant and enduring advantages. "This accumulated advantage," says Steinitz, "brings about a tension and this tension discharges itself like an electric current" which may set off a series of significant combinations.

ADJOURNMENT

The official suspension of a game in chess tournaments when it is impossible to finish a game in one session. Adjournments may be made for several hours in the same day or be carried over to the following day. During this period of adjournment, a player may analyze the game by himself but he is expected not to seek the help of others. The Laws of Chess specify the manner in which an adjournment shall take place as well as its resumption.

ADJUDICATION

The rendering of a decision by a recognized official or organization concerning a chess dispute which has been submitted for settlement. The highest official chess authority which is empowered to render official interpretations of the Laws of Chess is the Fédération Internationale Des Echecs. In the United States, chess difficulties should be submitted in writing to the Secretary of the United States Chess Federation. In match games and tournaments, the Match Referee or the Tournament Director adjudicates chess difficulties.

ADOLESCENCE, CHESS

Chess adolescence is the transitional period in the life of a chessplayer which occurs after a tyro has learned the rudiments of chess and ends when he becomes a mature chessplayer. It is an evolutionary period from the days of being a mere woodpusher when wild, chaotic moves were made, to the time when reasoned restraint earmarks every move. It is a period in the life of every chessplayer when threats are perceived quickly, and dangers are anticipated two or three moves in advance. Pawns and pieces are used more economically, and combinations are developed accurately and effectively. The time required for adolescent development depends entirely upon the individual capacity and ability of the student chessplayer, his enthusiasm and perseverance.

ADVANCED PAWN

Any Pawn which has advanced to the fifth rank or beyond. Any advanced Pawn, even though it may not be a passed Pawn, constitutes an invasion into enemy territory where with additional support it can exert a strong pressure on the opponent.

ADVANCED POST

By an advanced post is generally meant the occupation of a square on the fifth rank or beyond. Supporting Pawns and Knights are very useful in advanced positions; however, the Queens, Rooks and Bishops can work just as effectively from a distance.

ADVANTAGE IN CHESS

A superiority gained over an opponent which is favorable to a winning climax. An advantage gained may be either of a permanent or temporary nature. Everything else being equal as to such matters as mobility of the chessmen or a better command of territory, the player having more material has an absolute and permanent advantage. If, however, the number and value of the pieces are equal and a player has gained a superior mobility or is in possession of greater space, he is assured of a temporary advantage. A temporary advantage may be lost very quickly whenever the opponent makes a move sufficiently strong to seize the initiative. To force a win, a temporary advantage of superior mobility must be prosecuted relentlessly to a final victory.

AESTHETICS IN CHESS

Charming or beautiful performances of chessmen throughout the game. Aesthetic performance consists in making moves which captivate the spectators' attention and cause them to express their approval and enjoyment by such spontaneous remarks as "that was a spectacular move," or "that was a beautiful move." The players as well as the spectators may become emotionally overjoyed in observing how every move is a further step towards a decisive and startling victory. Such a beautiful performance occurs when the players view their chessboard as a stage on which their chessmen enact a human drama. Each and every move exhibits the player's intellectual performance. With controlled imaginative play, all moves can become beautiful in their possibilities and stimulating to the human emotions. See *Beautiful Game, Brilliancy* and *Initiative*.

AJEDREZ

Spanish name for chess.

AJEEB

The name of a mechanical chessplayer in which was concealed the real chessplayer. This automaton was developed by Charles Arthur Hopper of England, in 1868. It was dressed like an Egyptian and called "Ajeeb." This mechanical robot was exhibited throughout Europe and America. After several spectacular demonstrations at Coney Island, New York, Ajeeb was destroyed in a fire in 1929. An earlier mechanical chessplayer called the "Turk" was developed in the days of Catherine II of Russia. Another mechanical chessplayer was invented in England in 1878 which was called "Mephisto." See *Turk* and *Mephisto*.

ALAPIN'S OPENING

1. P-K4   P-K4;
2. N-K2

A perfectly safe opening which was introduced into tournament play at the Manchester British Chess Association Congress of 1890 by the Czechoslovakian chessmaster S. Alapin. White develops his Knight on K2 but at the same time blocks his own King's Bishop. This opening thus far is considered weak inasmuch as it is entirely too passive.

ALBIN–CHATARD ATTACK

An attack occuring in the French Defense opening. This attack consists of the first six moves, namely

1. P-K4	P-K3
2. P-Q4	P-Q4
3. N-QB3	N-KB3
4. B-KN5	B-K2
5. P-K5	KN-Q2
6. P-KR4	

After White's 6th move.

ALBIN COUNTER GAMBIT

1. P-Q4, P-Q4;
2. P-QB4, P-K4

Adolf Albin was born in Bucharest in 1848 and lived most of his life in Vienna where he died in 1915. He was a second-rate chessmaster but sufficiently influential to give his name to several openings. In the Albin Counter Gambit, Black offers a Pawn in favor of greater freedom for his pieces. White, however, can with further play (3 QPxP, P-Q5; etc.) obtain a better positional advantage. Fred Reinfeld is of the opinion that in this Albin Counter Gambit, Black's procedure "is premature and unsound."

ALBUM, CHESS

An ingenious book in which positions of a game of chess may be recorded, preserved and modified with the greatest of ease. The movable pieces for both Black and White are pictured on tough, long lasting pressboard or celluloid material. These slip into slots in the squares where they are held firmly in place. Opposite the pictured position of the game, a written record of the progress of the game may be seen. When a game is completed, the pieces can be disassembled, the used card replaced and a new game commenced.

ALEKHINE

Dr. Alexander Alekhine, distinguished World Champion chessplayer, was born in Moscow, on November 1, 1892, of a financially well-to-do family. He became a French citizen in 1929 and died in Lisbon, Portugal, in 1946. He learned to play chess from his mother when a mere child. At the age of nine, he began to play chess blindfolded. When he was sixteen, he attained the title of Master and in 1914 was a recognized Grandmaster. Having studied law, he served in the Russian Foreign Office but at the time of the Russian Revolution, he emigrated to France where he obtained the degree of Docteur en Droit from the University of Paris.

Alekhine won the title of World Champion by defeating Capablanca at Buenos Aires in 1927. He lost the championship temporarily in 1935 to

4

Dr. Max Euwe of Holland but regained the title in a return match two years later. He then retained the World Championship title to the time of his death in 1946. Not only did Alekhine distinguish himself in tournament matches but he was also an excellent blindfold chessplayer. At the Chicago World's Fair in 1932, he played 32 games blindfolded.

His superb quality of chessplay is summarized best by Irving Chernev when he says that Alekhine's "sensitive positional play was a joy to behold, while his combinations lit up the whole board with their radiance. His pleasing, graceful blending of profound strategy and lively tactics is particularly manifest." Fred Reinfeld observes: "No master, in any period whatever, even remotely approaches Alekhine in the consistency, artistry, profundity and dramatic richness of his achievements." And Dr. Reuben Fine considers Alekhine to be "the greatest Chess genius of the 20th century." For a fuller biographical account and some of Alekhine's chess performances, see *My Best Games of Chess,* 1908-1923; and *My Best Games of Chess,* 1924-1937, both written by Alekhine. See also his *World's Chess Championship,* 1937.

ALEKHINE'S DEFENSE

1. P-K4, N-KB3

A bold but challenging defense which Alekhine popularized in the 1920s. It was used earlier and can be traced to the 1862 International Handicap Tournament of London. The underlying wisdom of this defense seems to be to entice White's Pawns to move forward so that Black can attack them successfully. It presents White with a psychological pitfall whereby he will weaken his Pawns by advancing them prematurely. Dr. Lasker points out that this Defense "is not altogether logically satisfying." Fred Reinfeld observes that "Alekhine's Defense is most suited to

the needs of stronger players who are handling the Black pieces against weaker opponents."

ALEXANDER

C. H. O'D. Alexander, a British International Master, a chess writer and an influential officer of the British Chess Federation, was born in Cork, in 1909. He learned chess while attending King Edward's School. He has the honor of being the only chessplayer who has ever been both British Boy Champion and British Champion. In 1938, he won second prize at Hastings by finishing only a half point behind Reshevsky, and ahead of Fine, Flohr and other masters. In the 1947 Hastings event, he finished ahead of Tartakower.

Alexander is an active member of the British Chess Federation. He is not only a Life Member of this Federation but is also one of its vice-presidents and serves as a member of several important committees.

Reinfeld says that Alexander "is a first-class attacking player, rich in imagination and resourcefulness in the grand tradition of Blackburne and Yates. Like his predecessors, he has distinguished himself against some of the greatest masters of his time."

ALGEBRAIC NOTATION

A convenient, co-ordinate system of identifying each square on the chess-

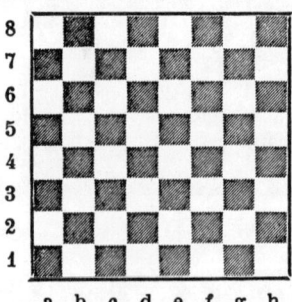

board. As shown in the diagram, the files are lettered from a to h from left to right, and the ranks are numbered from 1 to 8. The locations and moves of the men for both Black and White are always read from White's side of the board, or the lower side of the diagram. For example the White's Queen square is "d1" and White's King Rook square is "h1," whereas Black's King Rook square is "h8."

To record a move of a piece, the initial of the piece is given followed by the symbols of the squares of departure and arrival. A hyphen between the symbols indicates a move; a colon or an "x" indicates a capture. A similar procedure is followed to indicate a move or capture of a Pawn except that the initial P for Pawn need not be given. For example, Qd1—e2 means that the Queen moved from d1 to e2; and e2—e4 means that the Pawn on e2 moves to e4. Thus, the first few moves of the so-called Dutch Defense are recorded in the algebraic and descriptive notations:

Algebraic

1. d2-d4   f7-f5
2. e2-e4   f5-e4
3. Nb1-c3   Ng8-f6

Descriptive

1. P-Q4   P-KB4
2. P-K4   PxP
3. N-QB3   N-KB3

The algebraic or co-ordinate system, or, the "German system" of notation as it is sometimes called, is used in continental Europe (not in the British Isles). It is also used as a cable code for transmitting records of chess matches. Sometimes an abridged notation is used whereby only the square of arrival is given and when a move to a vacant square is given, the hyphen is also omitted. For example, e4 means a Pawn moves to the square e4; likewise, Rh5 means that a Rook moves to the square h5.

The advantages of this algebraic

system of notation are: 1) a reader need not re-orient himself between moves with reference to Black and White. 2) It is easily understood by peoples of different nationalities. This system is independent of languages. English speaking people, for instance, may readily understand the meaning of KKt2 or KN2, whereas non-English speaking people would understand much more readily the same designation as g2. This system also permits a more simplified record of a game. For the official use of this algebraic notation see *Laws of Chess,* Supplement No. 1. See: *Stamma.*

ALLGAIER GAMBIT

1. P-K4   P-K4
2. P-KB4   PxP
3. N-KB3   P-KN4
4. P-KR4   P-N5
5. N-N5

A variation of the King's Gambit named after Johann Allgaier, who was born in Swabia in 1763 and died in 1823. While serving as an officer in the Imperial army, Allgaier tutored the Emperor's sons in the art of chess strategy and tactics. Not only was he one of the greatest chessmasters of Vienna but he also became famous for

After White's 5th move.

two singular chess contributions. He published a book in 1795 in which chess games were arranged for the first time in tabular form. He also introduced the gambit which bears his name.

This gambit has been called the "All-gaier-Kieseritzki Gambit" by some chess writers because Kieseritzki favored this opening play and helped to popularize it. Freeborough and Ranken stated that in this gambit " a series of attacking moves is placed at White's disposal, and his success or failure will largely depend on the order in which they are made and how long he can keep up the pressure." Dr. Fine is of the opinion that "the Allgaier Gambit is unsound for White." For a brief presentation of the Allgaier Gambit procedure see *Practical Chess Openings* by Reuben Fine, or, *Modern Chess Openings,* Ninth Edition, by Walter Korn.

AMAUROSIS SCACCHISTICA

A Latin expression meaning "chess blindness." This Latin expression was used by Dr. Tarrasch when he referred to an oversight committed by an experienced chessplayer who had a mating position but lost the game by making a foolish move. See *Blindness in Chessplay.*

AMERICAN CHESS BULLETIN

A current chess periodical published bi-monthly, in New York City. It was founded in 1904 by its present editor and owner, Hermann Helms, who is sometimes referred to as the "Dean of American Chess."

The *American Chess Bulletin* expresses its dedication in its sub-title: "A Magazine Devoted to the Interests of all Branches of the Royal Game, Home and Abroad." Subscription price is $3.00 a year. It is obtainable by writing to its Executive and Editorial Offices, 150 Nassau Street, New York 38, N. Y.

AMERICAN CHESS CONGRESS, THE FIRST

The first assemblage in America of leading chessplayers who met and played in a tournament to determine the U. S. Chess Champion. Daniel Willard Fiske (1833-1904) was the originator and secretary of this first American Chess Congress. It was sponsored by the New York Chess Club which solicited the cooperation of chess clubs in all other states to send their best players to New York City where they were to compete with each other. The final winner was to be the recognized U. S. Champion Chessplayer. This Congress opened on the evening of October 5, 1857, and official play began the next day and concluded on November 10, 1857. Paul Morphy was the victor and was declared to be the first U. S. Champion Chessplayer.

AMERICAN CHESS FEDERATION

This Federation emerged in 1934 as a result of a felt need for broadening the scope of the Western Chess Association. The first championship tournament sponsored by this Federation was held in Chicago, in 1934. The first place honors were shared jointly by Reshevsky and Fine, who finished with a tie score. This tournament was the first real "Open" Tournament held in the United States. Since this time, the Open Tournament has become an American annual event. In 1939, this Federation united with the Western Chess Association and the National Chess Federation to form the present United States Chess Federation. See "The First American Chess Congress" by Jack Straley Battell, in *Chess Review,* October, 1957, pp. 318-320.

AMERICAN CHESS FOUNDATION, Ino.

An organization established in April, 1955, which is dedicated to the promotion and development of chess interests in the United States. An initial large sum of money which is to serve as the nucleus for starting a permanent fund has been established by a group of successful business men, all of whom are chess enthusiasts. The initial effort consisted in financing in June 1955, an expedition of U.S. chessmasters to Moscow for a series of international matches with Soviet masters. Eventually, the Foundation hopes to finance all activities pertinent to promoting the welfare of the game of chess.

The first officers of this Foundation were, Alexander Bisno of Beverly Hills, California, President; Rosser Reeves of New York, Vice-President; Maurice J. Kasper of New York, Treasurer; and Walter Fried of New York, Secretary. The Board of Directors consisted of the four officers and Lessing J. Rosenwald of Jenkintown, Pennsylvania; Jacques Coe of New York; and Mrs. Cecile Wertheim of New York. The address of the Foundation's headquarters is 1372 Broadway, New York City.

ANALYST

A chess analyst is a critical examiner of the various movements in a game of chess and, in the light of sound basic principles, points out the strong, the weak and the more or less placid features of the game. The analyst is concerned with the cold-blooded, logical display of what he considers to be the best moves for both Black and White. He does not report on the feelings, emotions, and other physiological and psychological reactions of the players. The chess analyst serves a very useful purpose but it should not be forgotten that as Horowitz and Reinfeld point out: "Just as postmortems can never bring a corpse to life, so the most beautiful analysis in the world cannot annul those deadly words "checkmate" or "resign." See *Annotator*.

ANDERSSEN

Adolf Anderssen was born in Breslau, Germany, on July 6, 1818, and died on March 13, 1879. He studied mathematics and philosophy and served as a professor of mathematics and German at the Breslau Gymnasium. In 1865 he received an honorary doctorate from the University of Breslau. He became a chess enthusiast during his student days and developed into a basically sound chessplayer. His extraordinary talents for chess combinations displayed the workings of a very lively imagination. For a while, he was a contributing editor to the *Deutsche Schachzeitung* and a noted chess-problem composer.

Anderssen was a Grandmaster and as such was recognized as the best chessplayer of his time. He won first prizes in various tournaments but when he won the first prize at the First International Master Tournament in London, in 1851, he was considered, unofficially (for there was no such title then in existence,) the World Champion. He maintained this honor from 1851 to 1858 at which time he was defeated by Morphy. One of Anderssen's games popularly known as "The Evergreen," has become famous in chess history.

Reuben Fine appraises Anderssen's chess play as "fresh, lively, full of ideas, happy inspirations, novelties, and surprises." His sacrifices, adds Fine, "were the main vehicle of his genius." See *Evergreen Partie*.

ANGLO-AMERICAN NOTATION

An abbreviated method, employed by English-speaking people, to record the names of the squares on a chessboard and the movements made by the players in a game of chess. The files are named in accordance with the names of the pieces which stand on them at the beginning of the game. The eight ranks are numbered from 1 to 8, counting from White's first rank for White, and from Black's first rank for Black. Consequently, every square has two different names, depending upon whether it is referred to as a

White or a Black maneuver. The names of the squares in this system of notation are indicated in the accompanying illustration.

BLACK

8	QR8	QN8	QB8	Q8	K8	KB8	KN8	KR8	1
7	QR7	QN7	QB7	Q7	K7	KB7	KN7	KR7	2
6	QR6	QN6	QB6	Q6	K6	KB6	KN6	KR6	3
5	QR5	QN5	QB5	Q5	K5	KB5	KN5	KR5	4
4	QR4	QN4	QB4	Q4	K4	KB4	KN4	KR4	5
3	QR3	QN3	QB3	Q3	K3	KB3	KN3	KR3	6
2	QR2	QN2	QB2	Q2	K2	KB2	KN2	KR2	7
1	QR1	QN1	QB1	Q1	K1	KB1	KN1	KR1	8

WHITE

In most British notations and in some American notations, the symbol "Kt" is used for the Knight, but for the sake of greater simplicity and less risk of confusion, this Dictionary is utilizing the simple letter "N."

In making a notation of a move, the following order is used: first, the number of the move is indicated; second, the letter of the chessman to be moved; third, the action taken by the identified chessman is given, a hyphen indicates a move, and an x indicates a capture; and fourth, the symbol of the square to which the chess unit is moved. Thus, 5. N-K5 means that White's fifth move was Knight moved to King's fifth rank. See *Notation*.

ANIMALS

Figurines of animals, in place of our chessmen, were used in the game of chess in various countries at various times. For example:

The Lion was used in place of our King in Tibet; the Tiger was used in place of our Queen in Tibet; the Camel or Elephant was used in place of our Bishop in Tibet; the Horse was used in place of our Knight universally; the Blackbird was used in place of our Rook in Arabia (probably); the Monkey was used in place of our Pawns in Burma.

In reading the history of chess, references can be found to the use of such other animals in the game as: the acanca, crocodile, dog, dragon, giraffe, and the unicorn. See *Great Chess*.

ANNIHILATION

Winning a game by exterminating all of the opponent's forces except the King. When a King is stripped of his army, he is rendered helpless. In earlier days this was the common method of terminating the game but since the late medieval days winning a game by checkmate was considered more praiseworthy than winning by annihilation. See *Bare King*.

ANNOTATOR

A chess annotator records games with critical, historical or explanatory observations regarding any phase, move, occurrence or detail affecting the game. A good chess annotator gives an awareness of what is going on and why it is going on. To be helpful, a chess annotator usually assumes the role of a friendly guide and points out the wisdom of the moves, explains new or revised theories at the moment they have practical application, and shows how other chessmasters handled similar situations. Hence, the services of a chess annotator are of great importance to a chessplayer who wants to improve his playing strength. See *Analyst*.

ANNOYANCES IN CHESSPLAY

Irritations which cause a chessplayer undue strain or force him to endure something obnoxious or unpleasant so as to upset his nerves or equilibrium and cause him to play poorly. Some annoyances are caused unintentionally while others are designed deliberately to disturb the opponent. The following annoyances have been cited in chess literature:

1. Seating the opponent so that he will be annoyed by the glare of the sun or other reflections.

2. Smoking foul cigars or blowing smoke into the opponent's face or across the chessboard.
3. Constantly shifting one's position, such as, swaying of the body or swaying on one's chair by sitting so as to rock the chair from its two back legs; or twitching with various parts of the body.
4. Displaying perplexing mannerisms so as to give false impressions as to the wisdom of moves, such as: grunting when a sacrifice or an exchange ·has been refused; or wringing or clasping one's hands to show elation of one's own move, or showing surprise at the stupidity of the opponent's.
5. Banging a piece down on the board with an air of great bravado and at the same time giving the opponent an hypnotic glare or "the eagle eye."
6. Continually combing one's hair, adjusting one's eye-glasses or clothing.
7. Tapping with one's finger, hand or foot.
8. Waving or hovering one's hand over chessmen to cause bewilderment.
9. Softly humming or whistling; muttering to one's self or uttering ejaculations under one's breath.
10. Chatting with spectators while making moves.

In correspondence chess games, chessplayers seem to dislike: overstepping the time limit in sending replies; receiving cold-blooded, unfriendly replies with only recorded moves; and "guys who never know enough to resign."

ANT

An "ant" in chess terminology is a bookworm. He is one who memorizes the games recorded in chess books with all the variations but is utterly lost when he plays a game with an opponent who deviates from the book and shows a little originality.

APPROXIMATE BALANCE OF POSITION

see *Balance of Position*

ARABIAN MATE

The earliest mate on record delivered by a Rook with the assistance of a Knight. While this is always an interesting possibility, this mate does not frequently occur in actual play.

ARTIST

An artist in playing a game of chess is one who by his skill and experience applies chess theory to the production of a beautiful game. A really true artist in chess transmits proven principles of chess from the region of scientific understanding to the region of those human emotions which unite the chessplayer and his observers in establishing a mutual bond of aesthetic enjoyment of the player's performance. Hence, artistic performance is more than the mere creation of pleasure or amusement. It must arouse the emotional delight and satisfaction which, in some manner, captivates the human mind and culminates in spiritual exaltation. See *Beautiful Game*.

ATTACK

A move or series of moves designed to win an advantage in material or check or checkmate. The essentials of making a successful attack consist in knowing *where*, *when* and *how* to attack and *having the manpower needed for an attack*.

1. *Where to attack.* There are two basic guiding principles, namely:
1) Attack the opponent where you have superior manpower, position and mobility.
2) Concentrate the attack where the opponent is weak; such as, where positions are sufficiently unguarded and the opponent has insufficient time to muster protective forces.

2. *When to attack.* Timing is extremely important in planning an attack. General principles indicate that an attack should be launched:
1) When some tangible superiority over the opponent can be exercised to advantage.
2) When sufficiently strong forces are stationed within striking range of the opponent's camp. The attack should be executed when coordinate action of the forces is assured.

3. *How to attack.* All techniques should be utilized which will weaken the opponent and bring about a final checkmate in a most effective and expeditious manner. Some of the more common techniques are: breaking-up the opponent's Pawn chain, paralyzing major pieces by the use of the "pin" and making sacrifices which will drive the opponent's King out in the open.

4. *Manpower needed for an attack.* In the words of Casablanca: "You must always try and defend your King with as few pieces as you can, and it is only when attacking your opponent's King that you must bring forward all the pieces you can. When attacking other pieces use just sufficient force to attain your object."

ATTACKING MOVE

A move which compels the opponent to defend his men or position. As a rule, the player who makes the first move against the opponent's forces or stronghold is said to have the "attack," and the second player has the "defense." See *Attack.*

ATTITUDE TOWARDS CHESS

A mind set or predisposition towards the game of chess. It is the mental framework which has been acquired from past experiences. These accumulated experiences influence a person's thinking and personal behavior as a chessplayer. For example, Doctor Emanuel Lasker's attitude towards chess was that chess offered an opportunity to unfold a dramatic conflict or struggle between two human beings who have agreed to abide by certain well-established rules. For Doctor Euwe, chess is an opportunity to find a solution to a problem. Some chessplayers have an attitude that chess offers them an outlet for demonstrating their superior powers, while others have a more congenial attitude and regard chess as an opportunity of recreational enjoyment or a challenge of wits. A chessplayer's attitude determines to a large extent whether or not he can take defeat with good grace.

AUTOMATON CHESSPLAYERS
see *Ajeeb, Mephisto* and *Turk*

A. V. R. O. TOURNAMENT

These initials stand for the name of the Dutch broadcasting system, *Algemene Verenigde Radio Omroep,* meaning the General Combined Radio Broadcasting Company, which sponsored a famous chess tournament at Amsterdam, Holland in November, 1938. In this tournament, the world's reputed eight best chessplayers competed with the understanding that the winner was to have the right to challenge Alekhine for the World Championship title. A tie was to be settled by the Sonneborn-Berger count. A tie did take place between Fine and Kérés. The Sonneborn-Berger tie-breaking method favored Kérés, but his match with Alekhine never took place. The A.V.R.O. final tournament scores were: Fine and Kérés 8½; Botvinnik 7½;

Alekhine, Euwe and Reshevsky 7; Capablanca 6; and Flohr 4½.

B

BABSON-TASK

A problem task developed by Joseph Ney Babson (1852-1929) which demonstrates the possibilities of Pawn promotions. This so-called "Babson-task" was awarded the first prize by Dr. Henry W. Bettmann in a 1926 problem-composers' contest. It illustrates how when a black Pawn is promoted to any one of the various major or minor pieces, White can counter successfully by promoting a Pawn to a similar major or minor piece. Thus, in the situation shown in the accompanying diagram, White first plays 1. P-QR8 which is promoted to a Queen. Now the effect of the Babson-task can be seen in operation by observing the following moves and the corresponding promotions.

White mates in three moves
Key: P-QR8(B)

If 1 .... PxB (Q); then White can respond with 2. P-KB8 (Q)
If 1 .... PxB (R); then White can respond with 2. P-KB8 (R)
If 1 .... PxB (B); then White can respond with 2. P-KB8 (B)
If 1 .... PxB (N); then White can respond with 2. P-KB8 (N).

BACK-RANK MATE

A checkmate taking place on the eighth rank. This mate may be ad-

ministered as a corridor mate, a smothered mate, a pawn promotion accompanied with mating possibilities or any other mating combination.

BACKWARD PAWN

A Pawn which lags so far behind its adjoining Pawns that they are unable to offer any protection in case of attack. A backward Pawn in an open file constitutes a positional weakness.

BAD BISHOP

A Bishop blocked by his own fixed Pawns which restrict his mobility. In the accompanying diagram, Black has a "bad Bishop" because it is hampered by its own Pawns, whereas, White has a "good Bishop" because it has greater freedom of action. One of the objections to Black's development in the French Defense is that Black's Queen-Bishop may very readily become a "bad Bishop" if it is hemmed in by too many black Pawns on white squares.

BAD MOVE

A faulty move, that is, one which violates a basic and well-established principle of chessplay. It is axiomatic that it is not only important to know what to do to win, it is equally important to know what *not* to do, so as *not* to lose. In chess, there seems to be an indisputable logical sequence of making moves, namely, the bad move which loses, is always the basis of the good move which wins. Fred Reinfeld observed that "before a player can begin to improve, he must clear away the faults that have been spoiling his games and deprive him of well-earned victories." To be helpful in eliminating and correcting bad moves, Reinfeld wrote a very practical book entitled: *The Second Book of Chess; The Nine Bad Moves of Chess,* which are:

1. Neglecting development of pieces.
2. Exposing the King to attack.
3. Making too many Queen moves in the opening.
4. Grabbing Pawns thoughtlessly.
5. Weakening the castled position.
6. Getting pinned.
7. Failing to guard against captures.
8. Underestimating your opponents threat.
9. Losing a won game.

BALANCE OF POSITION

An expression employed by William Steinitz to indicate a condition of a perfectly balanced or symmetrical position by both Black and White players in a game of chess. This condition exists at the beginning of the game but with additional moves an imbalance develops in either position or material. A balance of position may again be re-established during the game, which, however, is difficult to maintain for any length of time. A balance of position frequently occurs in the end-game when a battle royal may develop between an equal number of Pawns and the two Kings. This might easily end in a draw.

BARCZA SYSTEM

    1. N-KB3   P-Q4;
    2. P-KN3

An opening in which White makes noncommittal moves until Black has committed himself to a formation of some sort. During this time, White makes such waiting moves as P-KN3,

B-KN2, 0-0 (withholding P-Q4 or P-QB4). This will permit White, as

soon as Black's intention becomes known, to transpose into a variation of the Queen's Pawn Game, the Queen's Gambit, the Indian Defense, or into the Dutch or English Openings. For a presentation of the Barcza System and variations with accompanying notes, see *Modern Chess Openings,* Ninth Edition, by Walter Korn.

BARE KING

A King who, having been denuded of his forces, is the sole survivor. In some countries, like India and others, it was an early chess rule that a player whose King was stripped of all his men lost the game. In Icelandic chess, capturing all of the opponent's King's forces was considered an inferior form of victory. This distinction, however, was made; if a mate and a Bare King occurred on the same move, the game ended with "a Great Bare King," but, if the last capture was not accompanied with a mate, the game ended with a "Little Bare King."

"BASTARD" CHESS GAMES

A collective term applied by some chess writers to various types of modifications of the usual orthodox chess openings. See *Bird Opening.*

BATTERY

A term used in a chess problem situation where a white chessman shields the black King from immediate attack by another white chessman in the distance located on a direct line of attack. When the intervening white man moves off the line and the black King finds himself in a discovered check, the movement is spoken of as "firing the battery," and the intervening white piece whose move caused the discovered check is referred to as the "firing piece." For a fuller explanation and illustrations see *How to Solve Chess Problems* and *The Enjoyment of Chess Problems* by Kenneth S. Howard.

BEAUTIFUL GAME

A beautiful game of chess is the splendor of the truthful and faithful execution of well-established principles. A beautiful game is appreciated when the elegance of performance reveals the essential ingredients of beauty itself. These elements consist of:

Principles of Beauty

1. Principle of truth which is the basis of all beauty.
2. Principle of harmony of proportion.
3. Principle of economy.
4. Principle of profundity of goal-seeking.
5. Principle of rapturous satisfaction.

A Beautiful Game of Chess

1. Demonstrates mastery of basic principles.
2. Develops harmoniously all parts and phases of the game.
3. Moves are made with precision.
4. Attains pleasurable culmination of purpose.
5. Produces personal exaltation.

For a book which attempts "to convey something of the sheer beauty of Chess" see *The Pleasure of Chess,* by Assiac. See *Aesthetics in Chess* and *Artist.*

BEGINNER

One who is learning the A, B, C's of chess. He is learning the first steps of chessplay. He makes moves without a plan. He rushes into tactical play impulsively and carelessly. An advanced beginner develops some sense of

appreciation of planning and foresight. There are a number of excellent chess primers for beginners, such as:

1. *Chess for Beginners,* by I. A. Horowitz.
2. *First Book of Chess,* by I. A. Horowitz and Fred Reinfeld.
3. *A Primer of Chess,* by José R. Capablanca.
4. *Learn Chess Fast,* by Samuel Reshevsky and Fred Reinfeld.
5. *An Invitation to Chess—A Picture Guide to the Royal Game,* by Irving Chernev and Kenneth Harkness.

BENEFITS OF PLAYING CHESS

The special advantages an individual acquires by playing chess. Among the many claims made by chess authorities, chessplay disciplines one's intellectual behavior, cultivates social graces and provides a stimulating, purposeful and enjoyable activity. To paraphrase an early unknown writer, chess produces thinkers; it develops genius; it encourages mathematical calculations and fans the waning flicker of the dull interest into a flaming activity. It makes the young mind clear and the old mind young. It strengthens and nurtures the brain, and by its moral effect, preserves stability. It is that which makes for the quick eye, the calm spirit, the unruffled disposition. Finally, it provides a practical opportunity of gaining many of the benefits usually associated with a study, a profound problem, a mystery, a science and an art. See *Attitude Towards Chess.*

BENONI COUNTER GAMBIT

1. P-Q4   P-QB4
2. P-Q5

This is an aggressive but theoretically unsound counterattack. Black tries to split or to block White's center and to continue with a King-side attack. Among other things, the Benoni Counter Gambit suffers from a defective Pawn structure. This opening provides considerable chance for transpositions

to other Queen openings. For a presentation of Benoni Counter Gambit procedures with several variations see *Modern Chess Openings,* by Walter Korn, Ninth Edition, 1957.

BERGER

Johann Berger, an Austrian problemist and co-author of what is generally known as the Sonneborn-Berger System for breaking tournament ties, was born in Graz, in 1845. He was a strong chessplayer who always distinguished himself in international tournaments. He was also a gifted problem composer. He published many chess studies and in 1890, brought forth, in Leipzig, a book on end-games, entitled: *Theorie und Praxis der Endspiele.* In May, 1887, he had an article published in *The Chess Monthly* entitled: "On the Quality of Wins in Tournament Games." In it, he proposed an evaluation of tournament scores along the same lines advocated a few months earlier by William Sonneborn of London. Because this was an original contribution as far as both men were concerned, both names have been associated with their tie-breaking idea. Berger died in 1934. See *Sonneborn-Berger System.*

BERLIN DEFENSE

1.	P-K4	P-K4
2.	B-B4	N-KB3

An aggressive defense of the Spanish Game or the King's Bishop Game.

Instead of defending the Pawn at K4, Black answers with a counterattack which White cannot ignore.

BERNSTEIN

Ossip S. Bernstein was born in 1882 at Schitomir in the Ukraine. He obtained his Doctor of Law degree in Moscow in 1906 and after World War I, he emigrated to France where he was engaged in the practice of law.

He became a Grandmaster chessplayer and won the first prize at Ostend in 1906. Dr. Bernstein is in possession of one of the most interesting documents in chess history, which confers upon him the title "Chess Idiot." In a game with the Swiss champion Gygli, Bernstein had a winning position but made a blunder which resulted in his own defeat. When Bernstein recapitulated his blunder in the presence of Dr. Lasker the following dialogue took place:

BERNSTEIN—Am I not a chess idiot?

LASKER—That seems to be a reasonable explanation for that move of yours.

BERNSTEIN—Will you give me that in writing?

LASKER—Gladly.

A document in proper legal language was drawn up and signed by Emanuel Lasker.

Early in November, 1954, Dr. Bernstein, then 72 years of age, accepted an invitation from Monsieur Marcel

Berman, president of the French Chess Federation to participate in the 1954 UNESCO Chess Tournament in Montevideo, Uruguay. Here, Letelier from Chile won top honors, followed by Bernstein and Najdorf from Argentina in a tie for second place. Before leaving Europe to attend this tournament, a reporter from the Madrid Newspaper, *Informaciones,* conferred upon Bernstein an appropriate title which was incorporated in the newspaper caption: "An Audience with the Grandfather of Chess."

BIRD, HENRY

Henry E. Bird was born in London in 1830 and died in 1908. He was a respected accountant and an authority on railway finance.

He was one of the most brilliant English chessplayers from 1850 to 1900. Indubitably, he was a chess genius but lacked a working knowledge of positional play, which hindered him from becoming a masterplayer. He seemed to have been impatient with theory but delighted in waging an attack upon his opponents. He published several books, among which was his famous *Chess Practice* of 1882. When Bird found himself in a chess difficulty, he was quick to reply: "I'm sure the answer to that is in my book." The English chess writer, F. V. Morley, pointed out that Bird did get into difficulties when playing chess because he was a slashing fighter and "there was no *sitzfleisch* in his anatomy." Bird is remembered for the chess opening which bears his name.

BIRD OPENING

1. P-KB4

An interesting variation from the more orthodox openings. It foregoes the initial center Pawn move, and thereby offers Black the initiative for the control of the center. White's first move in this Bird's Opening is the same as Black's first move in the Dutch Defense. F. V. Morley comments on the Bird Opening by saying: "Old Bird!—not much remembered now, I fancy, but well enough respected in those days, and apart from other things the originator of Bird's Bastard, an opening still very pleasing in its old fashioned ding-dong way."

Bird's name is also attached to a defensive position in the Ruy Lopez where 3 . . . N-Q5 is the characteristic move. This opening proceeds as follows: 1. P-K4, P-K4; 2 N-KB3, N-QB3; 3. B-N5, N-Q5. This is known as the Bird's Defense.

BISQUIER

Arthur B. Bisguier, an International Grandmaster and Chess Champion of the United States (1954-1957), was born in New York, on October 8, 1929. His chess interest began when he was only seven years of age. Beginning modestly with third place in the Bronx-Empire Chess Club Championship of 1944, he soon achieved meteoric fame. Five years later, he became champion of the famous Manhattan Chess Club, of which he is a member. By winning the international tournament held at Southsea, England, in 1950, he was awarded the rating of an International Master. In the same year, he won the United States Open Chess Championship title at Detroit—a feat he repeated in Oklahoma City in 1956. In 1954, he not only became the Chess Champion of the United States by defeating Larry Evans in a tournament held in New York City, but he also won, in Hollywood, the Pan-American Championship title. In other tournaments at home and abroad, Bisguier makes a highly respectable showing of his skill at the chessboard. The title of International Grandmaster was conferred upon him by F.I.D.E. in the summer of 1957.

BISHOP

The Bishop is the mitered, minor piece, symbolized in chess notation as 🨝 and is recorded briefly by the letter B. In the opening position, White has two Bishops and Black has two Bishops. One is placed next to each

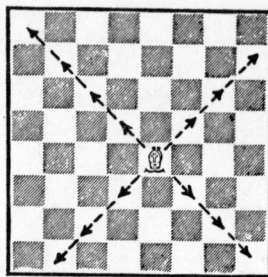

HOW BISHOP MOVES

This Bishop can move to any square indicated by an arrow. He always remains on white squares. His colleague moves in like manner on the black squares.

King and is referred to as the King's Bishop; the other is placed next to each Queen and is known as the Queen's Bishop. Each player has one Bishop which is always on a black square and one which is always on a white square. They remain on their respective colored squares throughout the game. Hence, a black and white Bishop complement each other; the action of one never duplicates, obstructs or interferes with that of the other.

How Bishop Moves. A Bishop moves diagonally in any direction over as many unoccupied squares as may be desired. If an opponent's man is in his immediate path, he may capture him by removing him and taking his place.

Advantages and Disadvantages. A Bishop has the advantage of making long or short moves and consequently controls all of the unoccupied squares in his immediate diagonal path across the board. In the hands of a skilled player, the two Bishops form powerful

defensive and offensive weapons. The obvious disadvantage of a Bishop lies in his inability to control the squares of the opposite color. This weakness of one Bishop, however, is neutralized by the presence and cooperation of the second Bishop, but when one Bishop has been captured, the other Bishop is by himself helpless in defending the total area in any given section of the chessboard.

Value of Bishop. A Bishop is usually given an equivalent value of three Pawns, and in general, is considered equal in value to that of a Knight. However, many experienced players regard the Bishop superior to a Knight in the end-game, especially when there are open Pawn positions.

Historically, the Bishop was represented in the Sanskrit literature of the game in India as an elephant, because not only were Bishops unknown in those days but elephant squadrons were very essential elements in the army of old India. In medieval chess, the elephant chess piece was changed to that of a court jester. In the days of Catholic Europe, the ecclesiastical Bishop became an important advisor to the royal family, and his position on the chessboard became desirable. Some historians see a resemblance between the two elephant's tusks and the two projections on the Bishop's miter. The present design of the Bishop was definitely established when Staunton designed chessmen in 1849. See "A Short History of Chess," Chapter 4, entitled: "The Bishop Was an Elephant," by Henry A. Davidson, M.D., in *Chess Review,* April, 1956, pages 110-111.

BISHOP'S OPENING

1.	P-K4	P-K4
2.	B-B4	

This opening gives an early indication that White plans to attack Black's King position. White's second move is not immediately dangerous. This gives Black an opportunity to seize the

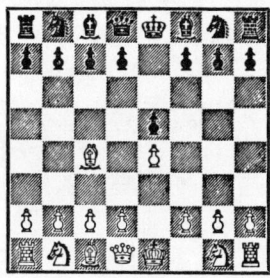

initiative. Reinfeld observes that the Bishop's opening is "old-fashioned and rarely played nowadays".

BLACK

The term applied to the chessplayer who plays with the dark colored chessmen. The dark colored chessmen are always called the black pieces and black Pawns as opposed to the light colored chessmen which are called the white pieces and white Pawns. See *How to Play the Black Pieces*, by Fred Reinfeld. See *White*.

BLACK BISHOP

The Bishop that moves along the black squares. See *Bishop*.

BLACKBURNE

Joseph Henry Blackburne, one of Britain's strongest chessplayers from 1870 to 1914, was born at Manchester, England, on December 10, 1841. He died in Lewisham, on September 1, 1924. Although he learned chess at the comparatively late age of nineteen, nevertheless, by the time he was twenty-six years of age, he was a professional chessplayer. In fact, for a time he was the champion chessplayer of England.

He played in his first International Tournament in 1862 and his greatest success came at Berlin where, in 1881, he finished in first place, ahead of Zukertort and others with the exception of Steinitz, who did not participate.

Again, in 1914, he took part in the British Chess Federation Congress at Chester where he tied for first place. Invariably, Blackburne won many high honors for British chess. In all, he participated in 53 tournaments, playing a total of 814 games. Of these, he won 62 per cent of the games.

Golombek indicates that Blackburne "curiously foreshadowed the most modern developments." He points out that Blackburne played the opening moves of the Nimzovitch Defense and Réti's opening moves before Nimzovitch and Réti were born. Philip Sergeant observes: "Blackburne will always be remembered with affection in his own country and probably was always so regarded in the many other lands he visited. He was a 'good mixer.' He was a very entertaining companion who had picked up much in life besides skill in chess."

BLACKMAR GAMBIT

1. P-Q4   P-Q4
2. P-K4

This close opening gambit was developed by the American master Blackmar. After Black accepts the gambit Pawn, White usually proceeds with 3. P-KB3. Hoffer is of the opinion that this gambit opening "is fundamentally unsound."

BLIND CHESSPLAYERS

People who unfortunately are deprived of vision can, nevertheless, play chess. They can even enter tournaments. A special chessboard and special chessmen are available for those who are blind. Each square on the board contains an aperture for holding chessmen in place. The rules of chess are the same for the blind as for the players with sight, with the following more practical applications. The Laws of Chess, Supplement No. 4, state:

"For the blind player the following exceptional rules shall apply:
  a) Touching a chessman is made only when it is taken out of its securing aperture.
  b) A move is carried out only when a chessman is placed in a securing aperture and, in the case of a capture, when the captured chessman is removed from the blind player's board.
  c) As soon as a move is made the player shall announce it to his opponent who must immediately transfer it to his board.
  d) A slip of the tongue in announcing a move does not render the teller liable to any penalty.
  e) When clocks are used the player shall stop his clock and start his opponent's as soon as the announcement is made.'"

BLINDFOLD CHESS

Playing chess without seeing the board or the chessmen. This requires the special ability to visualize in one's mind the lay-out of the board. This specialized skill plus a good memory of moves having been attained can be developed by practice and experience. Alekhine, Blackburne, Emanuel Lasker, Najdorf and others have excelled in blindfold chess play. On Dec. 2, 1951, George Koltanowski played fifty games blindfolded at the rate of ten seconds a move; winning 43, drawing five and losing two games. For a fuller explanation and a record of blindfold performances see *The Macmillan Hand-*

book of Chess by I. A. Horowitz and Fred Reinfeld, pages 130-141.

BLINDNESS IN CHESSPLAY

The inability to visualize for the moment an important and significant move or combination which seems obvious to others, such as, overlooking a possible mate, check or leaving unintentionally a piece *en prise*. Seemingly incredible oversights occur among the best of players. Masterplayers sometimes make "stupid blunders" which are very apparent, even to an amateur. When a master chessplayer does make such a blunder, it usually is such a rare event that the oversight becomes noteworthy. When, however, chess blindness appears as a chronic condition, it probably is not a case of genuine chess blindness but one of chess immaturity.

Chess blindness is often the result of physical and mental fatigue caused by prolonged concentration. It is not necessarily due to advancing age. In fact, there seems to be a negative correlation between chess blindness and age. However, psychological evidence does support the fact that an older person's brain tires more quickly than that of a more youthful one. For an interesting case of chess blindness, see *Bernstein.*

BLITZ CHESSPLAY

"Blitz" is a German word meaning "lightning." As applied to chess, it means playing chess with lightning speed. Blitz chessplay is a method of making a move-on-move, that is, making a move without hesitation or moving instantaneously. A premium is placed on active play. The advocates of blitz chessplay claim that it develops alertness and decisiveness. Quick perception of a situation is essential. The critical opponents point out that this method of chessplay is light-hearted, full of blunders and tends to be destructive of serious chessplay. In blitz tournaments, clocks are generally not used. In their place, a metronome is sometimes used or someone with a stop watch in one hand and a gong in the other gives the signal when the stipulated number of seconds, usually three, has elapsed for every move. Professional blitz players are inclined to give odds to those who are inexperienced in this form of chessplay. Samuel Reshevsky is one of the world's best lightning chessplayers.

BLOCKADED PAWN

A Pawn that is obstructed and cannot advance. This usually occurs when another piece or Pawn is stationed directly in front of it. Being immobilized, the blockaded Pawn is a weak Pawn. In the accompanying illustration, all Pawns are blockaded. The only solution is to get rid of a blockader which will then permit a Pawn to march on to its coronation.

BLOCK POSITION

A situation arising in a game or problem in which White can execute a mate for every possible Black move.

BLOCK THREAT

A block position arising in a problem wherein the key move constitutes a threat. See *Block Position*.

BLUMENFELD COUNTER GAMBIT

1.	P-Q4	N-KB3
2.	N-KB3	P-K3
3.	P-B4	P-B4
4.	P-Q5	P-QN4

This Counter Gambit occurs in the Queen's Pawn Game when Black plays 4 . . . P-QN4. This Gambit was named after Blumenfeld, a noted chessmaster of Moscow. It was first used in the Masters' Tournament at Pistyan in 1922. Fred Reinfeld considers this counterattack against White's Pawn position premature and "basically unsound."

BLUNDER

A blunder in chess is any move which violates some basic principle. It may be defined as a stupid mistake. Some of the more common blunders frequently made are: unnecessary Pawn moves, premature attacks, Pawngrabbing with the Queen, exposing the Queen to attack, and moving the same piece several times when one move would have sufficed. The consequences of a blunder may be costly, such as; the loss of material, loss of a favorable position, exposure of the King to checkmate, or giving the opponent an opportunity to seize the initiative whereby he may gain a greater advantage.

Very likely, a blunder may be found in every game of chess. Tartakower observed: "A winner in a game of chess is the man who made the next to the last blunder;" and Mason pointed out that "the root of brilliancy is blunder." See *Mistake*.

BOAT

A figurine used as a chesspiece in some of the oriental countries, such as Bengal, Java, Siam and others, where the principal means of communication is by water. The "Boat" has the same functions as our Rook.

BODEN-KIESERITZKY GAMBIT

1.	P-K4	P-K4
2.	B-B4	N-KB3
3.	N-KB3	NxP

This opening was developed simultaneously by the English master Boden and the French player Kieseritzky. This opening "is worthy of attention," according to Freeborough and Ranken, "as an example of the difficulty and occasionally dangerous position which may arise through the capture of an opponent's King's Pawn before your King has castled." They indicate that after the next two moves which usually are: 4. N-B3, NxN; 5. QPxN, P-KB3; White seems to have an overpowering attack but, to safeguard his King, he must castle. This gives Black time to organize a line of defense with his Pawns.

BODEN'S MATE

A mating maneuver in which two Bishops deliver the mate. In the accompanying diagram, the critical area is shown in which Black's King is in check and mated. This mating position was named after the English chess writer and chessmaster, Samuel Standige Boden (1826-1882), who popularized this mating position in official chessplay. Paul Morphy considered Boden the best chessplayer he met in England.

BOGOLJUBOW VARIATION

1.	P-Q4	N-KB3
2.	P-QB4	P-K3
3.	N-KB3	B-N5 ch

This Variation is a branch of the Queen-Indian game. It is named after Ewfim D. Bogoljubow, who was born on April 1, 1889, at Stanislawtzik, in the province of Kieff, now Ukraine. He was trained in an Orthodox Seminarium where a friend taught him how to play the game of chess. As a result, Bogoljubow became such a great enthusiast of the game that he made chess his life career.

His greatest chess victories began with the 1925 Moscow tournaments and continued to 1931. He had some successful encounters with Lasker and Capablanca, but not so with Alekhine, who defended his world title successfully. Bogoljubow experienced some difficulties when he played the younger chess giants. "The young people have read my book," he is reported to have said. "Now I have no chance." Nevertheless, Bogoljubow was a dangerous opponent in any game. He was a brilliant strategist who knew how to resolve complications with utmost simplicity.

Réti pointed out that Bogoljubow's characteristic style of play consisted in "employing an attack on one wing as a preparation for effecting a decision on the other. For example, by preparing an attack on the Queen's wing, he induces his opponent to set up such a grouping of pieces that will not permit a sufficient defense on the King's side."

BOHEMIAN SCHOOL OF PROBLEM COMPOSERS

A group of problem composers who follow the leadership of the Bohemian problemist Anton Konig (1836-1911) and his celebrated disciples Dr. Jan Dobrusky (1853-1907) and Jiri Chocholous (1856-1930).

The ideals of this Bohemian School were set forth by Joseph Pospisil (1861-1916) in his *Ceske Melodie* published in 1908, in the following words: "The Bohemian composer is pre-occupied mainly with three things. He desires to render two or more variations with a high degree of economical unity; he desires to secure model mates for his principal variations; and he desires to present an attractive initial setting, suggestive of freedom, without overcrowding or obviously unnatural arrangements." The typical Bohemian problem begins with an attractive setting. It offers its men great mobility of movement and a variety of ways of reaching the model mating positions. Modern Bohemian problems are principally three movers.

One of the most outstanding Bohemian problemists is Miroslav Kostal, or Havel, as he is better known among chessplayers. For a collection of 500 Bohemian chess problems see *Bohemian Garnets* by M. Havel, published in Stroud in 1923 by The Office of the "Chess Amateur."

BOOK-PLAYER

A chessplayer who slavishly memorizes and adheres to the moves recorded in a book of chess-games. He is a mechanical player who proceeds without contriving anything original. Lacking judgment and insight, this type of player may find himself completely frustrated when his opponent makes a novel move which changes the complexion of the game. Hence, a bookish chessplayer is one who relies completely on the recorded chessplaying experiences of others. See *Memorization of Games.*

BOTVINNIK

Mikhail Botvinnik, the world champion chessplayer, was born on August 17, 1911, in the city of St. Petersburg, now known as Leningrad. He became an electrical engineer and served his country in that capacity during World War II.

He learned to play chess at the age of thirteen. He became a member of the Leningrad Chess Club and by 1927, he achieved fame throughout the Soviet Union as a Master chessplayer. At the age of twenty, he was the champion of the U. S. S. R., and defended this title successfully on several occasions. In 1948 he won the World Championship title which he retained until 1957 when he was defeated by Vassily Smyslov. However, in May 1958, Botvinnik regained the title of World Champion Chessplayer, by defeating Smyslov by a score of 12½ to 10½.

Botvinnik plays chess with energy, patience and mathematical precision. He is critical of his own games; accepts success calmly and is not discouraged when defeated. He has a superb knowledge of theoretical openings. In the middle-game, he proceeds cautiously with his tactical maneuvers until the opportune moment presents itself—at which time, he lashes forth fearlessly and irresistably. "His endings," observes Fine, "are precise and on the highest technical level."

Kostick speaks of Botvinnik as a "very great master whose technical play is unrivalled." Dr. Fine observes: "All told, there is not a single significant weakness in his armour." For an account of Botvinnik's chess career and some of his games see: *Botvinnik The Invincible,* by Fred Reinfeld.

BOURDONNAIS

see *La Bourdonnais*

"BREAK-THROUGH"

Any separation of forces which creates an open file, rank or diagonal.

"BRIDGE, BUILDING A"

"Building a bridge" is an expression applied to the winning process in which the King is provided with a shelter as is illustrated in the Lucena's Rook and Pawn problem situation. See *Lucena's Mate.*

BRILLIANCY

The characteristic quality inherent in a series of moves which is capable of arousing a feeling of profound admiration at the intellectual resourcefulness and skill displayed by the chessplayer. It is essential that in a brilliant game of chess, the player expresses his intellectual ingenuity accurately and economically. These moves should also be interspersed with sparkling and sacrificial surprises. These four ingredients: ingenuity, accuracy, economy and sacrifice must be timed so as to produce a constantly accelerating climax of ecstatic satisfaction.

Prizes in chess tournaments have been awarded for this type of performance and are known as "Brilliancy Prizes." To be worthy of a Brilliancy Prize, the recipient must have produced a game which is a sparkling beauty. See *Beautiful Game.*

BRISTOL THEME

A mating idea developed in Bristol, England, by the famous chess problemist F. Healey (1828-1906). His theme consisted of utilizing the Key piece to clear a line and then relegating it into obscurity. For this startling theme of a line-clearance and the utter uselessness of the Key piece after its initial move, Healey was awarded the first prize in a Composing Tourney of the British Chess Federation held in the City of Bristol in 1861. An application of the Bristol theme is shown in the accompanying illustration. When, in a play, a piece takes two moves to make the clearance, the theme is referred to as a Hesitation Bristol. See *Key.*

White   Black
Key: R-QR1 If - K-B4
Q-N1 mate.

BRITISH CHESS ASSOCIATION

The first British Chess Association was formed in the 1860's. It was pointed out in an 1897 issue of the *British Chess Magazine,* that "after a somewhat fitful existence, the Association passed out of existence."

The idea of organizing a new British Chess Association was discussed in an article in the July 5th, 1884 issue of the *Field.* As a result, Mr. L. Hoffer, the chess editor of this magazine, sent out 500 circulars calling for a meeting of chessplayers. This meeting was held on July 24th, at Simpson's Divan, 101 Strand, and Mr. T. Hewitt, a founder of the Westminster Chess Club, presided. The proposal to organize a British Chess Association was adopted. The following were the first officers: Lord Tennyson, President; Lord Randolph Churchill, Sir Robert Peel, and John Ruskin, Vice-Presidents; and L. Hoffer, Secretary. On January 20, 1885, a Constitution was adopted, and six months later, this Association held its first chess tournament at Simpson's Divan. For a few years thereafter annual Chess Congresses were held, "but at length, like its predecessor, it died of inertia."

BRITISH CHESS FEDERATION

The official representative organization and voice of chessplayers in the British Commonwealth.

The British Chess Federation was organized in 1904, with Canon A. G. Gordon Ross presiding at the inaugural meeting. Its first Congress was held in the same year, at Hastings, England, when a British Championship, a ladies championship and a first-class amateur tournament were played. With a few exceptions, these competitions have been continued at the Congresses of the Federation.

As stated in its Constitution, the objectives of the Federation are:

(a) To encourage the study and practice of Chess in the British Commonwealth.

(b) To institute and maintain a British Championship.

(c) To promote National and International Tournaments and Matches in the British Commonwealth.

(d) To secure the interest of British players in Foreign Tournaments and Matches.

(e) To encourage British problem composers and solvers by instituting Tournaments.

(f) To arrange such contests, meetings, etc., as may be deemed desirable, and to provide and present to suitable organizations in the British Commonwealth, Trophies for Competition.

(g) To maintain and increase a Fund, to be permanently invested in the names of the Trustees in accordance with an approved Trust Deed.

Chessplayers can be affiliated to the British Chess Federation through their local Chess Leagues, Chess Unions, Chess Associations, or Chess Clubs, or they may apply for individual membership. A *Year Book* is published annually by the Federation which sets forth the organizational officers and the previous year's activities of its constituent units and counties.

BRITISH CHESS MAGAZINE

The oldest chess periodical in existence. It was founded in 1881 by John Watkinson, who felt that there was a need for a chess magazine which would be more than metropolitan in its outlook and more than national in its coverage. This has been the objective of this magazine throughout its long and uninterrupted period of service.

This *British Chess Magazine* is a monthly publication which keeps its readers alerted to current chess events throughout the world. It also presents interesting articles, annotated games, a problem department, a Fairy Chess department, and a section devoted to "Quotes and Queries" from its readers.

It is published twelve times a year. Subscription price is $4.00 a year. A special thin-paper edition for overseas air mail services is available for $5.70 a year. The address is: The British Chess Magazine, 20 Chestnut Road, West Norwood, London, S.E. 27.

BRONSTEIN

David Bronstein, champion U.S.S.R. chessplayer and contender for the World Crown, was born in Belaya Tserkov on February 19, 1924. When he was twenty years of age, he evinced a spectacular playing strength in chess which developed so successfully that by 1946, he won the Moscow City Championship and in 1949, won the U.S.S.R. Championship. Subsequently, he participated successfully in a number of international tournaments. In 1955, at an Inter-zonal Tournament, sponsored by the International Chess Federation, which was held at Goteborg in Sweden, Bronstein finished as the top ranking chessplayer; winning ten games, drawing ten, and losing not a single game. He was awarded the first brilliancy prize for his seventh round game with Keres. Now, Bronstein is a world championship contender.

Dr. Reuben Fine appraises Bronstein as a chessplayer in the following words: "Bronstein deserves to be ranked second to Botvinnik. His style is typical of the bold tactics adopted by the Soviet masters, with one exceptionally original twist—his attacks come right out of the openings, which he has studied more profoundly than his colleagues."

BUDAPEST DEFENSE

1.	P-Q4	N-KB3
2.	P-QB4	P-K4
3.	PxP	N-N5

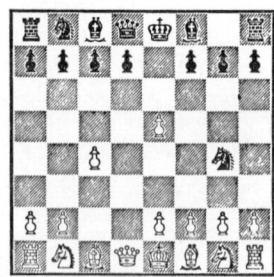

One of the "irregular" defenses which might have been named more accurately a "counterattack" or a "Budapest Gambit." It became popular about 1915-1920 but has steadily been conspicuous for its absence in recent master games.

The Budapest Defense is considered surprising, lively and catchy. Players of equal strength may shy away from this opening because as Horowitz points out: "When Black gives up a Pawn in the opening, its soundness rests, so as to speak, on a hair." Reinfeld suggests: "Try it only against weaker players who will be flustered by its intricacies."

BYE

A term applied to a contestant who, in an elimination type of tournament is by-passed and advanced to the next round of chessplay. For example, after pairing contestants in a Swiss tournament, there may be an odd player left over for whom there is no available partner. Since it is not the odd player's fault that he has no opponent with whom he may compete, he is given a "bye" with a full point of credit—just as though he won the game. He then awaits the next round of play. There are several methods of deciding which contestant will be given the bye. However, it is generally agreed that two basic rules be observed, namely: 1) A bye must be issued only when there is an odd player; and 2) No player should be given more than one bye in the same tournament. For the rules of the United States Chess Federation for issuing and scoring byes, see *The Official Blue Book and Encyclopedia of Chess*, pages 142-144.

C

CAFÉ DE LA RÉGENCE

A famous French historical rendezvous of Caissa's votaries. It was established in Paris during the government of the Duke of Orleans (1.747-93). Custom made this Café the Parisian headquarters of chess. It was a common occurrence that while sipping the Café's mocha, chessplayers would request the *garcon* to fetch the chess equipment and the loser of the game was expected to pay a small tribute. Many a famous chess tournament and games of brilliancy have originated in this renowned Café de la Régence. The Society of Amateurs which adopted and popularized Stamma's system of notation met regularly at .this Café. According to Staunton, this old Café de la Régence "was pulled down in 1855." Some of the celebrities who frequented this Café were Voltaire, Rousseau, Diderot, Robespierre, Napoleon, Richelieu, Benjamin Franklin, Philidor and many others—all of whom played chess. Reinfeld indicates that "during the period 1770-1800 the Café de la Régence was the Stork Club of the eighteenth century."

CAISSA

The alleged Goddess of Chess. This pleasing concoction of the nymph Caissa as the protecting Goddess of Chess dates from the sixteenth century poem *Scacchia Ludus,* by Vida. Later this dryad was popularized in English as a result of a poem entitled *Caissa* which was published by Sir William Jones in 1772.

CALABRESE COUNTER GAMBIT

1.	P-K4	P-K4
2.	B-B-4	P-KB4
3.	PxP	

A counter gambit of historical interest which has been out of fashion for over a hundred years. It has been named after Greco from Calabria. However, it was first mentioned by Polerio some forty years prior to Greco's compilation. This same counter gambit was also referred to as the opening "Gambit in der Ruckhand" by Allgaier at the end of the eighteenth

century. Fletcher points out that "when accepted this counter gambit is a strong weapon for the second player. Normally, however, it is declined by White's 3. P-Q3, and Black does not come out of the opening too well."

CAMBRIDGE SPRINGS DEFENSE

1.	P-Q4,	P-Q4
2.	P-QB4	P-K3
3.	N-QB3,	N-KB3
4.	B-N5	QN-Q2
5.	N-B3	P-B3
6.	P-K3	Q-R4

This Defense is identified by its characteristic move 6. . . . Q-R4. It derives its name from Cambridge Springs, in England, where in the 1904 chess tournament, this opening was used frequently. The underlying theory of this Defense is to be in a position for a counterattack on the Queenside by taking advantage of White's Queen Bishop's inability to return immediately to Q2 and thereby immobilizing

White's Queen Knight. This is considered a good, safe P-Q4 opening for Black. For a fuller presentation of this Defense procedure see *Modern Chess Openings,* Eighth or Ninth Edition, by Walter Korn.

CAMEL

A Camel is the Tibetan chess figurine used in place of our Bishop. See *Animals in Chess.*

CANADA,
THE CHESS FEDERATION OF

The Chess Federation of Canada is the official representative organization and voice of chessplayers in Canada. Its origin can be traced back to 1872 when it was known as the Canadian Chess Federation. In 1932, it was reorganized under the leadership of Bernard Freedman of Toronto and then became known under its present title. The aims of the Chess Federation of Canada are: (1) To weld into a united corporation every organized chess section of Canada for the purpose of carrying out national and international commitments. (2) To encourage consolidation of all unorganized chess sections of Canada. (3) To foster chess interests, friendship and understanding throughout the Dominion. Its official organ is the *Canadian Chess Chat,* a monthly magazine. The Chess Federation of Canada is a member of the Fédération Internationale des Echecs. Applications for membership in the Chess Federation of Canada may be sent to the Secretary, Mr. J. B. Beregvin, 311 Claremont Drive, Ottawa, Canada.

CANADIAN CHESS CHAT

The name of the official organ of the Chess Federation of Canada. This magazine was founded in 1947 by Daniel A. MacAdam, who retained its editorship to the time of his retirement in 1956. The Canadian chess champion, D. A. Yanofsky, was elected to succeed MacAdam.

The *Canadian Chess Chat* is published ten times a year. It is the only publication in Canada containing national coverage of chess events, games, personalities, announcements and articles of interest to chessplayers in Canada. Mr. Montgomery Major, former editor of *Chess Life* — America's Chess Newspaper — stated that "much of the solidity of Canadian chess is due to the unifying force of this readable and informative magazine." Subscription price is $3.00 a year.

CANDIDATES' TOURNAMENT

A qualifying tournament for the World Championship. This tournament is conducted under the auspices of F.I.D.E., every third year in a four year cycle. The winner in this "Candidates' Tournament" becomes the contender for the title of World Champion Chessplayer. See *Fédération Internationale des Echecs.*

CAPABLANCA

José Raoul Capablanca y Graupera, World Champion Chessplayer from 1921 to 1927, was born in the city of Havana, Cuba, on November 19, 1888. When he was eight years of age he showed at the Havana Chess Club signs of possessing an exceptional talent for chess. Four years later he became the Champion chessplayer of Cuba. Having attended Columbia University, he entered in 1913, the Cuban Foreign Service. His fabulous career ended at the famous Manhattan Chess Club where he had a heart attack. He was taken to the Mount Sinai Hospital where he died on March 8, 1942.

On his way to St. Petersburg, his first diplomatic assignment, he gave exhibitions of simultaneous chessplay in the cities of London, Paris and Berlin.

Later, when convenient, Capablanca also played successfully in many other cities, in Germany, England, France, Austria, Holland, Denmark, North America and South America. Some of the chess giants with whom Capablanca played were: Alekhine, Nimzovitch, Spielmann, Emanuel Lasker, Vidmar, Marshall, Znosko-Borovsky, Bernstein, Tartakower, Reshevsky, Keres, Fine, Euwe, Flohr and Botvinnik. He won the world championship at Havana in 1921 by defeating Dr. Lasker, but lost his crown to Alekhine in 1927.

For Capablanca each game he played was unique, every move he made was significant. He deviated from Morphy's principle that in the opening every move should develop another piece. He considered it a loss of time to proceed on a course of development for development's sake. He emphasized the importance of planning in every game. It was his theory that a piece should be moved when and where its development fits into the plan of the game which the player has in mind. He wrote three good books: *My Chess Theory*, 1920; *Chess Fundamentals*, 1921; and *A Primer of Chess*, 1935.

Capablanca will always be regarded as the genius par excellence of American chess. Horowitz and Kmoch observe that "A Capablanca game is like a Grecian temple." His biographer, Golombek, points out that Capablanca's games "breathe a serenity, a lucid crystal clarity, a type of model perfection present in no other master. Playing through a Capablanca game and fully understanding it after a close study constitutes a liberal education in the art of chess."

For an autobiographical sketch of Capablanca's chess life see his own book *My Chess Career*. See also *Capablanca's Hundred Best Games* by H. Golombek, and *World Chessmasters in Battle Royal* by I. A. Horowitz and Hans Kmoch.

OAPPED PAWN

A Pawn which is designated at the beginning of a game to give checkmate. Such a Pawn is generally identified by tying a ribbon or string around it. It is a method of giving odds occasionally employed by a strong player when he is confronted by a much weaker opponent. The recipient of this type of odds, which is about equal to giving a Queen odds, can win the game by either giving mate in the usual manner or by capturing this "capped Pawn." The giving of this type of odds usually occurs in friendly games. The "capped Pawn" is sometimes referred to as *Pion Coiffé*.

CAPTURE

The seizure of one of the opponent's chessmen. A capture is made by removing the hostile chessman from the board and replacing him with the attacking chessman. All pieces capture in the manner in which they move. If a piece can move to a square, it can also capture a hostile chess unit stationed on that square. Pawns, however, move forward in their respective files but capture diagonally to the right or left. When several pieces can be captured and recaptured, it is important to consider the quantity and quality of the attacking and defending chessmen. As a general rule, captures should be made in the order of relative values of the participating chessmen. In other words, whenever possible, first captures should be made by Pawns; then the minor pieces should be utilized, and finally the major pieces. However, the comparative quality of the tactical procedure must likewise be given careful thought. If the captures and recaptures produce an improved situation, even though a slight loss of manpower has been sustained, the struggle may be favorable in producing a final checkmate. In chess, a capture is always optional, except when a Pawn captures "en passant" or when a capture is the only legal move available. See *Exchange of Material.*

CARO-KANN DEFENSE

1. P-K4, P-QB3; (Invariably, the second moves are 2. P-Q4, P-Q-4).

After Black's second move.

This is an ancient defense mentioned by Giulio C. Polerio in 1590. However, it was not a favorite opening until Horatio Caro of Berlin and Marcus Kann of Pesth popularized it in the nineteenth century. Today, it is considered a safe, non-aggressive opening play in which Black's Queen's Bishop is not obstructed. Dr. Fine expressed it this way: "The basic idea underlying this defense is to get all the good features of the French defense without having to submit to the bad ones." Capablanca, Nimzovitch and Flohr used this defense. Dr. Lasker stated that this defense is "favored by conservative players who are anxious to curb the ambitions of aggressive players." For a fuller presentation of this Defense procedure and variations see *Modern Chess Openings,* Ninth Edition, by Walter Korn, or, *Practical Chess Openings,* by Reuben Fine, page 16-27.

CARRERA

Don Pietro Carrera, a chess compiler and an early advocate of modifying the standard game of chess, was born in 1571 and died in 1647. By profession he was a Syracusan priest. In 1617 he compiled *A Treatise of the Game of Chess* which was later published also in English. This work is basically a composite of the works of previous writers. Among the many ideas proposed by Carrera, was his suggestion that the game of chess could be improved by adding several new pieces and enlarging the chessboard. He advocated that two new pieces be added to the eight original pieces for both White and Black. One of these pieces was to be called *Campione.* This was to be placed between the King's Knight and Rook and be allowed to make a move which would combine the powers of the Knight and the Rook. The other piece was to be called *Centaur.* This piece was to be placed between the Queen's Knight and Rook and be allowed to make a move which would combine the powers of the Knight and Bishop. Two additional Pawns were also to be used by each of the players. The chessboard was to consist of ten files and eight ranks, making a total of eighty squares.

CASTLE

The word "Castle" is another name for "Rook." In past years, the word Castle was in common usage and is still used in many European countries today. In the United States, however, the term Rook is now generally employed. See *Rook.*

CASTLING

A combined move of a King and a Rook made to provide a greater degree of safety for the King as quickly as possible and at the same time to bring the Rook into a more active position. This is accomplished by *first* moving the King two squares along the first rank in the direction of the Rook that is to be used in the castling process and then moving the Rook to the other side of the King and placing it on the square immediately next to the King.

Position before Castling

Position after Castling
on the Queen-side

Position after Castling
on the King-side

Each player may castle once during the game at any time he pleases, provided:

1. Neither the King nor the Rook has been moved.
2. The King is not in check.
3. The squares between the King and the Rook are unoccupied.
4. The squares over which the King passes cannot be exposed to check. Castling is not forbidden if the Rook is under attack or has to pass over a square that is under attack.

Castling occurs in about ninety-five games out of a hundred, and in about ninety of these games, players castle on the King-side. Castling on the Queen-side usually takes place at a later stage of the game because the Queen must also be moved out of the way. Under normal conditions, castling with the King's Rook is preferable.

In chess notation, the symbol 0-0 is used to indicate castling on the King-side and 0-0-0 for castling on the Queen-side.

"In planning a game of chess," writes Rudolph Spielmann, "castling may well be said to be the most im-portant move, as two pieces are developed at one stroke. The King, to be sure, does not get into play thereby, but making the King secure is at least the equivalent of a strong developing move. Communication between the Rooks is established or prepared for, and this in due course provides for the central development of all the forces."

The original meaning of castling was that the King is retreating into a castle or fortress, away from the heat of battle. In the Middle Ages, mobile towers were important rolling fortresses into which the King might retire for his own protection. The idea of castling in chess was utilized by Ruy Lopez in 1561 and, by 1630, castling was a recognized chess maneuver in Britain, France and Germany. For a method of castling used in Italy and in some other countries, see *Free Castling*.

For further information on Castling see any basic book dealing with Principles of Chess, such as *Principles of Chess* by James Mason, *Manual of Chess*, by Emanuel Lasker, or *The Art of Sacrifice in Chess* by Rudolph Spielmann and *The Art of Checkmate* by Georges Renaud and Victor Kahn. For ninety-five illustrations of how a castled position may be weakened, see *1001 Brilliant Chess Sacrifices and Combinations*, by Fred Reinfeld, Chapter 20, entitled: "The Weakened Castled Position." For an illustration of how Black may prevent White from castling, see *Salvio Gambit*.

CATALAN SYSTEM

An opening which establishes a pattern of moves built around the idea whereby White develops P-Q4 and P-KN3 and fianchettoes his Bishop at KN2. There is no prescribed order of opening moves. However, to obtain the general effect, it is suggested that play proceed as indicated in the accompanying illustration. This System of moves combines the features of the Réti Opening and the Queen's Gambit games. Black is faced with the problem of neutralizing White's powerful fianchettoed Bishop but, as Reinfeld observes, "with minimum care, Black can obtain a satisfactory game."

"Watchful, resourceful waiting," he comments elsewhere, "must be Black's policy." For a fuller presentation of the Catalan System procedure and variations, see *Modern Chess Openings*, Ninth Edition, by Walter Korn.

After Black's fifth move.

1.	P-Q4	N-KB3
2.	P-QB4	P-K3
3.	N-KB3	P-Q4
4.	P-KN3	B-K2
5.	B-N2	0-0

CENTER

The four squares which enclose the mid-point of the chessboard, that is, the K4 and Q4 squares for both Black and White. Subsidiary to this basic center are the twelve surrounding squares, enclosed with broken lines in the accompanying diagram. In this subsidiary center, Bishops and Knights can function very effectively. Rooks usually are not stationed in the center but should be able to offer long range support when needed.

The total central area is considered the all-important nerve center of the field of battle because it serves as a network of interlinking paths useful for dispatching chessmen from one side of the board to the other. Pieces sta-

tioned in the center can exert their full power.

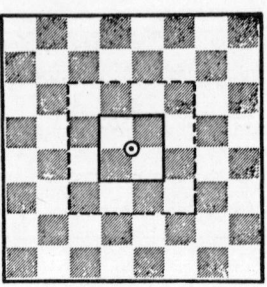

CENTER CONTROL

The power to possess, command or or regulate the center squares of the chessboard. This control is generally regarded as an essential feature of a complete and sound development. It is an essential pre-requisite to launching a successful direct attack against the opponent's King. Furthermore, this central control provides chessmen stationed there an opportunity to exercise their greatest power of mobility and to demonstrate their maximum usefulness in defensive and offensive activities. For example, a Knight stationed on K5 or Q5 can attack or defend eight important squares and as long as this piece cannot be driven away, it constitutes a tower of strength.

Actual occupation of the center may be desirable but it is not necessarily essential for its control. Tarrasch and his followers advocate that the early occupation of K4 and Q4 with Pawns constitutes "the alpha and omega of all opening strategy." Nimzovitch, however, was quick to point out that this control of the center was an advantage only as long as it could be maintained.

CENTER COUNTER DEFENSE
1. P-K4, P-Q4

The Center Counter Defense was first recommended by Lucena as early as 1497. Since then, it has had its advocates and its critical opponents. When White opens with P-K4, Black

immediately disputes this central position by attempting to control K5 and QB5 by playing 1 . . . . P-Q4. The wisdom of this opening has been questioned by many masters because of the early development of Black's Queen and retardation of his other pieces.

Dr. Emanuel Lasker thinks this opening is basically "an essentially sound idea." Horowitz also observes that "the strategic concept of the Center Counter Defense is laudable," but he is quick to point out that "its tactical execution is impossible of fulfillment . . . because (Black) is two tempi behind in development." Reinfeld is more vigorous in his appraisal of this opening by stating: "the Center Counter Defense is clearly inferior for Black and has no virtues that make it worth recommending." There are many "center-counter" defense plans which have been developed by chessmasters that have received a more favorable reception, such as the French Defense, the Caro-Kann Defense, the Sicilian Defense and others.

CENTER GAME

| 1. | P-K4 | P-K4 |
| 2. | P-Q4 | PxP |

This opening strives for an immediate control of the center and prepares for several developmental procedures which usually have been named after the players who utilized them in chess tournaments. Occasionally, these opening moves have been named after the location where they have been popularized.

After 1. P-K4, P-K4; 2. P-Q4, PxP; the so-called Center Game usually proceeds as is shown in the accompanying illustration. This opening has been recorded by Polerio as early as 1590 but it was not until 1737 when Stamma drew attention to 3. QxP. This early development of White's Queen nullifies White's initial advantage and leaves him in a somewhat cramped developmental position.

Walter Korn is of the opinion that the Center Game is "of no advantage to White and no longer offers him any chances of complications or surprises." Dr. Fine points out that "the early development of the Queen is such a serious breach of sound opening principles that (the Center Game) is a rarity in current tournament play."

After Black's fourth move.

1.	P-K4	P-K4
2.	P-Q4	PxP
3.	QxP	N-QB3
4.	Q-K3	N-B3

CENTER PAWNS

Center Pawns are the King's Pawn and the Queen's Pawn. Spielmann speaks of the center Pawns as "the shock-troops which open the battle."

CHAMELEON ECHO MATE

A picturesque term applied to echo mates in which the black King is mated on squares of different colors. In cases of echo mates where the black King is mated on squares of the same color, it is referred to as monochrome echo mate. See *Echo Mate*.

CHAMPION

A chess champion is one who has demonstrated successfully such superior playing strength that members of the chess fraternity recognize him as being worthy of the highest honor and acclaim they can confer upon him. Every chess club, city, state and nation may have its champion. In the United States, the organization known as the United States Chess Federation is now recognized as the authentic grantor of the national championship title. The World Championship title is now within the jurisdiction of the International Chess Federation. See *United States Champion Chess Players* and *World Champion Chess Players*.

CHARIOT

The figurine of a "chariot" is used as a chesspiece in Borneo, Burma, China, Japan, Korea, Malaya and Tibet in place of our modern "Rook."

CHATURANGA

An early game of India which is generally regarded as the forerunner of our modern game of chess. Chaturanga, however, was a game played by four persons. The very word chaturanga is a compound word of *chatur* meaning "four" and *anga* meaning "a member

or a component part." See *History of Chess*.

CHECK

An immediate and direct threat or attack against the King. In chess notation, check is written briefly as "ch." It is customary courtesy, though not obligatory, for a player giving check to warn his opponent of the impending danger to his King by saying "check." This practice may be traced to the early days of Persian chessplay when it was considered an act of courtesy and respect to His Majesty for an attacking player to call attention to the fact that the *Shah* (Persian word for King) was in danger. Today, we do not say *Shah* but "check" which is the equivalent of saying: "Sir, look to your King!" A player must always free his King from check immediately. This is known in chess as "the priority rule."

Any piece or Pawn may check the hostile King. A King can not check the opponent's King. Once a King is placed in check, he must be immediately removed from check or the game comes to an immediate end. A check may be parried in one of three ways: moving the King out of danger; capturing the checking unit; or, interposing a chessman between the King and the checking unit. If a Knight gives check, the opposing King must either move to safety or the Knight must be captured.

There is an old saying among chessplayers: namely, "Always check when you can, it may be mate!" For the official rules governing the use of "check" see *Laws of Chess*, Article 10.

CHECKERS vs. CHESS

Although checkers and chess may be played on the same checkered board, the two games are essentially different as to their objectives, materials utilized in play, and in their methods of play. More specifically these two games differ as:

Checkers	Chess
1. The object of this game is to capture the opponent's checkers.	1. The object of this game is to checkmate the opponent's King.
2. The game is played on the 32 dark squares.	2. The game is played on all 64 squares.
3. Each player starts with 12 checkers.	3. Each player starts with 16 chessmen.
4. At the opening, checkers occupy all the black squares on the three rows immediately before the player.	4. At the opening, chessmen occupy all squares, both black and white, on the two rows (ranks) immediately before the players.
5. Black moves first.	5. White moves first.
6. All checkers move and jump forward only until they are crowned "Kings."	6. The various chessmen have their own distinctive moves.
7. Checkers can be promoted to Kings only.	7. Only Pawns can be promoted. They may become Queens, Bishops, Knights or Rooks depending upon the choice of the player.
8. Capture or "to jump" is compulsory.	8. Captures are optional except when necessary to avoid checkmate.
9. Capture consists of leaping over the captured piece and removing the man that was jumped.	9. Capture consists of removing the captured piece and taking his position.
10. One or more checkers may be captured at one time.	10. Only one chessman may be captured at one time.

For a full explanation of these two games and many helpful illustrations see *Championship Chess and Checkers for All,* by Larry Evans and Tom Wiswell; and, *Chess and Checkers,* by Edward Lasker.

CHECKMATE

An attack upon a King from which there is no possible escape. The term checkmate, or simply mate, is a compound word of check and mate. Hence, while a check is a threat to the King, a mate is the pronouncement of his doom. A checkmate may result from 1) lack of the King's mobility; 2) exhaustion of forces; 3) brilliancy of play on the part of the winning player; and/or 4) blundering on the part of the loser. There are several excellent references on this topic, such as, *The*

Art of Checkmate, by Georges Renaud and Victor Kahn; *Chessboard Magic,* by Irving Chernev; *Mate in Three Moves* and *Mate in Two Moves,* by Brian Harley; and *Basic Chess Endings,* by Reuben Fine. See *Mate.*

CHECKMATE POSITIONS

Situations in which a King who is attacked cannot escape. Among the numerous situations in which a King is checkmated, it is sometimes necessary, especially in the end game, to checkmate a King with a minimum

34

number of pieces. How this may be accomplished with different pieces is illustrated in the accompanying diagrams.

Checkmate by
Queen and King

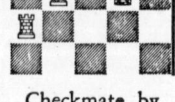

Checkmate by
Two Rooks

Checkmate by
Two Bishops
and King

Checkmate by
Rook and King

Checkmate by
Two Knights
and King

Checkmate by
Bishop, Knight
and King

CHERNEV

Irving Chernev, a prominent New York chessplayer, a chess bibliophile and a brilliant writer who has been referred to as the "Believe-it-or-not man of the chess world," was born in 1900. He participated in many State and National Championships and is known to possess an enormous library of chess books in his Brooklyn, New York, home.

He is the author of many chess books all of which have received the plaudits of chess critics. For example, Jack Straley Battell, the Executive Director of *Chess Review*, stated that "it is hard to imagine any one in the chess world not knowing of him." Some of the

books which Chernev has published are: *Chessboard Magic, Winning Chess Traps, The Russians Play Chess* and *1000 Best Short Games*. He also co-authored such books as the best seller *An Invitation to Chess* (with Kenneth Harkness), *The Fireside Book of Chess* (with Fred Reinfeld), and *Chess Strategy and Tactics* (also Fred Reinfeld). Chernev is also a Contributing Editor of *Chess Review*. In this "picture chess magazine," he conducts a section known as "Chernev's Chess Corner," which sparkles with the touch of an artist who knows how to present to his readers an easy grasp of chess problems.

Through his scholarly literary chess contributions, Irving Chernev has gained the respect of his chess colleagues. For example, Dr. Reuben Fine wrote: "Endings are an inexhaustible source of entertainment, an endless feast of delight. We can be thankful to Chernev for giving us a small store of jewels which will never tarnish." Jack Straley Battell pointed out that "there is something both of the brilliant and of the cheerful in all of his (Chernev's) books and works."

CHESS

Chess is a most fascinating intellectual challenge which finds its expression in the form of a game. It consists of a miniature battle between two opposing kingdoms conducted vigorously in a cultured manner according to national and international rules and regulations. The object of the game is to capture the opposing king. If, in the course of the game, the two kingdoms become so exhausted from their tactical and strategical maneuvers that neither one can annihilate the other, the contestants may agree to a truce, known in chess as a "draw."

The two opponents are called "Black" and "White." The game is played on a square board comprising

64 squares alternately light and dark in color. In the beginning of the game,

Black

White

the forces on each side are in every way equal and consist of 16 men for each player namely; A King, a Queen, two Rooks, two Bishops, two Knights and eight Pawns. The positions taken by these opposing forces at the outset of the game are shown in the accompanying diagram. "White" always moves first. Then each player moves alternately until the battle is won or terminated in a draw. For the rules and regulations of the game see *Laws of Chess*.

CHESS

The name of a magazine published in England. It was founded and edited by Baruch H. Wood in 1934. It contains games, problems and news of general interest to chessplayers. It also maintains a Postal Chess Club and a Postal Chess League with a combined total of over 2,000 members. *Chess* is published twenty-four times a year. Its subscription price in Canada and the United States is $4.50 a year; single copies 25¢ each. Its address is Chess, Sutton Coldfield, England.

CHESS ARCHIVES

A loose leaf encyclopedia of current chess theory and practice, edited by the former World Champion, Dr. Max Euwe. It is published fortnightly. Every issue consists of 16 pages which are punched for filing away according to a master code. Special binders are obtainable for keeping under permanent and organized control the various openings and their variations, games, and endgames as well as special features of the game. The publication of *Chess Archives* in English started in 1952. It was suspended for a while for reorganizational purposes. The so called "New Series" began on April 8, 1955.

Kester Svendsen, reviewing this publication in *Chess Life*, says that it is "the most thorough and useable system of classified chess knowledge in existence." The *British Chess Magazine* says that this is "the best chess publication in the world." Its price is $6.00 a year. It may be ordered through either George Koltanowski, 200 Alhambra Street, Apt. 9, San Francisco 23, California; or, Albert S. Pinkus, 1700 Albemarle Road, Brooklyn 26, New York.

CHESSBOARD

The chessboard is the battle-field where the game of chess is unfolded. It represents the framework within which two minds make visible their struggle for mastery of time, space and movement of material to accomplish the purpose of the game of chess.

The chessboard consists of a large square divided into 64 equally sized smaller squares which are alternately colored black and white. Some modern chessboards have other contrasting colors, such as, buff and brown.

The correct position of the chessboard is shown in the accompanying diagram. The board must always be placed so that the light square is always at the right hand corner nearest to the player.

Chessboards with accompanying chessmen are manufactured to meet the needs of various chessplayers. There are available the standard chessboards made of different sizes and materials; roll-up boards made of durable cloth; magnetized chessboards and chessmen; pocket sets and pocket wallets with a playing board and plastic chessmen.

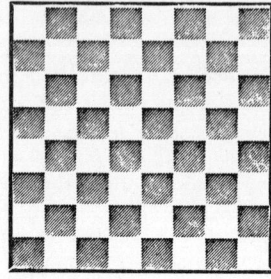

You are right if white is to your right.

CHESS CORRESPONDENT, THE

A magazine published by the Correspondence Chess League of America. Its purpose: (1) to report up-to-the-minute results on all CCLA-sponsored tournaments; (2) to publish good games played by CCLA members with annotations by a recognized expert and (3) to give its readers a constant coverage of new chess ideas, in the form of special articles, master games, and digests and translations from Russian, Dutch, and Latin American chess periodicals. Revised up-to-the-minute ratings of all CCLA members are given in every issue.

The Chess Correspondent is sent to all members of the CCLA and subscribers. Subscription price is $3.00 a year to non-members. It is published monthly except May through August, when it is issued bi-monthly. It is obtainable by writing to the Secretary and Business Manager of CCLA, 816 South Cecelia Street, Sioux City 6, Iowa.

CHESS LIFE

"America's Chess Newspaper" founded in 1945. It is published by the United States Chess Federation on the 5th and 20th of each month. It is sent to all members of the USCF and its subscribers.

Chess Life serves as the unifying organ of organized chess interests in the United States. It contains up-to-the-minute news of the activities of chessplayers everywhere, especially in the United States. Among other items of chess interest, the official chess ratings of all active chessplaying members of the USCF are published in *Chess Life,* semi-annually.

Its policy has been set forth by its editor, Mr. Montgomery Major, in the issue of January 5, 1956. Here it is stated editorially what the policy of *Chess Life* has been since the day of its founding. The first two statements indicate why *Chess Life* has been founded:

"First, *Chess Life* was established by the Federation as a vehicle of information whereby its members could be regularly advised regarding the activities and plans of the Federation in addition to receiving news reports concerning all interesting chess activity in these United States.

"Second, *Chess Life* was established primarily as the voice of the Federation . . . "

Subscription to *Chess Life* is included in the USCF $5.00 annual membership dues. Subscription to non-members is $3.00 per year. Single copies 15¢ each. Obtainable by writing to Kenneth Harkness, USCF Business Manager, 80 East 11th Street, New York 3, N. Y. As of January 1, 1958, Fred M. Wren of Gove House, Perry, Maine, is the editor of *Chess Life,* replacing Montgomery Major, who resigned.

CHESSMEN

A general term applied to all Pawns and pieces used in a game of chess. Each player begins the game with eight Pawns, two Knights, two Bishops, two Rooks (sometimes called Castles), a Queen and a King. The chessmen of one player are of a dark color and are referred to as the "black forces." His opponent's chessmen are of a light color and are referred to as the "white forces." The word "man" is used for any one of the 32 chessmen.

The Modern Chessmen
Designed by Staunton in 1849

King Queen Bishop Knight Rook Pawn

Symbols of Chessmen
Used in Chess Diagrams

White Men		Black Men	
♚	1 King	♚	1 King
♛	1 Queen	♛	1 Queen
♝ ♝	2 Bishops	♝ ♝	2 Bishops
♞ ♞	2 Knights	♞ ♞	2 Knights
♜ ♜	2 Rooks	♜ ♜	2 Rooks
♟ ♟ ♟ ♟	8	♟ ♟ ♟ ♟	8
♟ ♟ ♟ ♟ Pawns		♟ ♟ ♟ ♟ Pawns	

Chessmen exercise the following functions: 1) They guard and protect their King; 2) They come to the aid of each other; 3) They capture the opponent's men; 4) They obstruct other forces; 5) They restrict the mobility of the opponent's King and other pieces; and 6) They checkmate the opponent's King. For a discussion, with illustrations, of various shapes and styles of chessmen throughout chess history, see: *History of Chess,* by H. J. R. Murray, especially Part II, Chapter X, "Chessboards and Chessmen." See also *The Book of Chessmen,* by Alex Hammond, in which the author develops the influence of historic, military and religious conflicts of the design of chessmen. See *Staunton Chessmen.*

CHESS MONTHLY

The name of two different publications, neither one of which is now in existence. They were:

The Chess Monthly, of London; edited by L. Hoffer and J. H. Zukertort. It was published from 1879 to 1896.

The Chess Monthly, an American chess serial; edited by Daniel W. Fiske. It was published from 1857 to 1861.

CHESSOMANIA

A mental disorder characterized by excessive excitement about anything pertaining to chess. It is an abnormal condition in which the victim finds himself in a rage whenever anything or anyone interferes with his chess orgies. A chessomaniac is a chess madman. He may forego eating, sleeping, and other essentials of life to satisfy his chess cravings.

CHESSOPHRENETIC

A chess fanatic. One who possesses an inordinate craving for chess activities.

CHESS READER

A forthright magazine addressed in the main to chess bibliophiles and writers on chess subjects. It proposes to keep its readers informed about the vast amount of chess literature and help them "to form a fair opinion about individual books." The editor, Mr. Whyld, assures us in his first issue that a great effort will be made that his reviewers will *really review* books and not merely tell how they would have tackled the job had they been the authors. In addition to presenting critical reviews and compiling chess bibliographies, this magazine also includes answers to readers' queries; articles on some chess libraries, and correspondence on controversial topics.

Chess Reader is edited and published quarterly, although, strictly, there are no specific dates of publication because it is the intention of Mr. Whyld "to adjust publication to meet the flow of new books." The first edition (Vol. I, no. 1) appeared in the Spring of 1955. Subscription price is 3/6d (35¢) a year. The address is Chess Reader, 39 Charnwood Avenue, New Sawley, Long Eaton, Nottingham, England.

CHESS REVIEW

A chess magazine bearing the subtitle "The Picture Chess Magazine." It is edited and published by I. A. Horowitz with a host of such eminently famous contributing editors as: Irving Chernev, T. A. Dunst, Larry Evans, Dr. M. Euwe, Hans Kmoch, W. Korn, Fred Reinfeld, and Barnie F. Winkelman.

It reports on current events taking place on the international and local scenes which are of interest to its chess readers. Selected games from recent events are presented and annotated by experts. It also presents articles, stories, pictures, and cartoons. In addition, it contains sections devoted to Chess Quiz, Solitaire Chess, Chess Movies, Reviews of Readers, Games, and reports on the activities of Postal Chessplayers. The Magazine conducts a Postal Chess Club under the direction of the able organizer and manager Jack Straley Battell, executive editor of the magazine.

Chess Review is published monthly, 12 issues a year. Subscription rates: $5.50 annually; 2 years $10.50; 3 years $15.00. Address: Chess Review, 134 West 72nd Street, New York 23, New York.

CHESS REVIEW ANNUAL

A clothbound volume (8½" by 11") which contains all twelve issues of the *Chess Review Magazine,* published within the year. Obtainable from Chess Review, 134 West 72nd Street, New York 23, New York.

CHESS WEEK

A week of special activities proclaimed by some responsible individual. Such an official pronouncement is usually issued by the President or chief officer of a club, school, church, city, state or nation in connection with such special events as: the opening and dedication of a chess club; celebrating the arrival of an important personage; the holding of a Chess Tournament; or celebrating some other festive occasions. For example, in 1954, a city-wide "Chess Week" proclamation was issued by the Mayor of New Orleans which reads as follows:

PROCLAMATION

WHEREAS, the ageless and royal game of Chess has contributed to the mental stimulation and enjoyment of its followers in clean constructive sport and relaxation; and

WHEREAS, New Orleans has added a brilliant chapter to the Chess firmament with the late Paul Morphy of international Chess fame, generally considered world Chess champion of his era; and

WHEREAS, the New Orleans Chess Club now will be host to both the United States Chess Federation 55th annual Open Championship Tournament and the United States Women's Open Tournament August 2-14 inclusive, bringing approximately 200 Chess players and their families from all parts of the United States, Canada and Latin America to this city; and

WHEREAS, such contests as this promote good will and understanding between cities and nations:

Now, THEREFORE, I, de Lesseps S. Morrison, Mayor of the City of New Orleans, do hereby proclaim the period of August 2-9, 1954 as

CHESS WEEK

in New Orleans and urge our citizens to do everything possible for the enjoyment of our distinguished visitors.

Given under my hand and the seal of the City of New Orleans, on this the 23rd day of June, 1954.

de Lesseps S. Morrison
Mayor.

CHESS WORLD

A comprehensive Australian chess magazine containing annotated games, problems, accounts of chess events and other articles of interest to chessplayers. It was founded in 1929, by Cecil J. S. Purdy, the World Correspondence Chess Champion. It was originally known as the *Australasian Chess Review* but in 1946, the name was changed to its present title of *Chess World*. The office of this publication also conducts a chess shop which supplies chess goods and books. *Chess World* is published twelve times a year. Its subscription price is $3.00 a year; single copies 30¢. Its address is Chess World, 1 Bond Street, Sydney, Australia. In the United States, subscriptions may be sent to *Chess Life*, Editorial Office.

"CHESTNUTS"

A term employed by Charles Dickens when he referred to "chess problems."

CHILD

The word "Child" is used by the chess players in Tibet in place of our term "Pawn."

CHRISTMAS SERIES

A collection of 44 books on chess problems published between 1905 and 1936 by Alain C. White. As these books were issued, most of them were sent by Mr. White as Christmas gifts to his friends all over the world. This series of books is sometimes referred to as the A.C.W. Series. Mr. White (1880-1951) was an American composer and collector of chess games and problems. I. A. Horowitz regards him as "the greatest authority on chess problems of all time;" and D. J. Morgan of the *British Chess Magazine* states that Alain C. White was "the greatest patron and benefactor the chess problem has known." For an annotated bibliography of each of these books in this Christmas Series see *Chess Reader*, vol. I, no. 4, Winter, 1955-6; and Vol. II, no. 1, Spring, 1956.

CLASSICAL CENTER

The area of the chessboard which has been recognized as being most important for strategical and tactical maneuvering of a player's chessman. It consists of K4 and Q4 for both players. See *Center*.

CLASSICAL DEFENSE

A defense which has been accepted as the original or authoritative standard procedure. The term is used to distinguish the historically accepted procedure from variations which have grown out of more recent innovations and experiments. There are established "classical defenses" such as: the French Defense, Nimzo-Indian Defense, the Sicilian Defense and others.

CLASSIFICATION OF CHESSPLAYERS

Grouping chessplayers according to their playing strength. Every chess club and chess organization endeavors to classify its members into groups ranging from the strongest player to the lowly tyro. These players are generally rated according to some point system which serves as an index of their playing strength. This is done to provide players a means whereby they can match their own playing strength with other chessplayers of equal or better ability. It also facilitates the matching of players in tournament games and serves as a basis for awarding prizes and honors.

The United States Chess Federation classifies its active members as follows:

Grandmasters	2600 points and up.
Senior Masters	2400 to 2599 points
Masters	2200 to 2399 points
Experts	2000 to 2199 points
Class A	1800 to 1999 points
Class B	1600 to 1799 points
Class C	Below 1600 points

The Correspondence Chess League of America classifies its members into the following categories:

AA Class	1000 points and up.
A Class	800 to 999 points
B Class	600 to 799 points
C Class	400 to 599 points
D Class	200 to 399 points
E Class	20 to 199 points

A player new to a club or organization, usually begins on his own estimate of his playing strength. Then, as he wins or loses the games he plays, he is given a higher or lower rating according to an established rating system. See *Rating of Chessplayers.*

CLEARANCE

The removal of a piece from a square so that the square can be utilized by another unit which is more effective in bringing about a decisive attack. The piece removed may be sacrificed so as to prevent the opponent from rallying defensive reinforcements. The converse of "clearance" is "interference." For a brief statement of "clearance" and 37 illustrations see *1001 Brilliant Chess Sacrifices and Combinations,* by Fred Reinfeld, Chapter 9, entitled; "Clearance."

CLEVELAND CHESS LIBRARY

The largest public chess library in the world. This was largely due to the chess collection it received from John Griswold White, a lawyer of Cleveland, Ohio, who died in 1928, at the age of 83. Mr. White had spent more than sixty years assembling a collection of some 12,000 books, which included some rare items of inestimable value on the game of chess. He bequeathed this collection to the City of Cleveland and also provided for the purchase of fresh materials by the library. This chess library is part of the Cleveland Public Library.

CLOCKS, CHESS

Mechanical devices used by chessplayers to measure or to indicate the time they use while making their moves in a game of chess. Chess clocks now used in tournament games consist of two synchronized clocks, only one of which runs at a time. While one player ponders over his move, his clock runs. When he completes a move, he pushes a button which stops his clock and automatically starts his opponent's clock.

In club matches, usually a minimum of twenty moves is required to be made within an hour. In master tournaments, the minimum time is 15 to 18 moves per hour. Failure to complete the required minimum number of moves within the hour entails loss of the game.

The first official use of mechanical clocks occurred in the 1867 chess tournament held in Paris. Sandglasses were used earlier and were endorsed as late as 1852 by the English chess champion Staunton who recommended that a 3-hour sandglass be placed at each player's elbow with a friend nearby to turn it. For a historical account of the development of chess clocks see *A Short History of Chess,* by Henry A. Davidson. See also "Seventy-Five Years of Time" by R. Shilton in *The British Chess Magazine,* August, 1957, pp. 211-214. For rules governing the official use of chess clocks in modern chess tournaments see *The Laws of Chess,* Article 14. See also *The Official Blue Book and Encyclopedia of Chess,* pages 91-93.

CLOSED OPENING

A term applied to any opening which begins the game with anything other than a King's Pawn move, such as the English Opening (1. P-QB4) or the Réti Opening (1. N-KB3, P-Q4, 2-P-B4, P-Q5.) It is called "closed" because such an opening does not lead to many open lines and usually leads to a relatively quiet positional struggle. James Mason points out that "there are few closed games which do not sooner or later become open games." See *Open Game.*

CLUB, CHESS

An organization devoted primarily to the promotion of chess interests of its members. Non-member chessplayers are always welcomed. Edward Lasker, one of the leading American chessmasters and President of the famous Marshall Chess Club in New York City points out that "a chessplayer is received with open arms at chess clubs everywhere. He won't be lonely in any city in the world, even if he doesn't know a soul, as long as there are chessplayers in the city."

A chess club may carry on a variety of activities, such as:

1. Providing a meeting place for chessplayers.
2. Providing equipment for various types of chess matches and tournaments.
3. Providing a reading room containing chess books, chess magazines, and other chess literature.
4. Organizing and classifying its members according to their playing strength.
5. Promoting various types of matches, tournaments and chess exhibits.
6. Arranging for tournament matches with other clubs and organizations.
7. Inviting speakers, Chess Instructors, and Chess Demonstrators.
8. Sponsoring "Chess Week."
9. Editing a club bulletin or club newspaper.
10. Fostering good relations with the great chess fraternity by affiliating with regional organizations and the national United States Chess Federation.

The modern chess club is an outgrowth of earlier attempts of providing meeting places for chessplayers. These earlier meeting places have been called: Chess Resorts, Divans, and Coffee-Houses. For an account of the organization and operation of a chess club see *The Official Blue Book and Encyclopedia of Chess,* Chapter 5.

CO-CHAMPIONS

Sharing equally the honors of championship status by two or more players. As chess is organized at the present time, there is no rule, regulation or basic law of chess which prohibits more than one individual from being the recognized champion. When two or more individuals have attained the same final score in a tournament, some tie-breaking system is generally, but not necessarily, employed. Every organization has a right to decide on its own procedure in this matter. The United States Open Championship title was shared in 1934 between Reshevsky and Fine; in 1938, it was shared between Horowitz and Kashdan; and in 1942, between Steiner and Yanofsky. The State of West Virginia has a record of having five co-champions at the same time.

COCHRANE GAMBIT

1.	P-K4	P-QB4
2.	P-Q4	PxP
3.	QxP	N-QB3

A gambit opening introduced by John Cochrane of London who was an early nineteenth century chessplayer, noted for his brilliant and daring style of play. In 1822, he published in London *A Treatise on the Game of Chess* in which he incorporated many famous games. See *Salvio-Cochrane Gambit.*

CODE

A recognized system of symbols used to communicate briefly a chess situation or moves made by chessplayers. See *Notation.*

COLLE

Edgard Colle, a Belgian Chess Champion and proponent of a chess opening procedure, was born in Belgium in 1897. After winning the title of Chess Champion of Belgium in 1924, he became a prominent participant in many European chess tournaments. In a 1925 tournament, he finished ahead of Tartakower and Dr. Euwe. The year 1926 was a very active one in the chess life of Edgard Colle. In this year, he won first place honors at the international tournament at Merano. He also tied for fifth place at Hastings; seventh at Budapest; fourth at Bad Bartfeld; and, although he finished in the sixth place at Berlin, nevertheless, he was awarded the first brilliancy prize. In 1927, he won the first prize at the Scarborough Tournament. He died in 1932, when he was only thirty-four years of age. Dr. Fine considers him "one of the tournament stalwarts of the Alekhine era." Edgard Colle is probably best known for the opening named after him.

COLLE SYSTEM

This opening is named after the Belgian chessmaster Edgard Colle. As this game proceeds, this opening may branch off into many variations. Tartakower pointed out that "this quiet, but tenacious line of play . . . has the strategical object of preparing the central advance: P-K4, which will open up the game advantageously for the first player." However, the second player has many opportunities to equalize the

1.	P-Q4	P-Q4
2.	N-KB3	N-KB3
3.	P-K3	P-B4

game. Dr. Fine believes that the Colle system "packs a terrific wallop in spite of its placidity." Horowitz and Reinfeld consider this System of play "one of the best lines for inexperienced players."

COLORS REVERSED

see *Inverted Opening*

COMBINATION

A concerted action of two or more chessmen designed to achieve a specific objective, such as to gain material advantage, to win a more favorable position, or to effect a checkmate. A combination usually, though not necessarily, involves some sacrifice of material, and may occur anywhere and everywhere in the game.

The basis of a sound combination is a sound idea which, when correctly executed, results in a triumph of mind over matter. "The rough test of a sound combination," says the International Master Larry Evans "is whether it succeeds; if it fails, it is unsound. An unsound combination may succeed during the game, but if it is later refuted, it is termed unsound. A sound combination, on the other hand, may not succeed and yet be sound."

Inasmuch as Réti lays down the cardinal principle that a knowledge of a combination is the foundation of positional play, further knowledge may be developed by consulting such informative works as: *Elements of Combinations* by Fred Reinfeld; *Basis of Combinations in Chess* by J. DuMont; *The Art of Chess Combinations* by Znosko-Borovsky; and *Strategy and Tactics in Chess* by Dr. M. Euwe, (pages 58-170) where he discusses with illustrations: Mating Combinations, Open-Field Combinations, Compound Combinations, and End-Game Combinations. For a few examples of combinations see: *Fool's Mate; Scholar's Mate;* and *Smothered Mate.*

COMMAND A SQUARE

A chessman is said to "command" any square on the chessboard to which it can be moved legally. A piece is in command of a square, rank, file, or diagonal as long as it can capture the opponent's forces coming on any squares within its range. When a piece is placed in the center of the board and is not blocked by other pieces, its maximum power of command extends to 27 squares for the Queen; 14 squares for the Rook; 13 for the Bishop; and 8 for the Knight.

COMMANDO CHESS see Kriegspiel.

COMMENTATOR

One who, orally or in writing, observes and explains what is going on. He may or may not be critical or historical in his comments. He is the watchdog of present performance. In reporting on what is happening he may point out any physiological or psychological influence which might have an effect on the game, its players, spectators or readers. See *Analyst*.

COMMITTED PIECE

A piece placed in a position for specific purpose, such as, guard duty or protective duty. Once a piece is committed, its freedom of action is restricted and then it usually becomes an object of attack. In the accompanying

illustration, the Knight is definitely committed to protect the Pawn on Q4 from immediate attack of Black's Rook.

COMPENSATION, CONCEPT OF

The general theory of restoring loss of material or position by something of an equivalent value. For example, in general the loss of a Knight can be compensated by the capture of three Pawns; or, the loss of a Bishop is fully compensated by a capture of a Knight and a Pawn. See *Values of Chessmen*.

CONDITIONAL PROBLEM

A chess problem in which mate is to be given under certain prescribed restrictions. For example, at the outset, it is stated that a mate is to be given by a specified piece, on a specified square, or without moving certain specified chessmen. This kind of a problem, though once very popular, is now seldom encountered.

CONDUCT OF CHESSPLAYERS

The behavior of chessplayers engaged in a game of chess is prescribed in Article 18 in the *Laws of Chess*. Article 18, Section C. states: "Players are forbidden to distract or annoy their opponents in any manner whatsoever." For a list of annoyances commonly encountered by chessplayers see *Annoyances in Chessplay*. See also *Franklin, Benjamin* for his statement on *Morals of Chess*.

CONSULTATION GAME

A game in which one or both of the contending parties consist of two or more players who consult among themselves about the move to be made. This usually occurs, for example, when a team from one chess club plays a game by correspondence with a team from another club.

CONTINENTAL SCHOOL OF PROBLEM COMPOSERS

see *German School of Problem Composers*

CONTROLLING THE CENTER

The exercising of power over the vital central area of the chessboard. This can be accomplished either by actual occupation of the center or by stationing long-distance pieces (Bishops, Rooks, or the Queen) on squares from where they may attack the opponent's forces which move into this important central area. Since White has the first move, he has a good opportunity to be the first contender for controlling the center. The French Defense; 1 P-K4, P-K3; continued with a 2. P-Q4, P-Q4 indicates an immediate struggle for the control of the center. See *Center*.

"COOK"

A problemist's jargon for an alternative key which was not intended by the composer of the problem. Every sound problem should have one first move, or key which should lead to a mate in the prescribed number of moves. Hence, any problem cluttered up with any playable deviation from the composer's theme is said to contain a "cook" and the problem itself is said to be "cooked." For example, a problem with more than one key move is said to be "cooked." A problem is also said to be "cooked" when mate can be obtained in fewer moves than specified. The term is also applied by some writers to an impossible position or one having no solution. A "cooked" problem is an unsound problem. D. J. Morgan writing in the *British Chess Magazine* states that "the term 'cook' was originally used by Kling to signify the preliminary process that was necessary to fit his partner Horwitz's problems for the public table, and that was the original meaning of the term. It has no connection with the American composer E. B. Cook (1830-1915)."

COONS PAIRING SYSTEM

A system of controlling the matching of players in tournaments, devised by Everett A. Coons of Pittsburgh, Pennsylvania. The system was utilized in the 1954 Pennsylvania State Tournament and subsequently in other tournaments.

According to this Coons' Pairing System, all entrants in a tournament are divided according to their ratings, from highest to lowest, into four groups: Group I, comprises 25 per cent of the players having the highest ratings; Group II, 25 per cent of players having the next lower rating; Group III, those falling within the third lower quartile; and Group IV, the 25 per cent of players with the lowest ratings.

In Round 1. Players within each group are drawn against each other. Those rated in the upper half of Groups I and III play Black; whereas those in the upper half of Groups II and IV play White. In subsequent rounds, colors alternate for each player.

In Round 2. Players from Group I are drawn against players with like scores in Group II; and players from Group III are drawn against those with like scores from Group IV.

In Round 3. Players from Group I are matched with those with like scores in Group III; and similarly, Group II players meet those in Group IV.

In rounds thereafter. All players are paired with those of like scores. In each of these rounds, the players draw for alternation of color.

CO-OPERATION

The collective action of all chessmen needed to terminate the game successfully. The "principle of cooperation" whereby chess pieces work together toward a common goal is a simple corollary of the "principle of mobility." It is a means whereby pieces attain their maximum effectiveness. In chess, no one man, save the King, is all-important or self sufficient. To maintain the cooperation of pieces is of tantamount importance in every phase of the game; in attack, to strengthen each participating man; in defense, to protect each other; and in positional play, to complement each other.

CORKSCREW COUNTER GAMBIT

1.	P-K4	P-K4
2.	N-KB3	P-KB4
3.	NxP	N-KB3
4.	B-B4	PxP
5.	N-B7	Q-K2
6.	NxR	P-Q4

After Black's sixth move.

A risky variation of the Greco Counter Gambit which is now known as the Latvian Counter Gambit. This counter gambit was humorously named "the Corkscrew" counter gambit by Blackburne (1842-1926).

"It is surprising," says Fletcher, "that the excellent· trap which is the raison d'etre of this opening is so very rarely set, for the moves that allow White to stumble into it are very plausible."

CORRESPONDENCE CHESS

A method of playing chess whereby the players transmit their moves to each other via postal, telegraph, cable or radio facilities. Correspondence chess is utilized by a large host of chess enthusiasts, both men and women, in every walk of life. Many a correspondence chess player is an ailing or crippled shut-in. Some are inmates of prisons. Correspondence chess games are sponsored by various chess clubs. Some chess magazines like the *Chess Review* and the *American Chess Bulletin* and others maintain correspondence chess clubs, which anyone may join by paying a nominal fee. See *Correspondence Chess League of America* and *Postal Chess*.

CORRESPONDENCE CHESS LEAGUE OF AMERICA

The oldest and largest organization devoted exclusively to providing its members opportunities to play chess by mail. This CCLA was organized originally by Major J. B. Holt and William P. Hickok about fifty years ago for chessplayers within one hundred miles of Greater New York. In 1911, it was extended to include players "in all parts of the United States and Canada." In 1927, the organization was further enlarged by the addition of the Chess by Mail Correspondence Bureau; the National Correspondence Chess Association; and the Chess Amateur League (Canadian Branch). This composite organization became known as the Correspondence Chess League of America. This CCLA now extends its influence throughout the United States, Canada, Mexico and Cuba.

Its 1,500 members are classified and rated as follows:

AA Class	1000 points and up
A Class	800 to 999 points
B Class	600 to 799 points
C Class	400 to 599 points
D Class	200 to 399 points
E Class	20 to 199 points

New members may begin in any class they wish except the highest "AA Class." This top ranking class can be attained only by promotion from the "A Class." A new member notifies the Secretary of this League of his or her own estimate of playing strength. The Secretary then assigns to the applicant the medium number of points in the chosen class, namely: A, 900; B, 700; C, 500; D, 300; E, 90. From this point, each member then proceeds on his own merit. (See *Rating of Chessplayers.*)

This CCLA sponsors tournaments at home and abroad and offers prizes to finalists. It publishes *The Chess Correspondent,* an internationally recognized chess magazine. Application for membership, costing $4.50 a year, should be sent to Dick Rees, Secretary, 816 South Cecelia Street, Sioux City 6, Iowa.

CORRESPONDENCE CHESS LEAGUE OF AUSTRALIA

This League was founded in 1929 to unify chessplayers in far away places and give them an opportunity to play chess by mail. At that time Cecil J. S. Purdy, the World Correspondence Chess Champion, realized that Australian chess centers were separated by huge distances. Hence, he visualized this organization as the link which would bind together Australian chessplayers. Members are classified into six grades of chessplaying ability. Their activities are reported in *The C.C.L.A. Record* which is published quarterly by the League. For full details write to the Hon. Secretary, c/o Chess World, 1 Bond Street, Sydney, N.S.W., Australia.

CORRIDOR MATE

A mating situation in which the King can move only along the rank at the edge of the board and behind a group of Pawns from where he can not escape when attacked by a Rook or Queen. The rank along which the King can move serves as a closed "corridor." The critical area of a "corridor mate" is shown in the accompanying diagram.

COUNSELLOR

This was the original name for the Queen. Today, the Queen is still called a "Counsellor" in many of the oriental countries, such as Arabia, Borneo, China, Korea, Persia, Turkey and others. In Java, the term "Counsellor" is used in place of our Bishop.

COUNTERATTACK

Repulsing an attack by waging an attack on your opponent with an equal or stronger force, if possible. Marshall illustrates a counterattack by saying: "A man lifts his hand to give a blow and you knock him down before he can strike; this is counterattack." By and large, the most effective counterattack may be launched by 1) an attack against the King; 2) disrupting the opponent's forces; or 3) creating a sound counterplay elsewhere. A counterattack is the strongest and most effective defense.

COUNTER GAMBIT

Chess purists, like Emanuel Lasker and others, would define a counter gambit as the refutation of a proffered sacrifice by declining it and offering one in return. It is a "tit-for-tat" play made in the opening phase of the game for the purpose of a quicker development, such as the Falkbeer Counter Gambit.

More recently, L. Elliott Fletcher in his book entitled *Gambits Accepted,* published in 1954, would define a counter gambit as "those openings in which the second player (that is, Black,) offers the sacrifice." He stresses that "the side which offers the sacrifice is considered the gambit side: if White, the opening is called just a gambit; if Black, it is called a counter gambit."

COURIER

see *Runner*

COURIER GAME

A medieval game of chess, popular throughout Germany from the 13th to 19th centuries. This game was played upon a board having eight squares vertically and twelve squares horizontally across the board with 24 chessmen for Black and 24 for White. The board was placed with the longer sides adjacent to the players. Each player had the 16 chessmen now used plus 2 Couriers, 1 Counsellor or Man, 1 Schleich, and 4 additional Pawns. The opening position of these chessmen is shown in the accompanying diagram.

The pieces moved as follows. Only the Queen's Pawn and the Rooks' Pawns could make the double step for their first move. The *Courier* moved like our Bishop; the *Schleich* could move to an adjacent square in a vertical or horizontal direction, but not diagonally; the *Man* could move to an adjacent square, like that of the King, but without any of the King's limitations of freedom of move.

The game commenced by advancing the two Rooks' Pawns and the Queen's

The Courier Game (After Selenus)

C: Courier—a galloping man on horseback with a horn to his lips.
M: Man—a long-bearded sage:
S: Schleich—a fool with cap and bells.

Pawn two squares each, and then moving the Queen to her third square. The opponent did likewise. All subsequent moves consisted of single moves made alternately as in the ordinary game of chess.

CRAMPED POSITION

A combination of Pawns and/or pieces so cluttered up that their mobility is restricted. Cramped positions are weak positions. Tarrasch points out that a "cramped position bears the seed of loss." To ease the situation, it may be necessary to make exchanges. However, since in a cramped position the men involved are rendered more or less immobile, ineffectual and inconsequential, Réti observes that in such situations it is an important principle of attack "to avoid any not absolutely necessary exchange of pieces, in order not to give the opponent greater freedom of action." For a helpful explanation of how to avoid cramped positions and gain a "Command of Space and Superior Mobility" see *The Middle Game in Chess* by Reuben Fine, Chapter IX.

CRITICAL SQUARE

The square on which a long range piece (Rook, Bishop or Queen) interferes with the effectiveness of another long range piece. Before an offensive or defensive maneuver can be executed successfully, one of the pieces must first cross this square so that the force of the other piece can be felt. See *Grimshaw Interference*.

CRUISING RANGE

The maximum number of squares to which a piece may move from a given point of departure. The greater the number of squares to which a piece may move, the more valuable it becomes. By placing a piece in the center of an empty chessboard, it will be seen that the Queen has a choice to move legally to any one of 27 different squares. The Rook has a choice to move legally to any one of 14 different squares. The Bishop has a choice to move legally to any one of 13 different squares. The Knight has a choice to move legally to any one of 8 different squares.

CUNNINGHAM GAMBIT

1. P-K4   P-K4
2. P-KB4   PxP
3. N-KB3   B-K2
4. B-B4   B-R5 ch.

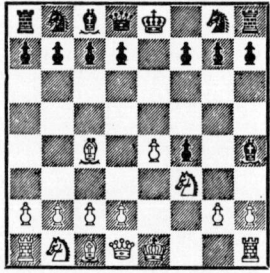

A King's Gambit opening in which Black makes the characteristic move 4 . . . B-R5 ch. There is a controversy as to which one of two Scotchmen in the early years of the eighteenth century, Alexander Cunningham or Andrew Cunningham, should be credited with this gambit opening. The fact remains that one of the Cunninghams made this opening playable and the so-called Cunningham Gambit appeared in *The Noble Game of Chess,* by Captain Joseph Bertin, published in London, in 1735. It also appeared in Stamma's work published likewise in London, in 1745.

The Cunningham Gambit is not used in modern tournament play. Horowitz comments that this Gambit "is too risky. On the face of it, it is doomed. Black can hardly afford to neglect his development." For a treatise on the Cunningham Gambit see Chapter 17 in *The Laws and Practice of Chess,* by Howard Staunton.

CZECH DEFENSE see **Slav Defense.**

D

DALTON THEME

A problem situation named after Dr. W. R. Ingle Dalton, an American chess problem composer who lived from 1841 to 1931. The theme consists of moving a white piece which unpins a black piece, but, in turn, this very same white piece is pinned when the same black piece which was unpinned makes its next move. In the accompanying illustration White makes the key move Q-K7. This unpins Black's Knight. Now any move this Knight makes immediately pins White's Queen and prevents White from making the next threatening move Q-QB5 mate.

Key move: Q-K7

DAMIANO DEFENSE

1. P-K4   P-K4
2. N-KB3   P-KB3

After Black's second move.

A defensive position sometimes called a gambit, was developed by Damiano, a sixteenth century apothecary of Odemira in southern Portugal. In 1512, Damiano published his *Libro da imparare Giocare a Scacchi* in which, among other things, he advised: "No move should be played aimlessly; when you have a good move look for a better one; do not play fast; with a winning advantage do not be tempted to disarrange your game to win a Pawn." This treatise was intended to facilitate the study of the game of chess. It was translated into English and published in London in 1562.

Hoffer observes that this Damiano Defense is not to be recommended because experience has shown that 2 ... P-KB3 "weakens the King side and impedes the development of the King's Knight." For some of the games played by Damiano see *The Works of Damiano, Ruy Lopez, and Salvio on the Game of Chess* by J. H. Sarratt. See also *Chess Openings* by James Mason.

DANISH GAMBIT

1.	P-K4	P-K4
2.	P-Q4	PxP
3.	P-QB3	PxP

After Black's third move.

This enterprising opening was played by a Danish jurist in Jutland in the 1830's; utilized by Dr. Lindehn, a Swedish player in an 1859 tournament match against Swanberg; and was popularized by Mr. From of Denmark. This gambit signifies a sacrifice of two Pawns in the hopes that their acceptance by Black will give White an advantageous development. However, Horowitz believes that with an accurate defense, "the attack peters out and the defender reaps his material reward." Tarrasch confirms this opinion by stating emphatically "the Danish Gambit is not recommended for White." For a development of the Danish Gambit see *Modern Chess Openings* (Ninth Edition), by Walter Korn, or, *Practical Chess Openings*, by Reuben Fine.

DEAD-DRAWN GAME

An emphatic expression applied to a game in which all Pawns and pieces have been eliminated and only Kings are left standing on the board.

DECIMAL CHESS

A modified form of chess utilized by some early Muslim chessplayers. The game was played on a board composed of 10 by 10 squares. Figurines of Camels were used for additional pieces. This game was also known as "Complete Chess." For other Muslim chess varieties see *Oblong Chess; Round Chess*, and *Great Chess*.

DECOY

To decoy a chessman is to lure him away from his position so that his opponent may have a freer range to launch his assault. For example, a piece may be decoyed when it is inveigled away from a square it was guarding or when it is enticed to move off a line where it was obstructing the opponent's forces. See *Roman Theme* as a specialized form of decoy.

DEFEATISM IN CHESS

A term employed by Tartakower by which he means "unnecessary resignation."

DEFENSE

The art of counteracting the attacking or threatening activities of hostile men. More specifically, Doctor Emmanuel Lasker defines defense as "the art of strengthening obstructions, of giving firmness to your position, and of averting the blow directed against you."

Defense is the correlative of attack. For example; the attacker seeks open lines, whereas the defender tries to keep vital lines closed. The attacker wants to induce weaknesses on the part of his opponent whereas the defender tries to avoid them. Generally, chessplayers prefer to play the role of the attacker than the defender, although Larry Evans maintains that "it is easier to defend *successfully* than to attack *successfully*." "When you come to think of it," observes Horowitz, "this reluctance to defend is a kind of spiritual laziness which we must all resist and overcome." He believes that "there is a solid thrill of satisfaction in defending resourcefully, skirting danger and living to tell the tale." It is his conviction that "when we school ourselves to become hard-boiled defensive players, we are not only better chessplayers but also better human beings as well." See *Attack*.

DESCHAPELLES

Alexandre Louis Honoré Deschapelles (1780-1847) was a recognized leading French chessplayer who was inclined to give odds to his competitors. It was his opinion that the study of chess opening analyses was a waste of time. The celebrated Louis Charles Mahé de la Bourdonnais was one of his pupils. Many chess clubs have been established and named in honor of Deschapelles.

DESCRIPTIVE NOTATION

A systematic method used by most English, French, and Spanish chess writers to describe chessmen, their positions on the chessboard, and movements made by chessplayers. It may be regarded as a descriptive "shorthand" method of chess recording.

The files are named in accordance with the names of the pieces which stand on them at the beginning of the game. The eight ranks are numbered from 1 to 8, counting from White's first rank for White, and from Black's first rank for Black. Consequently, every square has two different names, depending upon whether it is referred to as a White or a Black maneuver. For an illustration and diagram see *Anglo-American Notation*. For a statement of the official usage of the "Descriptive System of Notation" see *Laws of Chess*, Supplement No. 1.

DESPERADO

A term applied to a chess piece which inevitably is bound to be lost but, before being captured, causes its opponent as much damage as possible.

DEVELOPMENT

The process of moving chessmen into positions where they can play an active and aggressive role, either defensively or offensively. At the beginning of the game, the chessmen stand, as Frank Marshall describes "like troops in their barracks; their powers unorganized and uncombined, their mobility unawakened, affording little support to each other." To get the chessmen into organized, cooperative and active positions. as quickly as possible, is the essence of sound development. Used in this technical sense, development is a collective concept. It includes all chessmen needed in a strategic advance preparatory for the tactical maneuvers which subsequently take place.

To paraphrase Chernev and Harkness, good development consists of placing chess pieces on squares where they will be free from harmful attacks, where they cause a threat, attack a weak point in the enemy's position, or interfere with the opponent's development.

DIAGONAL

A row of squares running obliquely or slantwise across the board. These squares are of the same color. A diagonal can be short or long. The shortest diagonal contains two squares. A "long diagonal" is the line of eight squares extending from White's QR to Black's KR, or the one extending from White's KR to Black's QR.

DIAGRAM

A graphic presentation used in chess for recording and analyzing a chess position or problem. In all diagrams, unless otherwise stated, it is always assumed that White's position is at the bottom; Black's position is at the top. Black Pawns move down the diagram. White Pawns move up the diagram.

In solving a chess problem, James Rayner, former Problem Editor of the *British Chess Magazine,* advised that this be done from a diagram rather than from having the problem set on the chessboard, where one is then tempted to make movements at random until the solution has been found. Rayner points out many advantages to be gained by solving problems from diagrams. By using the diagram, he says, chessplayers are "compelled to exercise that reasoning, analytical faculty which is the true essence of solving a problem." He points out that "solving from the diagram secures accurate, thorough analysis, and, in an especial degree, increases the power of concentration, quickens the perception and strengthens the memory."

DICE IN CHESSPLAY

Dice were used in the early days of chessplay in most of the Oriental

countries and in many European countries. The Spanish work compiled by Alfonso X of Castile in 1283, sets forth the following interpretation given to the throws of the dice; namely 1 for the Pawn; 2 for the Bishop; 3 for the Knight; 4 for the Rook; 5 for the Queen; and 6 for the King. For a critical review of the use of dice in the game of chess see *A History of Chess,* by H. J. R. Murray.

DICKENS

Charles Dickens (1812-1870), the famous English novelist, was a chessplayer. One of his opponents was Miss Victoria Tregear. On one occasion, Dickens is reported to have observed: "The woman who grows up with the idea that she is simply to be an amiable animal, to be caressed and coaxed, is invariably a bitterly disappointed woman. A game of chess will cure such a conceit forever. The woman that knows the most, thinks the most, is the most. Intellectual affection is the only lasting love. Love that has a game of chess in it can checkmate any man." See Lasker's *Chess Magazine,* 1905.

DIRECTOR OF TOURNAMENT

The official in charge of a chess tournament. For a list of his duties see *Laws of Chess,* Article 19. See also *The Official Blue Book and Encyclopedia of Chess,* pages 89-90.

DISCOVERED ATTACK

A move producing two distinct and simultaneous thrusts at the opponent's forces. In the accompanying illustration, White's Bishop can capture the Pawn. This attack places the black King in check and at the same time exposes Black's Queen to capture by White's Rook. Since the priority rule must be observed, the black Queen is lost. For a brief statement and fifty-four illustrations see *1001 Brilliant Chess Sacri-*

fices and Combinations by Fred Rein-feld, Chapter 4, entitled: "Discovered Attack." See *Priority Rule.*

It is White's move.

DISCOVERED CHECK

A position in which a King who, not being in check, will however be placed in check when an obstructing or masking piece is moved. In the accompanying illustration, the black King is not in check. However, when White moves his Knight, a check given by his Rook, is immediately "discovered." Some writers would prefer to call this an "uncovered check." In chess notation, a discovered check is recorded as "dis. ch." For a brief statement and forty-eight illustrations, see *1001 Brilliant Chess Sacrifices and Combinations* by Fred Reinfeld, Chapter 5, entitled, "Discovered Check."

White to move.

DOG

A figurine of a "dog" is used as a chesspiece by Mongol chessplayers in place of our Queen.

DOMINATION

A term applied by some chess problemists to a situation in which all possible moves of a Black piece are so completely controlled that wherever it may move to, it is exposed to immediate capture. See *British Chess Magazine,* July, 1956, page 185.

DOUBLE ATTACK

Moving one of a player's chessmen so that two hostile units are threatened or jeopardized at the same time. Since the opponent can answer only one of the threats, the execution of the remaining threat wins material force. Every

A	B
The Knight makes a double attack, known as a fork. The Queen is lost.	The Pawn makes a double attack. The King is in check. The Queen is lost.

chessman, except a Rook Pawn, has the power to make a "double attack." A Knight making a double attack upon the opponent's King and Queen can be most devastating. A humble Pawn can be equally effective in a situation such as is illustrated in B in the accompanying diagram. For a brief statement and 114 illustrations, see *1001 Brilliant Chess Sacrifices and Combinations,* by Fred Reinfeld, chapter 3, entitled, "Double Attack."

DOUBLE CHECK

A check given by two pieces simultaneously. In chess notation, a double check is indicated as "dbl. ch." There is only one defense: move the King. In the accompanying illustration, White can move B-Q6 and "double check" the black King with the Bishop as well as with the Queen. The black King must move, with the result that his Queen will be captured. This

double check is a disastrous form of a discovered check. For a brief statement and twenty-four illustrations, see *1001 Brilliant Chess Sacrifices and Combinations*, by Fred Reinfeld, Chapter 6 entitled, "Double Check."

DOUBLE PAWNS

Two Pawns of the same color on the same file. Doubled Pawns are usually considered disadvantageous, as they are unable to defend each other. However, in the openings, when the Pawn is doubled especially towards the center, there is a compensation that often outweighs the disadvantage. Doubled Pawns open up a file which offers an opportunity for a powerful piece to come into action. The player who controls the file has an advantage, everything else being equal. The front Pawn in a double Pawn situation is called the "doubled Pawn."

DOUBLE ROOK

Two Rooks of the same color stationed on the same rank or on the same file, with no intervening chessman.

DRAGON VARIATION

A variation occurring in the Sicilian Defense when Black tries to develop pressure along the long diagonal by fianchettoing his King's Bishop. Walter Korn considers this variation to be "one of Black's strongest bulwarks." Early in the opening, the King's Knight Pawn is played to KN3 to make room for the fianchetto of the "Dragon Bishop" at KN2.

The origin of the term "Dragon Variation" cannot be traced with any degree of certainty but, as Horowitz points out, it is "most likely derived from Black's Pawn pattern in the early stages of play (where) it most definitely forms a serpentine outline." For a presentation of several procedural plays of this "Dragon Variation" see *Modern Chess Openings*, Ninth Edition, by Walter Korn, or see *Practical Chess Openings*, by Reuben Fine.

After Black's seventh move.

1. P-K4	P-QB4
2. N-KB3	N-QB3
3. P-Q4	PxP
4. NxP	N-B3
5. N-B3	P-Q3
6. B-K2	P-KN3
7. B-K3	B-N2

"DRAWING MASTER"

A nickname given to Karl Schlechter, the Viennese Master, who frequently terminated his games with a draw. Sergeant in his *Championship Chess* believes that this title has also "been earned by the young Czechoslovakian, Salo Flohr." See *Schlechter*.

DRAWN GAME

A game in which neither player wins nor loses. However, in tournament play it is scored a half-point for each side. A game is drawn in any of the following situations: 1) when the game ends in a stalemate; 2) when a player gives perpetual check to his opponent's King; 3) when the man-power of both players is so depleted that neither player can force a mate upon the other; 4) when the same position has recurred three times with the same player on the move; 5) when both players have made fifty moves each without making a capture or a Pawn move, unless it can be shown that more than fifty moves are needed to force a mate. Whatever the cause may be, a draw can always be declared by mutual agreement of both players when the conditions are such that a win for either side is unlikely. Sometimes, a strong player proposes that if the game ends in a draw, it shall be counted as a win for his weaker opponent. This is generally considered to be the least handicap a strong player can offer his opponent. See *Laws of Chess*, Article 12

DUAL

A generic term applied to problem situations where White has a choice of more than one mating move or when he can execute mate by one piece on several squares. "In an ideal problem," writes Brian Harley, "White should never have such a choice." For a fuller explanation see *The Enjoyment of Chess Problems*, and *How to Solve Chess Problems*, both by Kenneth S. Howard, and *Mate in Two Moves*, by Brian Harley.

DUB

A colloquial term which is sometimes applied to a bungling chessplayer.

Alfred Kreymborg in his *Chess Reclaims a Devotee* stated in a somewhat facetious manner; "Maybe I'm wrong but I think that the people who really enjoy chess are the *dubs* and the *duffers*, experts who have resigned their ambitions, those who play for pastime and the great fraternity of kibitzers."

DUFFER

As applied to chess, a duffer is an incompetent chessplayer.

DUMMY PAWN RULE

A rule prevalent in some foreign countries which permits a Pawn reaching the eighth rank to remain there as a stationary Pawn. This may be desirable when a player who seemingly is about to lose the game, can bring about a stalemate by advancing his Pawn to the last rank and leave it there as a motionless and powerless Pawn. In America, a player who advances his Pawn to the eighth rank has no choice in this matter. He is required to promote the Pawn to some major or minor piece.

DU MONT

Julius du Mont, a respected English chessplayer and chess writer, was born in Paris on December 15, 1881. He studied music at the Frankfort-on-Main Conservatoire and at Heidelberg and became a noted concert pianist and music teacher. When he was a young man, he moved to London, England, where he developed considerable talent for chess. He won and retained the championship of the strong Hempstead Chess Club for two years. In 1913 and 1915 he won the Middlesex chess championship. After World War I his interests were predominantly in chess journalism and chess authorship. From 1940 to 1949, du Mont was editor of the *British Chess Magazine* and for a time was also the chess editor of the *Field* and the *Manchester Guardian.* With the aid of Dr. Tartakower, he co-authored *500 Master Games of Chess* (two volumes). He translated Edward Lasker's *Chess Strategy* and Alekhine's *My Best Games of Chess* (first volume with M. E. Goldstein). Du Mont was also the author of *The Elements of Chess; The Basis of Combination in Chess;* and others. He died in a Hastings nursing home on April 7, 1956.

The *British Chess Magazine* paid the following tribute to his memory: "In the tournament room—where his presence was always welcomed—he was invariably quiet and courteous, and although gifted with a fine wit, he never used it unkindly," and "as long as a literature of chess remains, the name of Julius du Mont will not be forgotten."

DUTCH DEFENSE
1. P-Q4, P-KB4
The Dutch Defense is sometimes called the Hollandish Defense. Its origin has been traced back to 1775, when it was included in the *Traité des Amateurs.* It was elaborated upon in Stein's 1779 *Nouvel Essai sur les*

After Black's fifth move.

1. P-Q4	P-K3
2. P-QB4	P-KB4
3. P-KN3	N-KB3
4. B-N2	B-K2
5. N-KB3	0-0

Echecs. It has now been adopted by many masters, such as Botvinnik and others.

The Dutch Defense strives for a thorough-going control of the center. Tarrasch believes that the strongest reply is the Staunton's Gambit: 2. P-K4. Horowitz, however, suggests that the Dutch Defense be played as illustrated in the accompanying diagram. For other procedures and variations see *Modern Chess Openings,* Ninth Edition by Walter Korn, or *Practical Chess Openings,* by Reuben Fine.

E

ECCENTRIC OPENINGS
A general term applied to all openings which are away from the center. The term includes all openings other than a King Pawn or Queen Pawn opening move, such as, the Bird, Indian and Réti Openings. Reinfeld points out that "these openings are really suitable for adoption only by highly experienced players," because, as he observes among other reasons, "in many cases the opening moves are such that one opening can be transposed into others. This puts a premium on detailed knowledge of the openings." See *The Complete Chessplayer,* by Fred Reinfeld.

ÉCHECS
French name for chess.

ECHO MATE
In a very wide sense, the word "echo" is used in chess to mean a repetition of any particular element in a chess problem, such as, an identical type of play on squares in a different part of the chessboard. An "echo mate" is a mating position that is an "echo" or repetition of another mating position such as, a repetition of a mating posi-

tion in two or more lines of play. For a total of 300 such problems with accompanying explanatory notes and full solutions see *Tasks and Echoes,* by Alain C. White. See *Chameleon Echo Mate,* and *Monochrome Echo Mate.*

ECONOMICAL MATE

A term used by problem composers to indicate a mating situation in which every one of White's chesspieces on the board is utilized in some way, with the optional exception of the King and Pawns. See *Mirror Mate.*

ECONOMY OF FORCE

An expression first used by the famous chess problem composer Adolph Bayersdorfer (1841-1901) by which he meant the utilization of a minimum force sufficient to express an idea adequately. Whenever a given result in a problem could be obtained with fewer men or with less powerful ones, the problem is said to be constructed uneconomically. Material force must be used to the fullest extent. It is axiomatic that a major or important piece should not be used to do the work of a minor piece. Unless some additional meritorious feature is involved, a Rook, for example, should not be used to do the work which a Knight can accomplish, nor should a Bishop do the work of a Pawn. When several pieces can make a capture, the principle of "economy of force" would indicate that, everything else being equal, the capture should be made with the least powerful piece.

EDUCATION IN CHESS

Education in chess is essentially an education in independent thinking and judgment, developed as an intellectual form of relaxation and recreation. It is a type of education which is in conformity with what educators call *Worthy Use of Leisure Time*—one of

the "Cardinal Principles of Secondary Education." The goal of this form of education consists in equipping the individual with all those elements needed for the re-creation of body, mind, and spirit, and the enrichment and enlargement of one's personality.

Today, chess is considered an art as well as a science. As an artist, the chessplayer must learn how his performance on the chessboard will create emotional delight and satisfaction for himself as well as for those who observe and study his performance. As a scientist, the chessplayer must master the underlying principles and rules of the game. The eminent Dr. Emanuel Lasker pointed out in his *Manual of Chess* that "chess must not be memorized . . . You should keep in mind no names nor numbers, nor isolated incidents, not even results, but only *methods.*" Sooner or later, every chessplayer is on his own and he must then develop a creative science of his own.

To educate a person ignorant of chess so that he may attain the level of a successful player, Dr. Lasker recommends a course of study which would require:

5 hours devoted to learning
Rules of Play and Exercises

5 hours devoted to learning
Elementary Endings

10 hours devoted to learning
Some Openings

20 hours devoted to learning
Combinations

40 hours devoted to learning
Positional Play

120 hours devoted to learning
Play and Analysis

EFFECTIVE DEVELOPMENT

Moving pieces to squares where they have the needed mobility to do their best work. See *Development.*

ELEMENTS IN CHESS

The basic components of a game of chess, namely, force, space and time. *Force* is the strength and power needed for offensive and defensive maneuvers which makes itself felt through the players' chessmen. Other things being equal, the player who has the greatest force under his control, has a winning advantage. *Space* is the area, territory or terrain in which the chessmen operate. It is represented by the chessboard. The player who has his forces so well organized that they can maneuver in a larger area of the chessboard has, everything else being equal, a decided advantage over his opponent's forces which operate in a more restricted or limited space. *Time* or the speed with which a player's pieces are developed in the early part of the game constitutes, everything else being equal, a primary necessity for a successful prosecution of the game. Likewise, in the end-game, any move which gains time or saves time is always advantageous. In fact, speed in launching any attack before the opponent can mobilize his forces in the critical terrain is of paramount importance. For a further discussion on the importance of these "elements" and how they function, see *The Middle Game of Chess,* by Znosko-Borovsky.

ELEPHANT

A figurine of an "elephant" was originally used in place of our Bishop. The "elephant" is still used in Arabia, Borneo, Burma, Egypt, Ethiopia, India, Iran, Japan, China and some other oriental countries. In the Malay Islands, chess is sometimes referred to as *main gajah* i.e., the game of the elephant. See *Animals in Chess.*

END-GAME

The final phase of a game of chess. This final phase is characterized by 1) having relatively few pieces remaining on the chessboard; 2) pushing a passed Pawn on to its coronation; 3) having the King play an important offensive role; and, 4) proceeding now more cautiously than ever before in observing the all-important principle of utilizing the collective action of the remaining chess units. Nimzovitch pointed out that "eighty per cent of the whole of the end-game technique rests on combined play." Tartakower, who was considered to be one of the world's leading end-game experts, pointed out with many other chessmasters that a well-played opening game and middle game will merge imperceptibly into a satisfactory and decisive end-game. Many good books are available on this topic, such as *Manual of the Endgame,* by J. Mieses; *Basic Chess Endings,* by Reuben Fine; *How to Play Chess Endings,* by Znosko-Borovsky; *Practical End-Game Play,* by Fred Reinfeld, and many others.

ENEMY TERRITORY

Any section of the chessboard which is within easy range or under the control of the opponent. Moving onto the fifth rank is usually considered entering the enemy's territory. Moving onto the seventh and eighth ranks is regarded as being definitely within the enemy's territory.

ENGLISH NOTATION

see *Anglo-American Notation*

ENGLISH OPENING

1. P-QB4

The English Opening is the Sicilian Defense played by White. It is maintained that if the Sicilian Defense is good for Black then it should be more advantageous for White to initiate the game with this move. This opening, which was formerly known as "the Queen's Bishop's Pawn Game," became known as the English Opening because the English master Howard Staunton used it frequently in his opening plays. He used it in his matches with St. Amant of France. It was popularized by Staunton during the London Tournament of 1851.

In its strongest form, the English Opening leads by transposition into several variations. The wisdom behind this opening according to Reinfeld seems to be that "White deliberately refrains from advancing a center Pawn, partly in order to wait until Black's intentions are revealed." Reuben Fine indicates that "initially White makes no attempt to build up a Pawn center, but concentrates on speedy development." For a presentation of procedural developments of this English Opening see *Practical Chess Openings*, by Reuben Fine, or *Modern Chess Openings*, Ninth Edition, by Walter Korn.

ENGLISH SCHOOL OF PROBLEM COMPOSERS

A group of chess-problem composers in England who in general emphasized variety of play and stressed accuracy of construction to the point where it became a fetish and quite Victorian. Among the early problemists of this School who exerted a great influence were: Dr. Charles Planck (1856-1935) who published *The Chess Problem: Text-Book with Illustrations:* B. C. Laws (1861-1931) who was the problem editor of the *British Chess Magazine* for thirty-three years; and, A. F. MacKenzie (1861-1905) who lived in Jamaica.

"Mate in Three Moves" was the hobby of the earlier problemists of this School. They regarded a pure and economical mate as a mark of economical construction. Today, variety for its own sake is no longer stressed. It has given way to a greater emphasis upon the study of themes. For a fuller account of this and other Schools of chess-problem composers see *The Enjoyment of Chess Problems,* by Kenneth Howard.

EN PASSANT

A French expression meaning "in passing." The expression is used when a player exercises a capturing privilege which is exercised with one of his Pawns that has reached the fifth rank immediately after his opponent advances one of his Pawns two squares in an adjacent file. Capturing "en passant" is optional but, if exercised, it must be done immediately or not at all. In chess notation, "en passant" is recorded by the two letters "e.p."

In the accompanying illustration, White's Pawn has advanced to Q5. If Black now moves his Queen Bishop Pawn from its original position to QB4, White may then capture it immediately by saying "en passant." The effect is the same as though Black moved his Pawn to QB3 and White captured it on his next move.

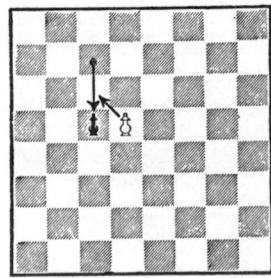

Black, on his last move, advanced his Pawn two squares. White may, on his next move, capture it, as illustrated.

This privilege of capturing "en passant" was first established about 1560, when the famous chess-loving Ruy Lopez adopted this procedure in his game. Subsequently, it was adopted in France, England and Germany. It is now in common usage. For an historical account of the capture of Pawns "en passant" see *Running the Gauntlet*, by Alain C. White, published in 1911.

EN PRISE

A French expression meaning "in taking." The term is applied to a chessman which is exposed to capture without compensation. If a player leaves a man unprotected, it is said to be *en prise*. Edward Lasker warns that "one should think twice before accepting the proffered gift." This is especially true when a strong player makes such an offer.

ÉPAULETTES MATE

The word *épaulettes* is from the French meaning "shoulder strap." An épaulettes mate is a mating situation in which the King is obstructed, on a rank or file by his own chessmen which are stationed to his right and to his left, as is shown in the accompanying illustration.

EQUIPMENT IN CHESS

The basic equipment needed to play a game of chess is a chessboard and thirty-two chessmen, sixteen of which are in a light color and sixteen in a darker color. Chessmen and chessboards are available in various sizes, colors and designs.

The importance of selecting the proper chess equipment has been stressed by all experienced chessplayers. For example, Larry Evans and Tom

Wiswell state: "We urge you to use the best equipment available. Checkers and chess are the finest hobbies and you should be proud to play these games—and show it by the paraphernalia you use." They state further that "a good player knows the value of good equipment in every sport—and refuses to use anything that is an insult to him and his pastime." They emphasize that with the expenditure of a few cents for good equipment, chessplayers "can derive a million dollars' worth of enjoyment." (From: *Championship Chess and Checkers For All*, by Larry Evans and Tom Wiswell. Copyright 1953, by A.S. Barnes & Company, Inc.)

"In selecting a board," advises Doctor Emanuel Lasker, "one with squares measuring between $1\frac{1}{2}$ and $2\frac{1}{2}$ inches will be found best suited to give a clear view of the whole battlefield. The color of the dark squares should be preferably black or a very dark brown or green, and that of the light squares should be a light tan or ivory. Very inexpensive boards of this type are obtainable in cardboard or linoleum. Naturally a wooden board is nicer, particularly if the squares are inlaid, but the cost of these boards is rather high. The same is true of chessmen. Wooden men have a nicer feel than plastic ones, but they cost more. Where the price is not a major consideration, lead-weighted men should be chosen, with the height of the King between 2 and $3\frac{1}{2}$ inches."

ETHICS IN CHESS

The science which deals with the moral goodness of human behavior during a game of chess and all other activities associated with its organization, promotion and performance. A code of ethics consists of a body of ethical principles which serves as a guide to human conduct. To be effective, a code of ethics must be formulated, accepted and respected by all those who are immediately concerned. Several individual attempts have been made to formulate a code of ethics that has immediate application to members of the chess fraternity. See *Etiquette, Chess;* and *Moralities of Chess.*

ETIQUETTE, CHESS

The display of good manners during a game of chess. Good manners consist of the observance of established rules of the game and the adherence to recognized social conventions without taking the liberty of making personal exceptions. The basic rules of chess etiquette are contained in the *Laws of Chess.*

Benjamin Franklin was the first American to express a code of chess etiquette which is contained in his *Morals of Chess,* published in 1779. In it, he states that "every circumstance that may increase the pleasure of (chess) should be regarded; and every action or word that is unfair, disrespectful, or that in any way may give uneasiness, should be avoided.

"Therefore, first, if it is agreeable to play according to the strict rules, then those rules are to be exactly observed by both parties, and should not be insisted on for one side, while deviated from by the other—for this is not equitable.

"Secondly, if it is agreed not to observe the rules exactly, but one party demands indulgencies, he should then be as willing to allow them to the other.

"Thirdly, no false move should ever be made to extricate yourself out of difficulty, or to gain an advantage. There can be no pleasure in playing with a person once detected in such unfair practice.

"Fourthly, if your adversary is long in playing, you ought not to hurry him, or express any uneasiness at his delay. You should not sing, nor whistle, nor look at your watch, nor take up a book to read, nor make a tapping with your feet on the floor, or with your fingers on the table, nor do any thing that may disturb his attention. For all these things displease; and they do not show your skill in playing, but your craftiness or your rudeness.

"Fifthly, you ought not to endeavor to amuse and deceive your adversary, by pretending to have made bad moves, and saying that you have now lost the game, in order to make him secure and careless, and inattentive to your schemes: for this is fraud and deceit, not skill in the game.

"Sixthly, you must not, when you have gained a victory, use any triumphing or insulting expression, nor show too much pleasure; but endeavor to console your adversary, and make him less dissatisfied with himself, by every kind of civil expression that may be used with truth, such as 'you understand the game better than I but you are a little inattentive;' or, ' you play too fast' or, 'you had the best of the game, but something happened to divert your thoughts, and that turned it in my favour.'

"Seventhly, if you are a spectator while others play, observe the most perfect silence. For, if you give advice, you offend both parties, him against whom you give it, because it may cause the loss of his game; him in whose favour you give it because, though it be good, and he follows it, he loses the pleasure he might have had, if you had permitted him to think until it occurred to himself. Even after a move or moves, you must not, by replacing the pieces, show how they might have been placed better; for that displeases, and may occasion disputes and doubts about their true situation. All talking to the players lessens or diverts their attention, and is therefore unpleasing. Nor should you give the least hint to either party, by any kind of noise or motion. If you do, you are unworthy to be a spectator. If you have a mind to exercise or show your judgment, do it in playing your own game, when you have the opportunity, not in criticizing, or meddling with, or counselling the play of others.

"Lastly, if the game is not to be played rigorously, according to the rules above mentioned, then moderate your desire of victory over your adversary, and be pleased with one over yourself. Snatch not eagerly at every advantage offered by his unskillfulness or inattention; but point out to him kindly, that by such a move he places or leaves a piece in danger and unsupported; that by another he will put his king in a perilous situation, etc. By this generous civility (so opposite to the unfairness above forbidden) you may, indeed, happen to lose the game to your opponent; but you will win what is better, his esteem, his respect, and his affection, together with the silent approbation and good-will of impartial spectators."

What constitutes *social decorum* among chessplayers may be gleaned also from what chessplayers point out as unbecoming or objectionable conduct during a game. See *Annoyances in Chessplay, Ethics in Chess,* and *Moralities in Chess.* See also *A Breviary of Chess,* by S. Tartakower, Chapter VI, in which he gives some "advice and observations" on the proper conduct during a game of chess.

EUWE

Dr. Machgielis (Max) Euwe, World Champion Chessplayer (1935-1937), was born in Watergraafsmeer, now part of Amsterdam, Holland, on May 20, 1901. His parents taught him the rules of chess at a very early age. From his eleventh year onward, he played in clubs and tournaments. In 1918, he entered Amsterdam University as a student of mathematics and received his doctor's degree in 1926. By profession, he is a professor of mathematics.

During his student days, he devoted his leisure moments to a thorough study of all phases of the game of chess. In August, 1921, he won the Chess Championship of Holland at Nymegen and since then he has played regularly in club tournaments and championship matches. In 1935, he defeated Alekhine in a match for the world championship title. He retained this World Championship for two years. In 1937, Alekhine re-captured the title.

Since the Second World War, Dr. Euwe has devoted himself entirely to chess. He travels all over the world, lecturing on chess, giving exhibitions and participating in tournament contests. He is a writer of books and numerous magazine articles. He is a scholar in chess openings, middle game and endings. He is a specialist and a recognized authority on chess openings. The product of his scientific studies appears in *Chess Archives,* a fortnightly publication. A few titles of books written by Dr. Euwe are: *Meet the Masters; Strategy and Tactics in Chess;* and *Judgment and Planning in Chess.*

Dr. Euwe's contemporaries are unanimous in bestowing high praise upon him as being a singularly warm, friendly gentleman, a thorough chess scholar, an artist at the chessboard, and a source of inspiration to novice chessplayers. Commenting on one of Dr. Euwe's tournament games, Dr. Reuben Fine stated that the game was "as graceful and pleasing as a Mozart symphony." C. H. O'D. Alexander observes that Dr. Euwe "has a scientific, unspectacular style which conceals a deep knowledge of every branch of the game, particularly the openings. His modesty and charm of manners make him universally popular in the chess world."

EVANS GAMBIT

1. P-K4	P-K4
2. N-KB3	N-QB3
3. B-B4	B-B4
4. P-QN4	

After White's fourth move.

A variation of the Giuoco Piano which has been named after Captain William Davies Evans who popularized this Gambit in the 1824 London-Edinburgh tournament. Captain Evans was born in Milford, England, on January 27, 1790. He was an officer in the British Navy. After his retirement, he lived a quiet life playing chess with notable people like the Grand Duke Nicholas of Russia. Captain Evans died on August 3, 1872.

The Evans Gambit occurs when White makes his fourth move: 4. P-QN4. The basic idea behind this move is, according to Dr. Lasker, "to win a move for the center, provided the proffered Pawn is taken." Tarrasch points out that "only if Black takes the Pawn, has the move any significance" for White. Reinfeld suggests that "Black's safest course is 4 . . . B-N3, seeking safety by refusing the Pawn." For an excellent use made of the Evans Gambit opening see *"Evergreen Partie."* For a discussion of the life and activities of Captain William Davies Evans see the *British Chess Magazine,* vol. 48, 1929, pages 6 to 18.

EVANS, LARRY

Larry Evans, the United States National Chess Champion of 1951-1954, an international grandmaster and chess writer, was born in New York City, on March 22, 1932. He was graduated from the College of the City of New York in 1954 where he majored in political philosophy and English literature.

Larry learned the game of chess from his brothers and loved to play chess during his school recess periods. He joined the Academy of Chess and Checkers on 42nd Street in New York City where he developed his chess-playing ability. When he was about thirteen years of age, he began to play chess more seriously. At that time he joined the famous Marshall Chess Club where he soon won the Junior Championship and before long, he became the Club's champion chessplayer. In 1948, he won the New York State Championship title. He won the United States "Open" Championship in 1951, 1952 and 1954. He also won the United States "Speed" Championship in 1950, 1951, 1952, 1953 and 1955.

Larry Evans also attained notable distinction in international chessplay. In 1950, he scored high in the Dubrovnik Olympics, in Yugoslavia. He was also a member of the 1952 United States Olympic team in Helsinki. He likewise represented the United States playing against a U.S.S.R. team in 1954 and again in Moscow in 1955. In 1956, he went at the invitation of the Yugoslav Chess Federation for a series of chess-play exhibitions in that country. On an average he won 80 per cent of his games. He was honored by the International Federation of Chess in 1952 by being awarded the distinctive title of "International Chessmaster."

During his various encounters in chessplay, he faced many Grandmasters across the chessboard, such as Mark Taimanov and David Bronstein of the U.S.S.R., and Samuel Reshevsky and Reuben Fine of the United States. The question has been asked "What distinguishes Larry Evans from the average chessplayer?" Evans replied by saying that although he is not especially combative by nature, nevertheless, in chessplay he attributes his success to "an extraordinary fierce will to win" and to the exercise of good judgment. "Judgment," he says, "consists in the ability to evaluate a position instinctively." He points out that most players "spend their lives struggling with how to win a won game, the master is concerned with how to get one." The Manhattan Chess Club *Bulletin* for February, 1955, recognizes and acknowledges the cleverness and resourcefulness of Larry Evans as a successful champion chessplayer.

Larry Evans has written several books, such as: *David Bronstein's Games of Chess; 1922 Vienna International Tournament; Trophy Chess*—an account of the Rosenwald Tournament, New York, 1954-55; and he co-authored with Tom Wiswell: *Championship Chess and Checkers For All.* He is a contributing editor of *Chess Life*—America's Chess Newspaper; and, *Chess Review*—the picture chess magazine.

"EVERGREEN PARTIE"

A poetic term, known in German as the "Immergrun Partie," was applied by Steinitz to a brilliant game by Adolf Anderssen in Berlin about a hundred years ago. (See *Partie.*) The game opens with the Evans Gambit and develops into what many chess writers and commentators hail as a game that has been played so brilliantly that it is second to none. In the *Cinéma des Echecs,* the French Master Alphonse Goetz wrote that every amateur should know this game by heart. Irving Chernev is of the opinion that beginning with the 19th move, Anderssen made that "wonderful first move of a combination which made history." Gottschall says that "this subtle and ap-

parently harmless (19th) move is the quiet key to the magnificent sacrifices which follow." Dr. Reuben Fine claims this to be "a magnificent conception, probably the most profound ever seen in over-the-chessboard at that time." This game *par excellance,* was played as follows.

1.	P-K4	P-K4
2.	N-KB3	N-QB3
3.	B-B4	B-B4
4.	P-QN4	BxP
5.	P-B3	B-R4
6.	P-Q4	PxP
7.	0-0	P-Q6
8.	Q-N3	Q-B3
9.	P-K5	Q-N3
10.	R-K1	KN-K2
11.	B-R3	P-N4
12.	QxP!!	R-QN1
13.	Q-R4	B-N3
14.	QN-Q2	B-N2
15.	N-K4	Q-B4
16.	BxQP	Q-R4
17.	N-B6 ch!	PxN
18.	PxP	R-N1
19.	QR-Q1!!	QxN
20.	RxN ch!	NxR
21.	QxP ch!!!	KxQ
22.	B-B5 db.ch.	K-K1
23.	B-Q7 ch.	K-Q1
24.	BxN mate.	

EXCHANGE OF MATERIAL

A capture and recapture of material. This give and take of material force usually signifies an even exchange. If the exchange has been profitable, the exchange is said to have been won; if not, the exchange is said to have been lost. Equal exchanges are generally in favor of the stronger party, provided there is no appreciable loss in position. Master chessplayers do not recommend exchanges unless some advantage can be gained. An exchange advantage may consist of 1) loosening up a cramped position; 2) seizing or opening a file; 3) reducing the strength of the attacker; 4) obtaining a more favorable position; or, 5) creating a discovered check which may lead to further advantages.

EXPERIENCE IN CHESS

Learning by doing. It is the acquisition of first-hand knowledge and skill from actually playing chess. Chess is easy to learn but difficult to play intelligently. When we profit from chessplay, we accumulate our chess experience. Experience can be obtained directly from our own efforts, or, vicariously, that is, profiting from the experiences of others. Direct, personal experience can be a hard and tedious way of learning; however, learning from others, either from teachers or books, can be a more economical method of learning. In the final analysis, books are silent teachers. They set down the *best* experiences of generations of experts. All of these accumulated experiences of others serve as a theoretical basis for our own experience. After all is said and done, personal experience is the final arbiter of all theory.

EXPOSED CHESSMAN

A chessman stationed on a square where he is laid open to attack. He is deprived of adequate protection.

F

FAIRY CHESS

A generic term used and popularized by the late T. R. Dawson of England. He applied this fanciful term to any type or form of chessplay which deviated from the conventional or orthodox equipment or procedure. According to Dawson, the name "fairy chess" was invented by H. Tate, of Melbourne. Chessplayers who experiment with novel chessboards or chessmen which function differently from what has been established and specified in the standard "Laws of Chess" are toying

with what Dawson would call "fairy chess."

To promote an interest in this type of of chessplay, T. R. Dawson founded *The Fairy Chess Review* which may now be obtained for 10 shillings per year (6 issues) by writing to The Fairy Chess Review, 49 Manor Street, Middlesborough, Yorkshire, England. See *Unorthodox Chess*.

FALKBEER COUNTER GAMBIT

1.	P-K4	P-K4
2.	P-KB4	P-Q4

This counter gambit was developed by the Austrian chessmaster Ernst Falkbeer, who was born in Brunn, in 1819 and died in Vienna, in 1885. This opening usually continues as is illustrated in the accompanying diagram. The wisdom behind this counter gambit is, as Horowitz points out, "for Black to ruin White's chances of establishing a strong center and of opening the King Bishop file and the normal diagonal of the Queen Bishop." Although Black loses a Pawn in this attempt, nevertheless, he is decidedly superior in the center. Marshall indicates that this opening "is considered by many leading players to give Black the better game." For procedural development of this counter gambit see

After Black's fourth move.

1. P-K4	P-K4
2. P-KB4	P-Q4
3. PxQP	P-K5
4. P-Q3	N-KB3

Modern Chess Openings, Ninth Edition, by Walter Korn, or *Practical Chess Openings,* by Reuben Fine.

FALSE MOVE

Moving a chessman contrary to the established procedure specified in the Laws of Chess; such as, castling when the King has been moved or is in check, or, moving a Rook diagonally. See *Illegal Move.*

"FAMILY CHECK"

A term employed by Bogoljubow when a Knight simultaneously checks and attacks a King and a group of several other pieces. This is illustrated in the accompanying diagram where the Knight is giving a check to the King and at the same time is attacking the Queen and the two Rooks.

FANTASY VARIATION

A move in the Caro-Kann Defense opening by which White (after 1. P-K4, P-QB3; 2. P-Q4, P-Q4) attempts to launch a gambit attack by playing 3. P-KB3.

FEATHERBED SOLDIERS

An expression sometimes applied to undeveloped pieces.

FÉDÉRATION INTERNATIONALE DES ÉCHECS

French phraseology for "International Federation of Chess." It is the highest official authority throughout the whole world of chess on all matters pertaining to international administration and interpretation of the Laws of Chess. The need for such an organization grew out of sheer force of necessity. Prior to the 1920' chess regulations applied to international tournaments and world championship matches, were left to the capriciousness of individuals. A world champion could decide whether he would accept, decline or ignore any chessplayer's request for a match which would challenge his world championship title. It became apparent that arrangements for championship matches should be removed from the whims and fancies of the champion and be vested in some governing body of the chess fraternity. In 1922, a body of Rules was drawn up in London which endeavored to correct this situation, but it applied only to the masters who subscribed to these London Rules. Hence, there was a felt need for a more universal and higher authority. As a result, at a chess Congress, held in Zurich in 1922, the Fédération Internationale des Echecs was established. The first President was Dr. A. Ruel from Holland. This F.I.D.E. grew in size, power and influence.

At present, it has as its members all of the official Chess Federations of about forty leading countries throughout the world. Each member federation pays to F.I.D.E. a fee which is calculated on the basis of its total membership. It is now the general practice to hold an annual congress at which the delegates from each national federation discuss the business of F.I.D.E. Since the Second World War, the F.I.D.E. has taken over the organization and procedure for finding the most promising candidate who might challenge the reigning World Champion. This is done in a four-year cycle. For administrative convenience, the International Federation has divided the chess world into various zones. In the first year of the four-year cycle, zonal tournaments are held throughout the world. Winners may participate in an inter-zonal tournament which is held the second year. In the third year, a "Candidate's Tournament" is held which is limited to the five finalists from each of the interzonal tournaments and the five highest scoring players from the previously held "Candidates' Tournament." The winner of this "Candidates' Tournament" plays a match, in the fourth year, with the World Champion for the World Championship title.

When the 23rd Congress of the Federation met in Stockholm in 1952, a final set of the "Laws of Chess" was adopted. These laws were amended at the 24th Congress which met in Schaffhausen, Switzerland, in 1953. This final version is now "strictly applied throughout the whole world of chess." The President of F.I.D.E. is (at the time this book goes to press) Mr. Folke Rogard of Kungstradgardagatan 16, Stockholm, Sweden.

FEGATELLO ATTACK

1. P-K4	P-K4
2. N-KB3	N-QB3
3. B-B4	N-B3
4. N-N5	P-Q4
5. PxP	NxP
6. NxBP	KxN

After Black's sixth move.

"Fegatello" comes from the Italian word *fegato*, meaning liver. Many use the term "Fried Liver Attack" in place of "Fegatello Attack."

This is an attack which occurs in the Two Knights' Defense. The critical move is 5 . . . NxP. This gives White an attacking opportunity, the defense to which is difficult. White sacrifices a Knight with the result that the black King is forced to journey out into the open where he is exposed to dangers.

FIANCHETTO

A term derived from the Italian word *fiancata*, meaning a "side or broadside blow." Ponziani (1719-1796) called every opening in which a side-wing Pawn was used, a fianchetto. Today, this term is applied to a flank or side development of a Bishop. A Bishop developed on N2 is said to be "fianchettoed." To play a Bishop to N2 is to "fianchetto a Bishop." Both the King's Bishop as well as the Queen's Bishop may be fianchettoed by moving the King's Bishop to KN2 and moving the Queen's Bishop to QN2. See *Queen's Indian Defense.*

The purpose of the fianchetto form of development is for the Bishop to control the vital center from the wing and to allow him to exert his influence on a commanding diagonal. The effectiveness of this development depends on the support the Bishop can receive from the rest of his fellow chessmen. By himself, the fianchettoed Bishop is relatively weak; with the cooperation of other forces, he is powerful.

F. I. D. E.

A short designation for "Fédération Internationale des Echecs" which is the official World or International Chess Federation. See *Fédération Internationale des Echecs.*

FIFTY MOVES RULE

The rule which states (*Laws of Chess*, Article 12, section 4) that "when a player having the move demonstrates that at least fifty moves have been made by each side without the capture of any man, or the movement of any Pawn" the game may be declared a draw. In practical application, Capablanca in his *Chess Fundamentals* points out "that at any time you may demand that your opponent mate you within fifty moves. However, every time a piece is exchanged or a Pawn advanced the counting must begin afresh."

FILE

A file is any one of the eight rows of squares running vertically between the two players. Each file receives its name from the piece standing on it at the opening of the game, as is illustrated in the accompanying diagram. Accordingly, the file on which the Rook stands on the Queen's side is always referred to as the Queen Rook's (QR) file; the file on which the Knight stands on the Queen's side is always referred to as the Queen Knight's (QN) file; and so on with the other files. Observe

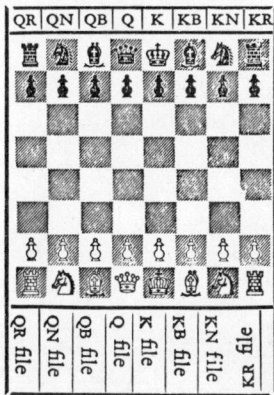

that the name of any file is always the same for both players. A Bishop's file, for example, is always called a Bishop's file regardless of where the Bishop moves.

Reference is frequently made to an "open file," a "flank file," and a "center file." When a file is unoccupied, it is said to be an "open file."

FINE

Dr. Reuben Fine, a Grandmaster chessplayer and one of the world's great authorities on chess, was born in New York City on October 11, 1914. By profession, he is a psychoanalyst. He received his Doctor of Philosophy degree in the field of psychology.

Dr. Fine learned to play chess when he was about ten years of age. Towards the end of his senior high school days, he joined the famous Marshall Chess Club in New York City, where he soon won the club's Junior Championship. After his graduation from the College of the City of New York, in 1933, he played successfully in city, state, national and international tournaments. From 1936 to 1939, Fine participated in numerous European tournaments and exhibitions. His major success came at the A.V.R.O. Tournament in Holland, in 1938, where he tied for first prize with Keres and won twice from the World Champion Alekhine. In 1942, 1943 and 1944, he won the United States Lightning Chess Championship, playing at the rate of ten seconds per move. He also demonstrated his tremendous chessplaying ability in the spring of 1933, when he played eight games blindfolded at the Old Hungarian Chess Club in New York City.

In addition to his note-worthy performances across the chessboard, he is also well-known for his significant contributions to the existing chess literature. Among the many books which Dr. Fine published in his own name are *Practical Chess Openings, Ideas Behind the Chess Openings, The Middle Game in Chess, Basic Chess Endings, Chess Marches On!* He has been Associate Editor of *Chess Review* since 1941. His writings are buttressed by innumerable examples and illustrations.

His chess colleagues hold Dr. Fine in high esteem. The profundity of his chess knowledge and his great love for the game are apparent throughout his writings. Edward Lasker, one of America's leading chess masters and President of the Marshall Chess Club, writes that Dr. Fine "is truly of World Championship caliber." See *Practical Chess Openings*.

FIRST AND SECOND PLAYER

The person who has the first move is called the first player and is usually said to play at the opening an offensive game. The one who moves next is termed the second player and is usually said to play at the opening a defensive game.

FIRST MOVE

The initial move made in a game by the player using the white chessmen. At the outset, it is customary for one of the players to take a white and a black Pawn in his hands and, after "shuffling" them, he holds one Pawn in each hand so that they are not visible, and then invites his opponent to select one of these Pawns. The color of the Pawn selected determines the color of his chessmen in the game to be played. In subsequent games, each player uses the chessmen of the opposite color. Other arrangements may be made. In many chess clubs, it is considered good etiquette that when a distinguished chessplayer visits the club, he automatically is offered, as an act of courtesy, the white chessmen so that he may have the first move.

FISCHER, ROBERT

United States Chess Champion (1958—) and chess prodigy of Brooklyn, New York. Bobby Fischer came into prominence as a strong chessplayer when he was twelve years of age by winning the Class B Trophy in the Greater New York Open Championship. His playing strength was noticeably augmented in subsequent tournaments held at Philadelphia, Oklahoma City, Washington, Milwaukee, San Francisco, and Cleveland where he won the U.S. (Open) Championship title.

In the last few days of 1957, the United States Chess Federation sponsored a United States chess championship tournament in New York City. Here, Bobby Fischer finished ahead of Reshevsky and others. Thus, at the age of fourteen, Bobby became the current U.S. Chess Champion chessplayer. In September 1958, Bobby qualified at Portoroz, Yugoslavia, as an International Grandmaster. "It is not mere magniloquence to suggest," comments Arthur Bisguier, "that he (Bobby Fischer) is the strongest fourteen year old chessplayer who has ever lived."

FISKE

Daniel Willard Fiske, chess organizer, author and journalist, was born in Ellisburg, New York, on November 11, 1831. He was educated at Cazenovia Seminary, Hamilton College and the University of Upsala, Sweden. When he was twenty years of age, he was associated with the United States Legation at Copenhagen. In 1852, he returned to the United States and accepted a position in the Astor Library in New York City. Five years later, he organized the first American Chess Congress which met from October 5th to November 10th, 1857, with Paul Morphy winning the first prize. A book containing a full account of this Congress with all games played and other items of interest was edited by Fiske and was published in 1859 by Rudd and Carleton of New York, and by Sampson Low, Sons and Company, in London. In 1861, Fiske became an attaché to the United States Legation in Vienna. In time, he traveled throughout Europe and eventually he returned to the United States where he joined the academic ranks of Cornell University as a Professor of North European Languages. After his wife's death, he lived in Florence, Italy. He died at Frankfort-on-the-Main, on September 17, 1904.

Fiske served as Editor of the *Chess Monthly* magazine. He was also influential in establishing a chess magazine in Iceland. Among his other chess writings, Fiske was the author of such books as *Chess in Iceland and in Icelandic Literature,* and *Chess Tales and Chess Miscellanies.*

FIVE-MINUTE CHESS GAME

A procedure of playing chess whereby both players agree at the beginning of a game that, when making a move, neither player exceeds his opponent's time by more than five minutes.

"FIVE-SQUARE-MOVE"

An expression of purely historical interest which was used before 700 A. D. It referred to a move made on the chessboard by the elephant which was then called in Sanskrit: *gaji.* This gaji, or elephant, could make a move which symbolically represented his five limbs, namely his trunk and four legs. Accordingly, the *gaji* could move to any of the five squares: one square forward or to any one of the diagonal squares. This square immediately in front was symbolic of the elephant's trunk and the four diagonal squares signified the animal's four legs. This, however, was later changed when the *gaji* was replaced by the modern Bishop and his moves were restricted to the diagonals of one color.

FLIGHT SQUARE

A square to which a King may flee to safety at a time of attack. In the position given on the accompanying diagram, Black's King is in check. He cannot capture White's Queen because it is protected by the Rook, nor can Black interpose a piece between the White's checking Queen and his King. His only possible move is to flee to R1, his "flight square." There is a tendency among some chessplayers to provide a "flight square" for the King, after castling on the King's wing, by moving P-KR3.

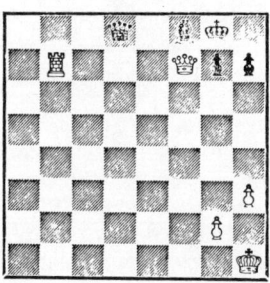

FLOHR

Salo Flohr, a Russian chessmaster, was born in Horodenka, Russian Poland, on November 21, 1908. During the first world war, he moved to Czechoslovakia but after the second world war, he became a naturalized citizen of the U.S.S.R. He began chess tournament play in 1929 and soon became conspicuous as one of the most formidable masters of his time. During his stay in Czechoslovakia, Flohr gained immense popularity. Dr. Fine observes in *The World's Great Chess Games* that there were Flohr pastries, Flohr cigars, and other items named after this national chess hero.

In his earlier years, Flohr developed tremendous skill at rapid chessplay, but in later years, he became an extremely cautious player, apparently making "safety first" his guiding principle. Reinfeld is of the opinion that Flohr is noted for his end-game technique, his almost flawless positional judgment, his patient maneuvering ability and his wonderful sensitivity to the slightest hostile weakness.

FOOL'S MATE

1. P-KB3, P-K4;
2. P-KN4, Q-R5 mate.

A name applied to a game of chess which is terminated in two moves without making a single capture. Tartakower refers to it as the "hara kiri" game of chess. In this game, White's moves have no logical plan, they do not develop his pieces, and above all, they ignore the most fundamental rule of chess, namely, "the King must be safeguarded at all times."

FOOT SOLDIER

The term "foot soldier" is used in place of our Pawn in China, Hungary, India, Iran, Japan, Korea, Poland and other countries.

FORCE

The power a chessplayer expresses through his chessmen. It is one of the basic elements in a game of chess. See *Elements in Chess*.

FORCED GAME

A game in which a player is caught in a position where no matter what move he makes, he can not escape certain defeat. A "forced game" is also referred to as a "forced won game." See *Maidens' Game* which in the history of chess, was also referred to as a "Forced Game."

FORCED MOVE

A move which a player is compelled to make. This may occur when there is only one possible move available for the King to get out of check, or, when there is only one legal move a player can make without going into check. The term is sometimes applied to a necessary move which will prevent a decisive loss of material or position.

FORCES

A broad collective term applied to the pieces and Pawns which each player has at his disposal. They are symbols of force and power. The term may be used to designate the different areas in which these men are used; the quality of the men, or their attachments, such as the center forces, superior or inferior forces, the White or Black forces, the King's forces, the Queen's forces, and others.

FORESIGHT

The ability to visualize in one's mind a number of moves and to analyze their consequences before the moves are actually made on the chessboard. Dr. Emanuel Lasker attributed the success of his chess career to this ability. He pointed out that "victory in a game of chess belongs to him who sees a little farther than his adversary." How far is "a little farther?" Znosko-Borovsky says: "It is impossible to foresee all future moves in a game of chess; be satisfied if you can conceive a more or less extended series of moves which represent a logical plan." Réti is of the opinion that to be able to calculate two moves ahead is enough to play like a master. Dr. Fine is of the same opinion. He says, "The best course to follow is to note the major consequences for two moves." When Janowsky was asked how far he saw ahead, he replied: "Only one move—the best move!"

FORK

A term used to describe a double attack made in different directions. Such a simultaneous attack can be executed by any piece or Pawn, except a Rook Pawn. In the accompanying diagram, the Queen has forked the Bishop and Knight. One of them will

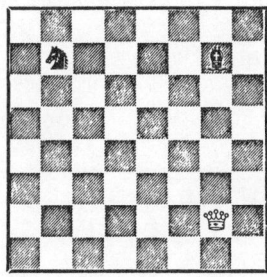

be captured on White's next move. A forking situation can be counteracted only by a violent move, such as, eliminating the threatening piece, launching a more devastating counter-attack, giving check, or threatening mate. For a brief statement and seventy-three illustrations of "Knight Forks" see Chapter 2, in *1001 Brilliant Chess Sacrifices and Combinations*, by Fred Reinfeld. See also an article entitled "Queen Forks" by Kenneth Harkness in *Chess Review*, June-July, 1946. See *Double Attack*.

FORKING CHECK

An attack upon a King and another chess unit at the same time. Since the rule of priority of check prevails, the King must be extricated from the "forking check" regardless of conse-

quences. In the accompanying illustration, Black's Knight has forked his

opponent's Queen and King. The King is in check. He must move. The Queen will be captured.

FORSYTH NOTATION

A "short-hand" method of recording positions on a chessboard without the use of a diagram. It was named after its inventor, David Forsyth, of Glasgow, Scotland, who eventually emigrated to New Zealand where he died at Dunedin on December 30, 1909. The method consists of recording what chess unit, if any is located on every square on every rank. When a square is occupied by a chessman, its symbol is written with a small letter for Black and a capital letter for White. Figures are used to record the number of vacant squares. For example, Black's fourth rank shows that beginning at the left, two squares are unoccupied, so the figure two is written in the Forsyth Notation; next, the Bishop is recorded by its symbol "b" (small letter for Black, capital letter for White); then one vacant square as 1; followed by

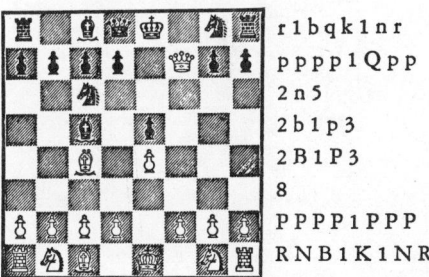

	r 1 b q k 1 n r
	P P P P 1 Q P P
	2 n 5
	2 b 1 p 3
	2 B 1 P 3
	8
	P P P P 1 P P P
	R N B 1 K 1 N R

a Pawn which is recorded as "p"; and, finally the three unoccupied squares are indicated by the number 3. Since every square must be accounted for either by a number or symbol of the chessman across the board, every rank must add up to 8. The accompanying illustration shows how the Forsyth Notation is used in recording the situation appearing on the diagram.

FOUNDATION, SOUND

A sound foundation is one which is laid in the opening phase of a game according to proven principles and procedures so that no structural weaknesses are present. The Pawn skeleton constitutes the basic foundation of a chess opening.

FOUR-HANDED CHESS

A game of chess in which four players participate as two groups of two partners each. They play as two allied nations waging a battle against two opposing allied nations. Each player begins the game with one King, one Bishop, one Knight, one Rook and four Pawns. There is no Queen. The opening position is shown in the accompanying diagram. The diagonal players are partners, that is, the Red and Yellow play as a team against the

Black

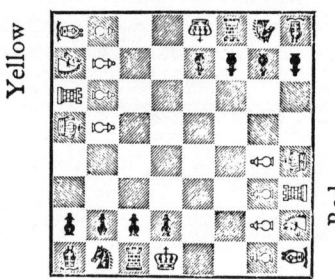

Yellow

Red

Green

Green and Black. When one player loses his King, his partner takes over the command of the remaining forces.

Whether Four-Handed Chess was the original primeval Hindu chess, known as *chatarrajah* is not known. However, Davidson in his *A Short History of Chess* states that the originator of the four-handed theory probably was Hiram Cox when he advanced this theory in an article on Burmese Chess published in *Asiatic Researches,* vol. 7, page 486, London,

1801. For a more detailed discussion of the earliest forms of "Four-handed Chess," see *A History of Chess,* by H. J. R. Murray, pages 58, and 69 to 75. See *Frere's Four-Handed Chess.*

FOUR KNIGHTS' GAME

1.	P-K4	P-K4
2.	N-KB3	N-QB3
3.	N-B3	N-B3

A solid, symmetrical opening which, as Reinfeld points out is a safe but dull opening and is very likely to lead to a draw. This opinion is confirmed by Horowitz, who adds that "this opening appeals to the conservative-minded player." Walter Korn in his MCO, Eighth Edition, comments that "first-class players have resorted much more to other openings where the problems to be faced create greater winning chances."

For an early index of the Four Knights' Game and variations see *Chess Digest* by Mordecai Morgan, Vol. 1, Part ii. For a more modern citation of the Four Knights' Game and variations, see *Modern Chess Openings,* Ninth Edition, by Walter Korn, or *Practical Chess Openings,* by Reuben Fine.

FRACTIONAL NOTATION

A method of recording the moves of a game whereby a White's move is written as the numerator and a Black's move as the denominator. The following three moves are recorded in columns and in the corresponding "fractional" method.

White	Black	Fractional Notation
1. P-K4	P-K4	1. $\dfrac{\text{P to K4}}{\text{P to K4}}$
2. N-KB3	N-QB3	2. $\dfrac{\text{N to KB3}}{\text{N to QB3}}$
3. B-N5	P-QR3	3. $\dfrac{\text{B to N5}}{\text{P to QR3}}$

FRANKLIN

Benjamin Franklin (1706-1790) was the first American to bring the game of chess into prominence in this country. Chess was one of his lifelong hobbies. Carl Van Doren reported that at times, Franklin became so absorbed in chess that he played it from six in the evening until sunrise. In 1779, Franklin wrote an essay entitled, *Morals of Chess,* in which he pointed out that by playing chess we learn that:

"The game of chess is so interesting in itself, as not to need the view of gain to induce engaging in it; and thence it is never played for money. Those, therefore, who have leisure for such diversion, cannot find one that is more innocent . . .

"The game of Chess is not merely an ideal amusement; several very valuable qualities of the mind, useful in the course of human life, are to be acquired and strengthened by it, so as to become habits ready on all occasions, for life is a kind of Chess, in which we have points to gain, and competitors or adversaries to contend with, and in which there is a vast variety of good and ill events, that are, in some degree, the effects of prudence, or the want of it. By playing chess then, we learn:

"1st. Foresight, which looks a little into futurity, and considers the consequences that may attend an action; for it is continually occurring to a player, 'If I move this Piece, what will be the advantage or disadvantage of my new situation? What use can my adversary make of it to annoy me? What other moves can I make to support it, and to defend myself from his attacks?'

"2d. Circumspection, which surveys the whole Chessboard, or scene of action—the relation of the several Pieces, and their situations; the dangers they are repeatedly exposed to; the several possibilities of their aiding each other; the probabilities that the adversary may make this or that move, and attack this or that Piece, and what different means can be used to avoid his stroke, or turn its consequences against him.

"3rd. Caution, not to make our moves too hastily. This habit is best acquired by observing strictly the laws of the game; such as, if you touch a Piece, you must move it somewhere; if you set it down, you must let it stand . . .

"And lastly, we learn by Chess the habit of not being discouraged by present bad appearances in the state of our affairs; the habit of hoping for a favorable change, and that of persevering in the search of resources. The game is full of events, there is such a variety of turns in it, the fortune of it is so full of vicissitudes, and one so frequently, after contemplation, discovers the means of extricating one's self from a supposed unsurmountable difficulty, that one is encouraged to continue the contest to the last, in hopes of victory from our skill; or at least from the negligence of our adversary; and whoever considers, what in Chess he often sees instances of, that success is apt to produce presumption and its consequent inattention by which the loss may be recovered, will learn not to be too much discouraged by any present success of his adversary, nor to despair of final good fortune upon every little check he receives in the pursuit of it." See *Etiquette, Chess* for a statement of Franklin's views on the conduct to be observed in playing a game of chess.

FRATERNITY, CHESS

Chess fraternity is a broad collective concept which embraces all chessplayers and lovers of the game of chess.

FREEBOROUGH

Edward Freeborough, an English chess compiler, theorist and writer, was born in Hull, England, on August 18, 1830. He was an accountant by profession, and after gaining some experience as an employee of several concerns, he eventually started his own business.

The Town of Hull was a leading chess center which attracted many chess notables. In time, Freeborough became a very active member of the Hull Chess Club which he served as its Secretary and subsequently as its President. Eventually, the Hull Chess Association was founded and Mr. Freeborough was elected as its President and re-elected on three subsequent occasions. In 1868, he entered the Chess Problem Tourney of the Paris Congress where he was ranked as the fourth best chess problem composer.

As a chessplayer, Freeborough displayed distinct individuality. He developed brilliant combinations and was fond of developing masked attacks. It was said that he played with his brain rather than from memory. In a word, he was a player with chess ideas.

As a chess analyst, he earned the respect of the great chess fraternity. He devoted six years to the study of the literature of the game and chessplay. His chief reputation rests upon his contributions to the literature of chess openings and chess endings. In col-

laboration with the Reverend C. E. Ranken (1828-1905) he published *Chess Openings—Ancient and Modern*. It was stated in the *British Chess Magazine* that this compilation "is wonderfully accurate, while on nearly every page are signs of originality and independent research and study." In 1896, Freeborough published a book entitled: *Chess Endings*. He also wrote a series of articles for the *Gentleman's Journal*, and was also a contributor to the *British Chess Magazine*.

His death on September 14, 1896, was considered "a loss to the chess world." The *British Chess Magazine* commented that as "a brilliant writer with a rare power of phraseology and a wide general knowledge, Mr. Freeborough has enriched the pages of the *British Chess Magazine* with many lively contributions."

FREE CASTLING

A method of castling adopted by Roman chessplayers sometime after 1600. Accordingly, the King was free to move to any square along the first rank up to and including the Rook square, and the Rook was then to be placed on the other side of the King up to and including the King's square. In the seventeenth century, it was fashionable to move the King's Rook to KB1 and the King to KR1. This castling privilege could be exercised as long as the King remained unmoved and subject to the restrictions of not giving check. Nor could the King or Rook take up a position of attacking any hostile man during the process of castling. This "free castling" technique is also referred to by some writers as the *"Italian method of castling,"* or *Free rochade.*

FREEING MOVE

A move which releases a chessman which has been pinned, or, a move which opens up a cramped position so as to give mobility to the hampered chessmen. Nimzovitch, however, warns that "there is no such thing as an absolute freeing move."

FREE ROCHADE
see *Free Castling*

FRENCH DEFENSE
1. P-K4, P-K3

This opening has been mentioned by Lucena in his treatise published in 1497. D. G. Morgan, writing in the *British Chess Magazine,* indicates that the name of the French Defense can be traced back to the correspondence match between London and Paris in 1834. A member of this Parisian team was a strong amateur named Chamouillet, a chess habitué of the Café de la Régence. He persuaded his team that when the English team plays 1. P-K4, the French team should reply with "King Pawn one square." Morgan stated that "this was done. Paris won the game and the opening gained its name."

After Black's second move.

1. P-K4   P-K3
2. P-Q4   P-Q4

The French Defense opening initiates a struggle for the center. If the play continues, as it frequently does, with 2. P-Q4, P-Q4 (see diagram), then White obtains an advantage in that both of his Bishops have outlets for action, whereas, Black's Queen Bishop is immobilized for a time. Although

Black's position is temporarily cramped, he has a stable position and possibilities for counterplay. Horowitz and Reinfeld point out that the French Defense is more conservative than the Sicilian and that "the French is well-suited to the style of tenacious defensive players."

Since, as stated above, this opening often continues with 2. P-Q4, P-Q4; the game may then branch out into several variations, such as, to mention only a few:

Albin-Chatard Attack: 3. N-QB3; N-KB3; 4. B-KN5, B-K2; 5. P-K5, KN-Q2; 6. P-KR4..

McCutcheon's Variation: 3. N-QB3, N-KB3; 4. B-KN5, B-N5;

Winawer Variation: 3. N-QB3, B-N5;

Nimzovitch Variation: 3. P-K5;

Tarrasch Variation: 3. N-Q2.

For further procedural development of this French Defense and many more variations, see *Modern Chess Openings,* Ninth Edition, by Walter Korn; or, *Practical Chess Openings,* by Dr. Reuben Fine.

FRERE'S FOUR-HANDED CHESS

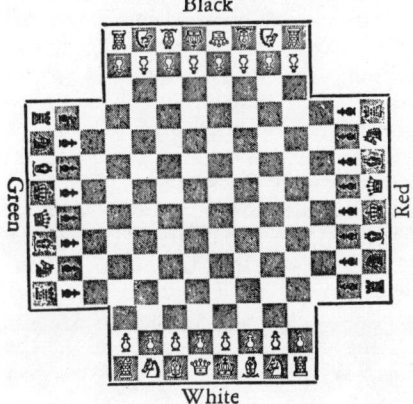

A four-handed game of chess recorded in Frere's *Chess Hand Book* published in 1858. It is played on a

board of 160 squares. Each of the four players has his own set of regular chessmen. The opening position of the game is indicated on the accompanying diagram. In the opening, the Kings are always placed on the same file as their partner's Queens—each King faces his partner's Queen. Black and White are partners and play as allied nations against their opponent allies who play with the Red and Green chessmen. White always has the first move, then Green, Black and Red; that is, the move always passes to the player at the left.

The object of the game is to checkmate both of the opponents' Kings. A partner must come to the aid of his allied partner whenever danger threatens. When a King is in check, his partner must, if he can, get his friendly King out of check. If this can not be done, the next player will mate the King and remove him from the board. The remaining forces retain their positions and become part of the allied King's forces.

Pawns move only one square at all times. They move straight ahead and capture to the side. When a partner's Pawns meet each other in the same file, they are allowed to jump over the allied Pawn, without removing it, and continue as usual. When a Pawn reaches his allied King's rank, he becomes a "Capped Pawn." (Tie a string around the Pawn.) A "Capped Pawn" moves back, one square at a time, in the direction from where it started at the beginning of the game. It is then "de-capped" and moves forward again as it did in the very beginning. Should a Pawn reach any of the extreme end squares of the enemies' territories, it becomes a Queen.

FRIED LIVER ATTACK

see *Fegatello Attack*

FRINGE PIECE

A term in common usage among chess problemists when they refer to a chess piece which is not essential to the solution of a problem. A "fringe Piece" is generally used to complicate a problem. It may be removed without affecting the basic soundness or the thematic development of the problem.

FRINGE VARIATION

Any variation which utilizes one or more "fringe pieces." Such a variation has no relation to the theme of the problem nor does it spring spontaneously from the chess pieces needed to present the theme of the problem. It has no effect upon the solution of a problem.

FROM'S GAMBIT

A center gambit which Mr. From of Denmark popularized. Martin S. From (1828-1895) was a strong chessplayer and chess analyst. In 1865 he organized the Copenhagen Chess Club and served as its first President. The From Gambit is more generally known as the Danish Gambit. Commenting on this gambit, Howard Staunton says: "This conception is highly ingenious, but against the best defence the attack succumbs." See *Danish Gambit*.

FRONTIER

An imaginary line of departure from which a Pawn enters into enemy territory. It may be said to run in the open-

The Frontier Line

ings of all games between the fourth and fifth ranks of the chessboard, as is indicated in the accompanying illustration.

G

GAMBIT

An opening maneuver by which a Pawn is offered in order to obtain a better position, to break up the opponent's center, or to set the stage for an early and/or more effective attack. A gambit is usually associated with a Pawn sacrifice although occasionally a piece may be involved.

In offering a gambit, the player assumes a calculated risk. He sacrifices material for the gaining of time or space or for some other subsequent advantage. Dr. Euwe points out that "the outstanding feature which characterizes a true gambit is that neither side knows for a certainty what he will be up against." Hence, some writers suggest that "as a general principle, it is always best to accept a gambit," on the other hand, some believe that it is preferable to decline a gambit when one has a choice, because accepting it means spending time upon the capture of a Pawn instead of development.

The term gambit was brought into chess vocabulary by Lopez, who originally applied it to the Damiano Gambit. The word itself is derived from the Italian word *gamba,* meaning a leg; and *gambitare,* meaning to set traps. Italian wrestlers speak of *gambitare,* by which they mean to set traps to catch the legs. For a historical survey of gambits in chess, dealing with their classifications, themes, sequences and traps, see *Gambits Accepted: a survey of opening sacrifices,* by L. Elliott Fletcher.

GAMBIT PAWN

The Pawn sacrificed by the first player in the opening game. In a game which opens: 1. P-K4, P-K4; 2. P-KB4, PxP; the Pawn advanced by White at his second move, is called a "Gambit Pawn."

GAMBITTO GRANDE
see *Kieseritzky Gambit.*

GELBFUHS SYSTEM
see *Sonneborn-Berger System*

"GENERAL"
The term "General" is used in some oriental countries (China, Korea, etc.) in place of our King. In other countries (Burma, Japan, etc.) it is used in place of our Queen.

GENERALITIES IN CHESS
Common ideas which, when everything is considered in a game of chess, are believed to be the best serviceable guides. These ideas have come into common usage as a result of tried and tested experiences of master chessplayers who have accepted the same basic objectives in chess procedures. "Generalities" serve as the backbone of chess theory and not as specific rules of routine procedure. Hence, when making practical and specific application of generalities in a game of chess, every phase of the game and every move must be considered on its merits.

GERMAN NOTATION
see *Algebraic Notation.*

GERMAN SCHOOL OF PROBLEM COMPOSERS
A group of chess problem composers who followed the precepts and influence of German problemists. Because of a change of emphasis in their presentations, these problemists may, for descriptive convenience, be grouped into 1) the Old German School; 2) the Transitional School; and 3) the Modern German School.

1. The Old German School emphasized the artistic element of a problem. They stressed "art for art's sake" in chess problems. Their main line of play consisted in presenting elaborate compositions in which they combined strategic maneuvering, difficulty of solutions and purity of mate. Their chief advocates were Dr. Johann N. Berger (1845-1933); Dr. Conrad Bayer (1828-1897); Philipp Klett (1833-1910) and their disciples. In 1884, Dr. Berger published the ideals of this School in his book: *Das Schachproblem, und dessen Kunstgerechte Dartstellung.* These German problemists were soon joined by the Rev. J. Jesperson (1848-1914) of Denmark; Emil Pradignat (1831-1912) of France and others from nearby countries. This led some writers to refer to this entire group of problemists as "The Continental School of Chess Problem Composers."

2. The Transitional School emphasized the aesthetic element of a problem. The adherents of this School were led by Johannes Kohtz (1843-1918) and Karl Kockelhorn (1843-1914). They maintained that the development of a theme was of paramount importance to a problem.

3. The Modern German School emphasized the intellectual element of a problem. These modern, twentieth century composers are more concerned with the development of critical moves in strategic themes rather than with the format of a problem.

For a fuller explanation of this and other schools of problem composers, see *The Enjoyment of Chess Problems,* by Kenneth Howard. See *Schools of Chess.*

GIANUTIO

The inventor of the Two Knights' Defense and a sixteenth century author whose writings contain what had already been published by Damiano and Lopez.

GIMMICK IN CHESS

A clever tricky play or situation such as a trap, pitfall or swindle which seems sound and logical but has a catch to it. It is a cunning way of luring a player to make a move which will result in disastrous consequences. On the surface, a chess gimmick usually seems to be a plausible exception to a generally accepted principle. Horowitz and Reinfeld devote an entire book to chess gimmicks under the title of *Chess Traps, Pitfalls and Swindles.*

GIUOCO PIANO

1.	P-K4	P-K4
2.	N-KB3	N-QB3
3.	B-B4	B-B4

One of the earliest recorded openings which dates back to the time when fifteenth century Italian chessplayers were most active and influential. The name of this opening consists of two Italian words; namely, *giuoco* meaning: game; and *piano* meaning soft or quiet. Hence this is a quiet opening game in which strategical development of the forces proceeds in a methodical and easy manner for both sides. Dr. Fine

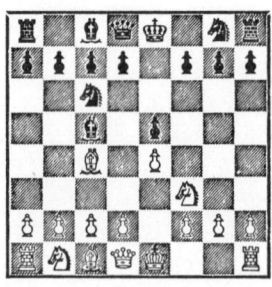

points out that this opening is not seen often in modern tournaments "because Black has too much defensive latitude." Horowitz believes that this opening "should appeal to the type of player whose imagination occasionally runs rampant." For a fuller presentation of the procedural development of this opening see *Modern Chess Openings*, Ninth Edition, by Walter Korn; or *Practical Chess Openings*, by Reuben Fine.

"GO"

A Japanese game which is considered by some writers as a competitor of the game of chess, and by others as a Japanese version of our game of chess. Actually, GO differs from chess in the following respects:

GO	SYOGI (Japanese word for Chess)
1. GO is played on a square board having 19 equidistant parallel lines which are crossed at right angles by 19 similar lines.	1. Syogi is played on a square board which contains 64 equally sized squares and which are alternately colored "black" and "white."
2. Each player has 181 "stones" or disks which are placed on unoccupied points where the lines intersect.	2. Each player has 16 chessmen, not all of which have the same function.
3. GO is democratic in spirit. There is no distinction between one "stone" and another. One and the same value is given to all stones.	3. Syogi is aristocratic in spirit. Chessmen differ in rank, power and value.
4. The game is started with the idea that the board represents "no-man's land," free and open to be conquered.	4. As a preliminary condition for the contest, the chessmen are lined up facing the opposing forces for battle.
5. The purpose of the game is for each player to extend his own territory over the virgin land.	5. The purpose of the game of chess is to mate the opponent's King.

Edward Lasker who believes GO to be an ideal game for a mathematical mind, describes this game in full, with illustrations, in his book, entitled: *Modern Chess Strategy*, pages 370-440. See also the pictorial brochure entitled: *Japanese Game of "GO"* by Hukumensi Mihori, translated by Z. T. Iwado, published by the Board of Tourist Industry, Japanese Government Railways, 1939.

GOLOMBEK

Harry Golombek, International Chess Master and British Chess Champion in 1947-49-55, was born in London, in 1911. He was educated at London University. When he was eighteen years of age, he became the boy champion chessplayer of London and soon developed into one of Britain's leading chess performers. He won various prizes in British as well as in many Continental tournaments. He was awarded the title of International Chess Master by the F.I.D.E. In 1952, he was chosen to be the captain of the British team which played at the Helsinki International Chess Tournament. Likewise in 1954,

he was the captain of the British chess team playing at Amsterdam. The International Federation of Chess honored Golombek by asking him to act as a judge at the World Championship matches held in 1954, 1957 and 1958.

Golombek is a highly respected chess author. He has written many books on various aspects of chess, such as: *The Game of Chess; Réti's Best Games;* and game books, such as: *World Chess Championship, 1954;* and *XXII U.S.S.R. Chess Championship, 1957.* He is Chess Correspondent of *The London Times* and *The Observer.* He is also the Games and Overseas News Editor as well as one of the Directors of the famous *British Chess Magazine,* Golombek is also a Life Member and one of the Vice-Presidents of the British Chess Federation.

GOOD BISHOP

A Bishop who can exercise his functions without being blocked by his own forces. To enjoy freedom of action, a "good Bishop" is referred to as one who operates on squares which are of a different color from those on which his fixed Pawns are posted. See *Bad Bishop.*

GOOD CHESSPLAYER

A broad term applied to any careful chessplayer who having grasped an understanding and appreciation of sound basic principles of the game of chess is not disheartened by unexpected events. He is one who is ready for every emergency and makes the best of a difficult situation.

Apropos of the frequently repeated observation that "chess is played with the mind and not with the hands" Davidson points out that the prime ingredients of a good chessplayer are: "visual imagery, patience, self-restraint, deliberateness, good memory and sufficient associative reasoning." Other chess authorities advocate similar qualifications with a few additional requisites such as foresight, concentration and good sportsmanship. See *Player in Game of Chess.*

GOOD COMPANIONS

A popular term applied to members of the *Good Companion Chess Problem Club.* This club was an organization of problem composers founded in 1913, by J. F. Magee of Philadelphia. Its register numbered more than six hundred members, some of whom were internationally famous problem composers. It was disbanded after a decade of activity. The modern chess problem of "Mate in Two" moves was emphasized and developed by this club.

GOOGOL

A term sometimes used by chess writers to indicate in a very general way the countless number of possible moves that may be made in a game of chess. The word was coined by Kansner and Newman in their *Mathematics and the Imagination.*

GOTTINGEN MANUSCRIPT

A chess publication of unknown authorship which probably made its appearance about 1485. It is believed to have been the first publication of the "new chess era" which grew out of feudalism and came to be accepted as the earliest record of modern chessplay. The appearance of this manuscript coincided with the development of Humanism in northern Europe.

GRANDMASTER

A title bestowed upon a chessplayer who is considered to be a top ranking star. Dr. Ossip S. Bernstein stated that "the title, Grandmaster, was introduced in the international tourney at Ostend in 1907, in which I shared first prize with Akiba Rubinstein." The title "Grandmaster of Chess" was first conferred in 1914 by the Czar of Russia on the five finalists of the St. Petersburg Tourney. They were Lasker, Alekhine, Capablanca, Tarrasch and Marshall. In the earlier days, to be called a Grandmaster was an honorary title, but now it has been given international recognition by F.I.D.E. In the United States Chess Federation, a chessplayer who, in accordance with the established classification system, has gained a playing strength of 2600 points and up, is identified as a Grandmaster. See *Classification of Chessplayers.* For a listing of International Grandmasters see *The Official Blue Book and Encyclopedia of Chess,* page 286.

GRASSHOPPER

A term sometimes applied to a chessplayer who aimlessly jumps around the chessboard. He has no planning ability, no foresight, no appreciation of the consequences of his actions.

GREAT BARE KING

see *Bare King*

"GREAT CHESS"

A title given to earlier forms of chess. Murray in his book entitled *History of Chess* accounts for three varieties of the "Great Chess" game.

1. One form of this "Great Chess" game was invented originally by early Muslim Chessplayers. This game was played on a rectangular board of eleven by ten squares with two additional *"citadels."* (Murray, page 344).

2. Another form of the "Great Chess" game was described in a Turkish encyclopedia of 1805-6. This game was played on a board of 13 by 13 squares with 26 chesspieces on each side. In addition to the usual number of chesspieces it also utilized five additional pawns, a *Great Ferz,* two rhinoceroses, and two antelopes. (Murray, page 346)

3. Alfonso X of Castile refers to another form of "Great Chess." This game was played on a board of twelve by twelve squares. The game was played with or without dice. A die having eight faces was especially designed for this game. The numbers on the dice indicated the chesspiece to be moved, namely, 1 Pawn; 2 Giraffe; 3 Crocodile; 4 Lion; 5 Rook; 6 Unicorn; 7 Acanca; and 8 King. The numbers also indicated the relative value ascribed to each piece. (Murray, page 348.)

GRECO COUNTER GAMBIT

1. P-K4   P-K4
2. N-KB3   P-KB4

This Counter Gambit was founded on the principle that the strongest defense is a counterattack. It was developed by Gioachino Greco (1600-1634), a celebrated Italian chess genius. He was supposedly a native of Morea but spent his youth in Calabria in the Kingdom of Naples, whence he became known as the "Calabrese" or

"Calabrian." His education in chess was developed in the clubs of Italy. When he traveled through Rome, France, Spain and England, he collected manuscripts of games of chess which he ultimately organized and published. In 1669, a French edition was published in Paris. Later, more than forty editions were published in many other languages.

Chess writers point out that this Counter Gambit is theoretically unsound. Reinfeld indicates that "Black's counterattack against White's center is premature and generally leaves White with a considerable lead in development." This Greco Counter Gambit is a variation of the King's Gambit played by Black with a move behind. Today, the Greco Counter Gambit is generally referred to as the Latvian Counter Gambit.

GRID CHESS

An unorthodox or Fairy type of chess in which the chessboard is divided into a network of cells consisting of four squares each as shown in the accompanying illustration. Attacking moves are playable only when they cross at least one grid line. This also applies to checks. Consequently, a King is in check only when the checking piece or Pawn makes an attack from another "cell," that is, it must cross a grid line. Hence, in the given illustration, the white King is not in check from the black Bishop, but, if it were Black's

next move, then the Bishop could capture the Pawn and the white King would then be in check. Opposing Kings may move into one another's grid cell and there occupy adjacent squares without giving check—because they are considered to be in a friendly territory.

GRIFFITH

Richard Clewin Griffith, a highly respected English chess devotee, Champion chessplayer and chess writer, was born in London on July 22, 1872. He was educated at Charterhouse School and at the Royal School of Mines. He was a metallurgical chemist by profession and eventually became a senior partner of Daniel C. Griffith Ltd., Assayers to the Bank of England.

Chess was a part of the Griffith home environment where Richard Griffith learned chess from his father, who had founded the Hempstead Chess Club. In time, Richard became one of the best chessplayers in this club. In 1912, he won the British Championship at Richmond, and in 1941 he won the Middlesex Championship. He was also respected for his simultaneous and blindfolded chess performances. As a chess-

player, he displayed "steadiness rather than audacity."

After years of study and research, Griffith collaborated with J. H. White and produced in 1912 the first edition of *Modern Chess Openings,* and in 1920 they published the *Pocket Guide to the Chess Openings.* Griffith was also Editor of the *British Chess Magazine* from 1920 to 1938. From time to time, he served as secretary, treasurer, match-captain, and president of the London Chess League, the Middlesex County Chess Association and the Hempstead Chess Club. He retired in July, 1946, and took up residence at St. Leonards-on-Sea. His interest in the game of chess now found expression in the nearby Hastings Chess Club. He died on December 10, 1955.

GRIMSHAW INTERFERENCE

A chess problem in which two black pieces interfere with each other. This is illustrated in the accompanying diagram, where, after White's key move, Black can move either his Rook or Bishop to K3. In either case, the move of one piece interferes with the effectiveness and mobility of the other. When a composer arranges an inter-

Key: Q-K7

ference between two pieces which result in two different mates, it is then said to be a *mutual interference.*

The Grimshaw Interference was developed in 1850 by Walter Grimshaw (1832-1890) a noted chess problem composer of Yorkshire, England.

GRUENFELD DEFENSE

1. P-Q4	N-KB3
2. P-QB4	P-KN3
3. N-QB3	P-Q4
4. N-B3	B-N2

This Defense is a variation of the King's Indian opening which was developed by the Austrian master Ernst Gruenfeld, who was born in 1893. It has been said that Gruenfeld knew more about chess openings than any other player. He was a prize winner in nearly all tournaments in which he participated in his earlier years but eventually his games displayed his conviction that every game should, if

properly played, terminate in a draw.

The Gruenfeld Defense is a hypermodern defense in which, according to Reinfeld, "Black is perfectly willing to let White set up a broad, formidable-looking Pawn center," and then hopes "to take pot-shots at this Pawn center by fianchettoeing his King Bishop." Horowitz is of the opinion that this Defense has an appeal to all those who wish to get away from drab defenses. For a presentation of the procedural development of the Gruenfeld Defense with its variations, see *Modern Chess Openings*, Ninth Edition, by Walter Korn; or *Practical Chess Openings*, by Reuben Fine.

GUARD

A chessman placed in a defensive position where he can protect one of his own pieces, or where he may capture a hostile man in the event of immi-

nent danger. For a brief statement and seventy-two illustrations on "Removing the Guard" see Chapter 8 in *1001 Brilliant Chess Sacrifices and Combinations* by Fred Reinfeld.

GUÉRIDON MATE

A mating situation in which the pieces are stationed in a position which is suggestive of a small table. Hence, the use of the French word *guéridon,* meaning a stand or small table. This may be visualized as a T-shaped table in the accompanying diagram where the two squares behind the King's right and left are occupied by friendly pieces and the white Queen next to the King controls the unoccupied squares adjacent to the King who is mated.

H

HAMPPE OPENING

1. P-K4	P-K4
2. N-QB3	

An opening named after Herr Hamppe, who was a distinguished Viennese chessmaster and contemporary of Steinitz. In the eighteen-seventies, he popularized with Steinitz the idea of developing the Queen's Knight before the King's Knight. Inasmuch as 2. N-QB3 was used so frequently in the Vienna Tournament of 1873, this opening became known as the Vienna Opening, or the Hamppe Opening. See *Vienna Opening.*

HANDICAP

A method of equalizing the opportunity of winning a game when one of the players is superior to the other. This is usually accomplished by giving some sort of odds which will serve as a disadvantage to the superior player and conversely will favor the inferior player. The wisdom for doing so is that a good strong chessplayer is more alive to the combinations inherent in various positions throughout the game. See *Odds*.

HANGING PAWN

A single disconnected Pawn or a separate group of Pawns which can not be guarded by other Pawns. A "hanging Pawn" is frequently found dangling by itself in the middle game or end game. In the middle game hanging Pawns can constitute an advantage provided they are supported by minor or major pieces and the opponent is not ahead in development. But, in the end-game, says Dr. Euwe, "hanging Pawns are nearly always weak."

HARKNESS

Kenneth Harkness was born in Scotland, where he learned to play chess in his boyhood days. He came to the United States in 1918 and worked as a designing engineer and writer in the radio field. From 1941 to 1947, Mr. Harkness was managing editor and co-publisher of *Chess Review* —the picture chess magazine. Since then he has devoted his energies wholly to the promotion of the welfare of the chess fraternity and that of the United States Chess Federation. In 1952, he was appointed Business Manager of the Federation. He also served the USCF as its membership secretary, rating statistician, and Chairman of the Rules Committee. He is also a highly respected chess organizer and director of chess tournaments.

Mr. Harkness made distinctive contributions to the chess world. He is the originator of efficient pairing and tie-breaking systems which are now used in tournaments conducted by the United States Chess Federation and many of its affiliates. He also formulated a body of Tournament Rules which contain specific regulations for the organization and conduct of chess tournaments. He also developed a method of classifying and rating chessplayers which has been adopted in the United States, Canada, Great Britain and other countries.

Kenneth Harkness has enriched the chess literature by his many writings. With Irving Chernev, he co-authored *An Invitation to Chess*. His latest monumental contribution is *The Official Blue Book and Encyclopedia of Chess*.

HARKNESS PAIRING SYSTEM

A system originally proposed by Kenneth Harkness for matching tournament chessplayers according to their official national ratings in the first round and thereafter by the changes resulting from each round of play. This procedure was adopted in the United States Open Championship Tournament conducted in Long Beach, California, August, 1955. For a discussion of the mechanics of this Harkness Pairing System, with illustrations, see *The Official Blue Book and Encyclopedia of Chess*, pages 185 to 196.

HARLEY

Brian Harley, a noted authority on chess problem composition, was born at Saffron Walden, Essex, England, on October 27, 1883. Apart from his war service, he spent his entire professional life as an actuary with the National Provident Institution. He retired in 1947. He was throughout his lifetime a Latin scholar, a devotee of Charles

Dickens' writings, a keen bridgeplayer and a musical instrumentalist (piano). He died on May 18, 1955.

He became interested in chess problems during his boyhood days. In 1916, his interest was aroused in what became known in chess parlance as the "mutate." In 1919, he was appointed chess editor of the *Observer*, where he did much to popularize the "mutate" in his regular chess columns. In addition to his journalistic work, he was also the author of *Mate in Two*, 1931, and *Mate in Three*, 1943. From 1947 to 1949, he served as the President of the British Chess Problem Society.

Harley considered the ideal chess problem as "a mixture of art, science, humor and puzzlement." He maintained that a key move becomes more meritorious when it possesses one or more of the following characteristics, namely, 1) sacrifices; 2) flight giving opportunity; 3) self-pinning of a white man; 4) unpinning of a black man; and, 5) allowing a black check. Harley's name is remembered as having coined the word; "mutate."

At the time of his death, everyone spoke in glowing and affectionate terms of Brian Harley's work. The *British Chess Magazine* stated: "His passing leaves an unfillable gap." See *Mutate*.

HARRWITZ

Daniel Harrwitz, famous chessplayer of the nineteenth century, was born in Breslau, Germany, in 1823. He lived in England for seven years and in 1856 he moved to Paris where he became the undisputed "King of Chess," at the Café de la Régence. He was also a famous blindfold chessplayer. During his chess career, he encountered Morphy, Staunton, Anderssen, Lowenthal, Kolisch and other chessmasters. He retired to Bozen, Austrian Tyrol, where he died in 1884.

HAVEL

Miroslav Havel, chess name of a Bohemian chessmaster, whose real name was Miroslav Kostal. He was born on November 7, 1881, at Teplitz, Bohemia, living most of his life in Prague. He was educated in the Prague Technical High School. After the establishment of the Czechoslovakian Republic, he became an official in the Government's Railway Ministry. On May 1, 1898, he published his first chess problem and before long he was recognized as one of the most influential chess problemists in the Bohemian school of chess. He was awarded thirty-eight prizes, sixteen of which were first prizes. He also received many honorable mentions. For a good example of Havel's classical style of simplicity and delicacy in solving chess problems see his *Bohemian Garnets*—A Collection of 500 Chess Problems, published in 1923 by the Office of the "Chess Amateur."

HIPPOPHOBIA

A term sometimes applied to chessplayers who dread the presence of Knights on the chessboard. The word is derived from two Greek words: *hippos*, meaning horse; and *phobos*, meaning an inordinate fear. Chessplayers who are afflicted with hippophobia are known to take great risks so as to eliminate their opponents' Knights.

HIPPOPOTAMUS

A figurine of a hippopotamus has been used in place of our Rook in some of the earlier forms of chess in several foreign countries. For a list of these countries see *A Short History of Chess*, by Henry A. Davidson. For the use of other animal figurines used in chess, see *Animals in Chess*.

HISTORIES OF CHESS

Books in which the authors have recorded their findings of an inquiry into the records pertaining to the origin and development of chess. Those available in the English language are:

1. *A Short History of Chess,* by Henry A. Davidson. New York: Greenberg Publisher, 1949.
2. *Early Chess in America,* by Alfred Klahre. Middletown, New York: Whitlock Press, 1931.
3. *History of Chess,* by H. J. R. Murray. Oxford, London: Clarendon Press, 1913.
4. *History of Chess,* by Duncan Forbes. London: William Allen, 1860.
5. *History of Chess,* by Richard Lamb. London: J. Wilkie, 1765.

HISTORY OF CHESS

Historians are not in perfect agreement as to the time and place of the origin of chess. It is generally assumed that Asia is the cradle of man as well as the cradle of the chessmen. There are records in Sanskrit that chess was played in western India and that many ideas used in the game can be identified as elements in the early Indian army. For example, the original chessmen represented chariots, horses, elephants and foot soldiers. These were the four basic elements of the Indian army. Furthermore, there was a game prevalent in the early days of India known as *chaturanga* (meaning: four member army) which is said to have contained the germ idea from which our modern game of chess may have originated.

Due to commercial and cultural intercourse between the merchants of Persia and India, the game was brought to the Persian homeland. Here a chess literature developed which became the foundation of many ideas and usages observed in modern chess. With the development of the commercial and political life between the land of the Shahs and the Byzantine Empire, many Persian customs were introduced into the life of the people of Constantinople, and chess is believed to have been one of the imported luxuries adopted by the Turks. Likewise, the Arabs are believed to have learned chess during their invasion of Persia.

Mohammed was known to have been opposed to games of chance, but approved games of war. Since the game of chess was an image of war and since it was possible to play chess as a mental exercise, many caliphs themselves became ardent chessplayers. When Moslems invaded southern Europe, they brought the game of chess with them. The Moors developed the game in Spain and the Saracens developed it in Italy. Thereafter, the game of chess spread from country to country until now, when it has become an international pastime.

If history can be a study of the lives of great men, as Thomas Carlyle once said, then the history of the game of chess is no exception. In 1561, a Spanish priest, Ruy Lopez, published a textbook on chess. Improvements followed. Masterplayers came into prominence. Among the more influential was Philidor, who defeated Stamma in 1747. Deschapelles succeeded Philidor. Chess supremacy eventually passed into English hands. At the Great Exhibition in the Crystal Palace in London, in 1851, Adolf Anderssen emerged as Europe's leading chessmaster. In 1857, Paul Morphy from New Orleans crossed the Atlantic and defeated Anderssen. After Morphy's withdrawal from active play, Wilhelm Steinitz assumed the title of world champion. In 1894, Dr. Emanuel Lasker defeated Steinitz in a New York tournament. Noteworthy contemporaries of Lasker's era were Pillsbury, Marshall, Tarrasch, Schlechter, Janowski, Rubinstein, Capablanca and Alekhine, to be followed by more modern players.

Dividing history into epochs is to a large extent a matter of convenience. Accordingly, the period prior to the seventh century might be called the prehistoric days of the game of chess. Then followed a long period of growth and development. Beginning with the days of Ruy Lopez, there emerged a classical period in the history of chess. Then, Steinitz applied to the game of chess what the Germans call *Strengwissenschaftliche Methode*—a vigorous scientific method. This was called the scientific period in the history of chess. Then came the so-called romantic period which extended to the time of the death of Alekhine in 1946. Modern chess, with its emphasis on strategy and tactics, and the psychological development of the game, gave the chess world such outstanding masters as Dr. Euwe, Nimzovitch, Réti and Tartakower. Present-day notables include Reshevsky, Botvinnik, and a host of promising young experts.

For a more complete discussion see the references given in the previous definition: *Histories of Chess.*

HOLE

An opening in a Pawn structure which provides a square where an opponent's chessmen may be placed without fear of immediate capture. The term was coined by Steinitz. In the accompanying diagram, Black has two

"holes," one at KB3 and the other at KR3. In either place, White's forces could establish themselves without the

possibility of being dislodged by Black Pawn moves. Horowitz says that "a hole is a weakness in the Pawn structure," and that "it is a haven for an enemy piece—an outpost for an enemy attack."

HOLLANDISH DEFENSE

see *Dutch Defense*

HOLZHAUSEN INTERFERENCE

A problem situation named after Baron Walther von Holzhausen (1876-1935) in which two pieces of like motion interfere with each other when they are placed in positions from where they can make similar directional moves. In the accompanying diagram, such an interference occurs when Black moves 1 . . . Q-K2. Here the black Queen interferes with Black's Bishop which is guarding Black's Rook.

HOROWITZ

Israel Albert Horowitz, one of America's most outstanding chessmasters, three times United States "Open" Champion chessplayer, author, publisher and editor of *Chess Review* magazine, was born in Brooklyn, New York, on November 15, 1907. He learned to play chess at the age of five and developed his chessplaying ability in various recreational centers. He was an active chessplayer throughout his high school and college days. He captained the New York University chess team to victory in the intercollegiate tournaments during 1927 and 1928. In fact, Horowitz has been one of the leading American chessplayers since the 1920's. He was a member of the United States chess teams which won the world championship in the International Tournaments held at Prague in 1931, at Warsaw in 1935, and at Stockholm in 1937.

Horowitz has written a number of books, such as, *The Macmillan Handbook of Chess, Modern Ideas in the Chess Openings, How to Win in Chess Openings, How to Win in the Middle Game of Chess* and many others, some of which have been co-authored with Fred Reinfeld as well as with Hans Kmoch. In 1933, Horowitz founded *Chess Review*—the picture magazine, which has become the leading American chess journal.

As a chessplayer and chess writer, publisher and editor, Horowitz has earned the respect of the American chess fraternity. Dr. Fine observes that Horowitz is well known "for his over-the-board exploits." Chernev and Harkness report that "in a recent rapid transit (ten seconds a move) tourney, chessmaster I. A. Horowitz actually gave odds of a Queen, Rook, Bishop and Knight to one of his opponents— and won!"

Horowitz has taken an active interest in developing and promoting a lively enthusiasm in chessplay among the young people by giving chess exhibits in schools and clubs throughout the country.

HORSE

Another name for a Knight. It was the original and one of the most frequently used names for the Knight. The Croatians, Czech and Polish chessplayers call the Knight their "Little Horse."

HORSEMAN

An earlier name for a Knight. In medieval days, when chess was viewed as a royal entourage proceeding against an enemy, the chess piece we now call a Knight was characterized as a rider seated on a horse. Hence, this piece became known as the "horseman." In time, only the head of a horse was used as the simplified and distinctive feature of this chesspiece.

HUNGARIAN DEFENSE

1.	P-K4;	P-K4
2.	N-KB3,	N-QB3
3.	B-B4	B-K2

This Defense was named after the Hungarian chessplayers who followed this procedural opening in their correspondence match between Paris and Pesth which was played from November, 1842 to January, 1846. Actually, this Defense dates from Cozio (1766) but it has received comparatively little attention from chess writers. In fact, Staunton, Wormald, Gossip, Bird and Cook do not mention it as a regular opening.

Black's third move is the characteristic move of this Defense and marks a departure from the Giuoco Piano and the Evans Gambit. This Defense favors White. Reinfeld points out that "Black's pieces are cramped; they cannot be freed; and they cannot be given any respectable scope." Hence, concludes Reinfeld, "White can simply proceed to tie up Black systematically, depriving him of more and more terrain." For a procedural development of this Hungarian Defense see *Mod-*

ern Chess Openings, Ninth Edition, by Walter Korn, or, *Practical Chess Openings,* by Reuben Fine.

HURDLE CHECK

A term used by Hanauer in his book entitled *Chess for You and Me.* The term is applied to a situation in which a King is placed in check but, when the King moves out of check, the checking piece captures the hostile piece stationed further along the same line. Other writers refer to the same situation as a "Skewer attack." In the accompanying illustration White moves R-N4ch. After the King moves, the Rook will capture the Bishop. See *Skewer.*

HUTTON

Reverend G. D. Hutton, the originator of the Cross-Pairing System used in tournament chessplay, was born in Scotland, in 1866. He was educated at the University of Edinburgh and became a clergyman. He served as a minister in Edinburgh, Scotland; Melbourne, Australia, and in 1883, he returned to Scotland where he served at Bathkenner, Stirlingshire, until he retired in 1919. He died in Scotland in 1929.

He was a member of the Falkirk Chess Club and the Edinburgh Chess Club. He participated in several Scottish Associational Chess Congresses with no great success. His main contribution consisted in developing a method of pairing an odd number of teams in chess tournaments and thereby avoiding the use of byes. In 1922 he suggested the principle of inter-pairing teams to L. P. Rees who was then the Secretary of the British Chess Federation. According to W. Ritson Morry, writing in the British Chess Federation Yearbook for 1954-1955, this "Hutton Pairing Method" or "Jamboree Pairing Method," as it is sometimes called, "involves arranging for all teams in a competition to meet on the same day. Each player plays only one game because the teams are inter-paired so that each team meets a composite team from the remaining contestants. This pairing is arranged so that all top boards inter-pair, all second boards meet each other, and so on down the teams. The conditions of the competition must require all teams to have the same number of players." For a full explanation with illustrations as how this method operates, see "The Hutton Method of Pairing for Team Events," by W. Ritson Morry, in the British Chess Federation *Yearbook, 1954-1955,* pages 198 to 210.

HYPERMODERN CHESS

A style of chessplay which was tremendously popular during the nineteen-twenties and early nineteen-thirties. Richard Réti, Nimzovitch and Tartakower were among the chief exponents of this school of chessplay. There was no change in fundamentals between the modern chessplayers and the hypermodern players. There was, however, a change in the style of playing which, as Capablanca observes, was "not always for the best at that." The hypermodernists agree with the modernists as to the importance of center control. The hypermodernists, however, developed a new tactical procedure for gaining this control. Instead of actual occupation of the center, they advocated controlling the center from a distance, creating spheres of influence, and using the fianchetto as the principal elements of their *plan de campagne*. In short, the long-term plan of the hypermodernist was to allow the enemy to occupy the center and then to demolish him later. "The idea, of course," says Horowitz, "is good, if it works. There are, however, so many factors which come into play, that, at best, it is a tenuous procedure;" or, as Horowitz says elsewhere, "There is such a thing as pressing one's luck too far. Even a hyper-modernist, cool and calculating as he is . . . is sometimes foolhardy." See the *Gruenfeld Defense* as an example of a Hypermodern Defense.

I

IDIOT, CHESS

The term "Chess Idiot" was used by Ossip S. Bernstein and applied to himself for losing a game in which he had a winning position. Dr. Emanuel Lasker endorsed this appellation. See *Bernstein*.

ILLEGAL MOVE

A move which is contrary to the established "Laws of Chess" as stated in the "Official Code" of the *Fédération Internationale des Echecs* or in the Official American Translation published by The United States Chess Federation.

As soon as an illegal move has been discovered, the last correct position must be reestablished, and the offending player must make, if possible, a move with the same piece with which the illegal move has been made.

If castling is made illegally, the correct position must be reestablished and the offending player is then required to move his King, provided this can be done without placing the King in check.

It is reported that Napoleon was a champion when it came to making illegal moves. He was a very poor loser. When a losing position presented itself, he would move, for example, a Bishop on to a diagonal of the wrong color. See *Laws of Chess*, Article 9.

IMPORTANCE OF CHESS

The "importance of chess" can be defined in terms of the inherent qualities in chessplay which the contestants exercise while playing a game of chess. Chess experts have cited numerous reasons why they consider chess to be one of the most important, if not the most important of all pastimes. Marshall says: "Chess is not only the most cosmopolitan of all games, but it is the most democratic. A chessplayer is welcomed in every part of the world, regardless of his social or financial status."

Tarrasch says: "Chess is a form of intellectual productiveness, therein lies its peculiar charm. Intellectual productiveness is one of the greatest joys—if not the greatest one—of human existence. It is not everyone who can write a play, or build a bridge, or even make a good joke. But in chess everyone can, everyone must, be intellectually productive and so can share in this select delight. I have always a slight feeling of pity for the man who has no knowledge of chess, just as I would pity the man who has remained ignorant of love. Chess like love, like music, has the power to make men happy."

Fiske quotes: "It (chess) affords a keen delight to youth, a sober pleasure to manhood, and a perpetual solace to old age."

Zweig writes that the game of chess tends "to slay boredom, to sharpen the senses, to exhilarate the spirit."

Grover says: "The Royal Game offers rich dividends,—a keen and alert mind, a higher appreciation of values, a sense of proportion, a more mature understanding of life itself and of our fellow-man."

Reinfeld says: "I can honestly say that I learned a great deal from chess: how to be patient, how to abide my time, how to see the other man's point of view, how to persevere in uncompromising situations, how to learn from my failures." See *Virtues Inherent in Chessplay* and *Universality of Chess*.

IMPURE MATE

A mating problem situation in which, at the time of the mate, any one of the squares around the black King (a) is guarded by more than one of White's men; or, (b) is occupied by a black man and also guarded by a white man. See *Pure Mate*.

INDIAN ATTACK

1. N-KB3, P-Q4

This is the Indian Defense in reverse. It was first employed in official tournament play by Dr. Emanuel Lasker in 1924, although Nimzovitch and Réti made use of this opening in 1923. As this opening progresses, Réti offers a warning that "attacking moves which are justified by an extra tempo, and which bring an advantage, can fail in a backward development and bring a disadvantage." For an example of how a famous master used this Indian Attack, see *Réti Opening*.

INDIAN DEFENSE

1. P-Q4, N-KB3

A defensive opening named after the country where the game is said to have

originated and where leisurely and non-aggressive games were played. Black's reply is conservative and with

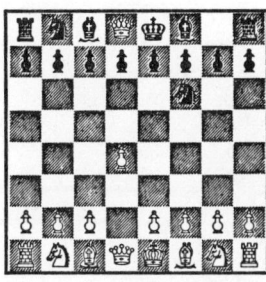

further development may lead to other well-known opening procedures. See: *Queen's Indian Defense, King's Indian Defense, Gruenfeld Defense* and *Nimzoindian Defense*.

INDIAN PROBLEM

A term applied to a problem in which White manipulates his pieces so that he may become victorious by depriving Black of a stalemate. Such a situation is presented in the accompanying diagram, to which there are several solutions. In the suggested solution, it can be seen how White's second move blocks the action of his Bishop. This provides Black with a move which prevents him from being stalemated. Thereupon, White uncovers his blocked piece and produces

A Solution:

1. B-QB1	P-N4
2. R-Q2	K-B5
3. R-Q4 dble check and mate.	

a discovered check, a double check and mate.

This problem is generally credited to the Reverend Loveday (1815-1848) an English clergyman living in India. It was first published anonymously in the *Chess Player's Chronicle,* in 1845, and became known as the "Indian problem."

INITIATIVE

The right or power to begin action. "Initiative" implies having an advantage of time and action. At the outset of the game, both sides begin with the same position and the same amount of material. But White has the first move. Therefore White has the "initiative" at the beginning of the game. A slight blunder can be sufficient for a player to lose the initiative. This gives the opponent an opportunity to seize the initiative and commence a counterattack. The player who has the initiative, and can retain it, has the advantage and should win, everything else being equal.

INTELLECTUAL GAME

A term frequently applied to the game of chess. This idea has been developed largely because chessplay is essentially a process of the intellect. The moves themselves merely give a visual indication of the mental reaction to the problematic situation presented on the chessboard.

There is also a historical basis for calling chess the "Intellectual Game." In the eleventh century, chess writers of India made a distinction between their original *chaturanga* and a newer development of the game associated with *buddhi,* the enlightened or intellectual. This game became known as *buddhidyuta* or "The Game of the Enlightened" or "The Intellectual Game."

There is some limited statistical evidence that there is a close correlation between chessplaying ability and general intelligence. By using the Spearman ranking method, Davidson in his *A Short History of Chess* reports that there is a positive correlation of .72 between these two factors. His statistical world consisted of the following cases:

Individuals	Chessplaying ability rank	Intelligence rank
A....................	1	1
B....................	2	2
C....................	3	5
D....................	4	4
E....................	5	6
F....................	6	3
G....................	7	7

INTERCEPTION CHESS

One of the chess varieties used in Japan. This game, known as *Hasami-shogi,* is mentioned by H. J. R. Murray in his book entitled *History of Chess.* Murray points out that in this game "each player arranges his nine *Fuz* upon his back row. Each man can move any distance forwards or laterally. When two men occupy the two squares adjacent to that occupied by an opposing man, in either a horizontal or a vertical direction the opposing man is captured."

INTERFERENCE

A situation in which a player hinders his own progress by obstructing one of his files, ranks, or diagonals. This may occur when a player has a choice of moving two pieces to a critical square. By moving one piece he may obstruct the action of the other piece. Problemists speak of the interference of long-range pieces, namely the Queen, Rook and Bishop. An obstruction of a Pawn move is usually referred to as a "block" or "blocking;" except in the case of the initial double move of a Pawn where its progress may be hindered by an "interference" of a man on the next rank. The converse of "interference" is "clearance." For a brief statement and forty-three illustrations see *"1001 Brilliant Chess Sacrifices and Combinations,* by Fred Reinfeld, Chapter 10, entitled: "Interference."

INTERNATIONAL CHESS MAGAZINE

The name of a monthly chess magazine which was published in New York City from January, 1885, to December, 1891. It was edited by Wilhelm Steinitz, who was universally recognized as the chief exponent of the modern scientific school of chess. See *Steinitz.*

INTERNATIONAL POSTAL CHESS NOTATION

A numerical method of transmitting moves to chessplayers located in foreign countries. As shown in the accompanying diagram, the files are numbered from 1 to 8 from left to right, and the ranks are numbered from 1 to 8 beginning with White's first rank. Consequently, each square is identified by a number of two figures, the first indicating the file and the second indicating the rank. Thus, the same number assigned to each square is utilized by both players.

BLACK

WHITE

A move or capture is recorded by combining the numbers of the square of departure and arrival of a chessman.

For example, 7163 means that the man on square 71 moves to or makes a capture on square 63. Castling is recorded as a move made by the King; thus, if White castles on the King's side, the move is recorded as 5171. The only time a name is used in this notation system is when it is necessary to indicate the piece to which a Pawn is promoted; thus, 5758 (Queen) means that the Pawn moving from square 57 to 58 is promoted to a Queen.

This system of notation is authorized by the International Federation of Chess. Since this system is independent of language, it can be easily understood by chessplayers in any foreign country. The first few moves of the Indian Defense may be recorded as follows:

White	Black
4244	7866
2133	4745

INTERNATIONAL TOURNAMENT, FIRST

The first international chess tournament was played during the great International Exposition in London in 1851.

It was organized under the leadership of the British chessmaster Howard Staunton. On May 22, 1851, a Committee of Management was organized to summon an assemblage of all those who proposed to take part in a masters' tournament. It was stipulated that the first prize was to consist of a sum not less than one-third of the net amount of the funds collected. Other cash awards of lesser amounts were to be awarded to the next five winners. Chessmasters from many foreign lands attended. Adolf Anderssen from Breslau, Germany, won the first prize and became the recognized World Champion Chessplayer. See *Staunton, World Champion Chessplayers,* and *Fédération Internationale des Echecs.*

INTERPOSE

The process of relieving the King of check or safeguarding a valuable piece from attack by moving another chessman between the King or the threatened piece and the hostile man.

INTERPRETATION OF
THE LAWS OF CHESS

Explaining or clarifying the meaning of any part or section of the established and recognized Laws of Chess. The highest organization recognized throughout the chess world which is empowered to render official decisions regarding any question pertaining to the meaning or application of the Laws of Chess is the World Chess Federation (Fédération Internationale des Echecs). In the United States, questions pertaining to the meaning and application of the Laws of Chess should be referred to the Secretary of the United States Chess Federation, which is the American Unit of the World Chess Federation.

INTER-ZONAL TOURNAMENTS

Qualifying tournaments for the World Championships. These tournaments are held under the auspices of F.I.D.E., every second year in a four year cycle. The five highest chessplayers are permitted to enter the "Candidates' Tournament" which is held the following year. See *Fédération Internationale des Echecs.*

INVERTED OPENING

An opening in which White proceeds in a manner that has generally been recognized as a defensive formation played by Black. The advocates of "inverted openings" or "reversed openings" as they are sometimes called assume that if the opening is good for Black, it should be equally good, if not better, for White who has the advantage of the move. Thus, the English Opening is an inverted Sicilian Defense.

Colle System is an inverted Slav Defense.

Réti Opening is an inverted Indian Defense.

IRREGULAR OPENING

Any opening which deviates from what has been regarded as the classical opening of central Pawns. "Irregular openings" are employed less frequently and come under the heading of "closed games." See *Closed Openings.*

ISOLATED PAWN

A Pawn which has no Pawn of the same color on either of its adjacent files. Due to the fact that, first, an "isolated Pawn" is deprived of the potential support which united Pawns can offer to each other, and second, that it must be guarded by a major or minor piece, it is generally considered to be a disadvantage to its owner. An "isolated Pawn" is frequently referred to as an "isolani."

ITALIAN CASTLING
see *Free Castling*

ITALIAN DIAGONAL

White's diagonal: QR2-KN8. It is called "Italian Diagonal" because of the effective use made of this diagonal in the Giuoco Piano Opening (3. B-QB4) where White's King's Bishop is developed quickly for an early attack.

ITALIAN GAME
see *Giuoco Piano*

J

"J'ADOUBE"

A French expression meaning "I adjust." This expression is used by a player to notify his opponent that he intends to touch a man merely to adjust his position. A player is expected to say "j'adoube" *before touching* the man to be adjusted. Saying "j'adoube" does not entitle a player to take back an indifferent or bad move which has been made.

JAMBOREE PAIRING METHOD
see *Hutton*

JANOWSKI
David Janowski, a world champion contender and a champion chessplayer of Paris, was born in Lodz, Poland, on May 25, 1868. He emigrated to France where he became one of the regulars of chess tournaments. He is remembered for his wild attacking style of play. His difficulty seemed to have been that he knew perfectly well how to attack but not when to attack. As Dr. Bernstein observed, "Janowski was no chess scientist or theoretician. He knew what he had to do on the chessboard; but he did not know, or could not explain why it had to be done." Nevertheless, Janowski's bold and dashing play earned for him many brilliancy prizes. He did a great deal of pioneering work in the Queen's Gambit opening. Eventually, he developed a variation which became known as the "Janowski Defense." Its characteristic move was 3 . . . P-QR3.

In official chessplay Janowski was more concerned with playing chess than in the outcome of the score. Hoffer stated that "Janowski has an inherent contempt for the score. I have seen several occasions when he could have secured a higher prize by drawing a game, but he tried to exact the utmost out of the position even at the risk of jeopardizing his place, notably at London, 1899, and at Cambridge Springs, 1904."

As a chessplayer, Janowski exhibited two cardinal weaknesses: underestimating his opponents and a seeming in-

ability to learn from his own mistakes. He was so self-confident and got so excited in a won position that, as Emanuel Lasker observed, he could not bring the game to a victorious con-

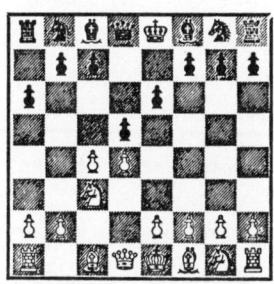

Janowski's Defense

1. P-Q4	P-Q4
2. P-QB4	P-K3
3. N-QB3	P-QR3

clusion. Dr. Bernstein pointed out that during a chess game, Janowski "did not so much as look at his opponent. All his thoughts were rapt upon his game. But, once the game was over and he had happened to lose, he often lost his temper and became intolerable."

Writing in *Chess Review*, Dr. Bernstein concludes his account of "My Encounter with Janowski" by saying that "Janowski's last years were very difficult. He was ill, had few friends. He died in 1927, almost forgotten."

JAPANESE CHESS
The Japanese call their chess *shogi*. At the opening of the game, the major and minor pieces are stationed on the first rank, the second rank remains vacant, and the Pawns are placed on the third rank. The pieces are flat rectangular shaped counters. On the face of each piece appears its name and on its reverse side its "promotion-name." In this game a captured piece may become one of the victor's forces whenever the player desires its services. A stalemate is illegal.

There are several varieties of chess found in Japan, such as; Jumping Chess; Interception Chess; Shaking Chess; and Receiving Chess. See *History of Chess* by H. J. R. Murray. See also *British Chess Magazine,* vol. 16, 1896, page 200.

JEROME GAMBIT

1. P-K4	P-K4
2. N-KB3	N-QB3
3. B-B4	B-B4
4. BxP ch.	

An opening developed in America in the latter part of the nineteenth century by Mr. Jerome and analyzed by S. A. Charles of Cincinnati, Ohio. Some chess writers would extend the so-called Jerome Gambit to include 4 . . .KxB; 5. NxPch, NxN. The opening starts quietly with the Giuoco Piano. This is

After Black's fifth move.

followed by White sacrificing two pieces in quick succession in return for two Pawns and the possibility of displacing Black's King and having him drawn into the center of the board. The Jerome Gambit is not recommended by the experts.

JESTER

"Jester" was the royal clown, a name given to our Knight by early Greek chessplayers. In some European countries, the Bishop was designated as the court jester and was represented on the chessboard as a clown bedecked with cap and bells.

JUMPER

The English translation of the German word "springer" which is used for our Knight.

JUMPING CHESS

One of the chess varieties used in Japan where it is known as *tobi-shogi.* It is played more like our game of checkers than chess. In this game, each player arranges eighteen men upon the first and second ranks. All men are of equal value. Each man moves straight ahead or laterally, and captures as in the game of checkers or draughts. The game is reported by H. J. R. Murray in his book, entitled: *History of Chess.*

K

KEMPELEN, VON

Baron Wolfgang von Kempelen, a nobleman of Pressbourg, Hungary, was a celebrated engineer at Vienna's imperial court where he also served as the Aulic counselor on Mechanics to the Royal Chamber. He was noted for his mechanical genius and many notable inventions, especially a chess automaton.

Great excitement was caused at the Royal Palace in Vienna when it was announced that the Baron would build and exhibit a machine that would not only amuse Empress Maria Theresa but would also astonish everyone with its intellectual powers. The machine was invented in 1769. It was submitted to the scrutiny of assembled scientists and exhibited before Empress Maria Theresa of Austria-Hungary, as well as Empress Catherine II of Russia and Emperor Joseph II of Germany.

This automaton appeared as a life-sized figure, dressed as a mustachioed Turk, clothed in Oriental costume with a turban on his head. He was seated at a large box the top of which served as a chessboard. This mechanical robot, which became known as "The Turk," was ready to play a game of chess with any challenger from the audience.

After the inventor's death, this mechanical chessplayer was sold to Johann Nepomuk Maelzel, a Bavarian musician, and eventually was resold and exhibited in many of the larger cities of Europe and America. Finally, "the Turk" was placed in the Chinese Museum in Philadelphia, Pennsylvania, where, at the age of 85, it was destroyed in a fire. See *Turk*.

KERES

Paul Keres, Grandmaster chessplayer, Estonian Chess Champion and a professional chessplayer, was born at Narva, a small town in Estonia, on January 7, 1906. He learned the elements of chessplay from his father at the age of four and developed his chessplaying ability by playing with his three-year-older brother. He began to specialize in mathematics but the war altered his plans and he developed into a professional chessplayer. In 1931, he became interested in postal chess, playing as many as 150 games at a time. In 1934, he played for the Estonian championship title. He displayed extraordinary brilliancy in chessplay in a number of tournaments. In 1936, he tied with Alekhine for the first prize, and, in 1937, he captured the first prize ahead of such eminent players as Capablanca, Fine and Reshevsky. In 1938, he was the top ranking winner at the famous A.V.R.O. Tournament (see *A.V.R.O. Tournament*). In a 1940 chess match, Keres defeated Euwe, a former World Champion.

Chess observers note that Keres is conspicuously impassive at the chessboard; that he takes the bitter with the sweet with equal calm. Dr. Fine notes that "Keres essays gambits in serious play, and is responsible for many crucial innovations in them." Fine also observes that "his great forte remains in the area of sudden unforeseen attack."

KEY

The first move in a chess problem is called a "key move" or briefly a "key." This move should, according to the theory of good problem construction, be the least obvious move on the board. Problemist Rayner stated that "the object of the key move should be carefully concealed, and should not be apparent until the mating move is made." Problemist Howard observes that "ordinarily (the key) should be an apparently aimless move; one which on the surface does not seem strong from a playing point of view." Hence, a good key move would be one which withdraws a piece from a strong position and moves it to a seemingly useless one. A move which offers the opponent's King greater freedom of action before being mated is considered a good key move. On the other hand, a key move is considered to be weak when it is too obvious, gives check, captures an important piece, or restricts Black's forces. In a word, obviously strong or aggressive moves do not make the most desirable key moves.

KEY PIECE

The White piece which makes the key move in a chess problem. See *Key*.

KIBITZER

When applied to chess, a kibitzer is a meddlesome spectator who offers gratuitous advice or makes witty remarks during a game of chess. A chessplayer may, however, be his own "kibitzer" by developing his own kibitz, or witty expression, which is repeated frequently by himself and others. In such a case, the chessplayer is usually pleased when he is identified by his own pet kibitz and feels honored when others repeat his crisp, humorous remark. Serious chessplayers, however, usually dislike kibitzing during a game.

KIESERITZKY GAMBIT

1.	P-K4	P-K4;
2.	P-KB4	PxP
3.	N-KB3	P-KN4
4.	P-KR4	P-N5
5.	N-K5	

An old fashioned gambit which was popularized by the French chessplayer Kieseritzky, who died on May 18, 1853. It was first mentioned by Polerio more than four and a half centuries ago and was known by Italian players as the *Gambitto Grande*.

According to Fletcher, this opening takes on "the mantle of perpetual youth," because, as he states, there are within it a large number of good refreshing Black defenses to counteract the vigorous White attack. Marshall stated that "here we have an opening which is supposed to be unsound theoretically, but in practice the chances would appear to favour White." Modern theory recommends that Black might prefer to play 3 . . . P-Q4 rather than to exploit his King-side Pawns by playing 3 . . . P-KN4.

KING

According to the standard Staunton design (See *Chessmen*), the King is the tallest chess unit on the chessboard.

He wears a crown which is superimposed with a cross. In chess notation, he is symbolized as ♚, and is briefly recorded by the letter K.

How the King Moves. The King always moves gravely, one step at a time, to any square adjoining the square he occupies, provided he is safe there from an immediate attack. The two Kings, that is, the black and white Kings, can never be on adjoining squares. There must always be at least one square between them. Once during the game, each player has the privilege of castling which automatically increases the King's safety. (See *Castling*.)

Value. His Majesty, the King, is the most important of all chessmen. In fact, he is the only indispensable man in a game of chess. Strictly speaking, a King is never captured; he is mated. (See *Mate*.) To mate the opponent's King is the object of the game. When a King is mated, the game is terminated. Hence, the King's safety is of paramount importance at all times.

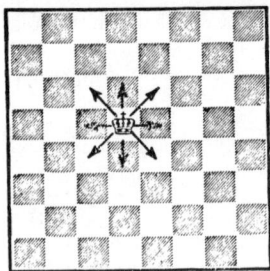

How King Moves

The King may move to any square adjoining the one he occupies as indicated by the arrows, provided he is safe there from immediate attack.

His functions; advantages and disadvantages. In the beginning of the game, the King usually plays a defensive role, but in the end-game, when most of the forces have been eliminated, the King by force of necessity assumes an offensive role. Interestingly enough, the King can attack any one of the opponent's pieces which is unprotected, save the Queen. He may capture her, but never threaten her. To do so, would mean his own demise—mate.

Historically, the importance of the King's position has always been recognized. His method of movement, powers and functions have remained unchanged for more than twelve centuries. For a more complete treatise see "A Short History of Chess," Chapter 2 entitled, "The King Never Dies," by Henry A. Davidson, M.D., in *Chess Review,* March, 1956, page 76.

KING'S BISHOP OPENING

1. P-K4, P-K4; 2. B-B4

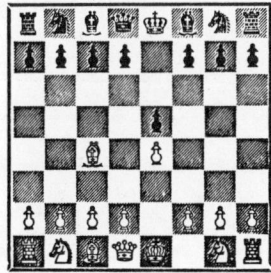

This King's Bishop opening has been preferred by Philidor and has been regarded as a mere transposition of the King's Knight opening. Advocates of this opening have claimed that 2. B-B4 does not interfere with the advance of the KB Pawn. Modern chessplayers, however, consider the King's Knight opening stronger and safer. One of the chess rules which has been sponsored by many modern chessmasters states that Knights should be developed before Bishops. From the King's Bishop Opening, such games as the following may develop.

Berlin Defense—
    2 . . . N-KB3; 3. P-Q3

Boden-Kieseritzky Gambit —
    2 . . . N-KB3; 3. N-KB3, NxP;
Classical Defense—
    2. . . . B-B4;
Lewis Counter Gambit—
    2 . . . B-B4; 3. P-QB3, P-Q4; 4. BxB
Lopez Gambit—
    2 . . . . B-B4; 3. Q-K2, P-Q3; 4. P-KB4
McDonnell's Double Gambit—
    2 . . . B-B4; 3-P-QN4, BxP; 4. P-KB4

KING'S FIELD

The area composed of the square on which the King stands and the ones adjacent to it. When the King is cornered, his field consists of four squares: the one on which he stands and the three surrounding squares. When the King is out in the open in the middle of the board, his field comprises nine squares: namely, the one on which he stands plus the eight surrounding squares. The term "King's field" is frequently used by problem composers.

KING'S GAMBIT

1. P-K4, P-K4; 2. P-KB4

The King's Gambit opening which Jaenisch in 1842 styled "an imperishable monument of human wisdom," was first mentioned by Ruy Lopez in 1561. Its chief advocates have been Italian chess writers.

In sacrificing a Pawn, White gains

control of the center and opens the King's Bishop file for his Rook. The early advance of the King's Bishop Pawn is questionable. In fact, Tarrasch states very positively: "I maintain it to be a decisive mistake." Horowitz believes that because complications generally come thick and fast in this opening, "the King's Gambit ought to be part of the repertoire of every chessplayer." For a development of the King's Gambit opening see *Modern Chess Openings,* Ninth Edition, by Walter Korn; or *Practical Chess Openings,* by Reuben Fine.

KING'S GAMBIT DECLINED

Schemes for declining the proffered Pawn in the King's Gambit were proposed by Lopez as early as 1561. Many modern masters recommend that for better development, Black should decline White's proffered Pawn and get his minor pieces out quickly so as to gain a tempo. This may be accomplished by playing (after: 1. P-K4, P-K4; 2. P-KB4) 2 . . . B-B4. Black may also proceed with 2 . . . N-KB3 or with the Falkbeer's Counter Gambit by playing 2 . . . P-Q4. As to the actual merits of accepting or declining the King's Gambit Pawn, Horowitz is of the opinion that "they are about on a par."

KING'S INDIAN DEFENSE

1.	P-Q4	N-KB3
2.	P-QB4	P-KN3

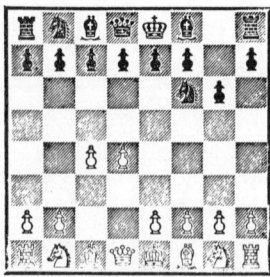

In this defense, Black avoids actual

occupation of the center but endeavors to control it by fianchettoing his King Bishop and playing . . . P-K4 later on. About a hundred years ago, Louis Paulsen pioneered with this defense. Nevertheless, he did not think very highly of it and for a quarter of a century, it was considered a dubious line of defensive play. Lately, however, it has gained the attention of chessplayers.

Reinfeld points out that this Defense "yields interesting chess, rich in possibilities despite the theoretical drawbacks for Black." Although White has a comfortable development, a strong Pawn center and considerable mobility, Black, on the other hand, has ample maneuvering opportunities for his men. Walter Korn indicates that the King's Indian Defense "is suited to all styles of players." For a procedural presentation of this Defense with its variations see *Modern Chess Openings,* Ninth Edition, by Walter Korn; or *Practical Chess Openings,* by Reuben Fine.

KING'S KNIGHT OPENING

1.	P-K4	P-K4
2.	N-KB3	

A safe and sound opening which is merely preparatory to any one of the following openings.

Ruy Lopez or Spanish Game—
  2 . . . N-QB3; 3. B-N5
Giuoco Piano—
  2 . . . N-QB3; 3. B-B4, B-B4
Ponziani —
  2 . . . N-QB3; 3. P-B3
Evans Gambit—
  2 . . . N-QB3; 3. B-B4, B-B4;
  4. P-QN4
Scotch Game—
  2 . . . N-QB3; 3. P-Q4
Two Knights' Defense—
  2 . . . N-QB3; 3. B-B4, N-B3
Petroff (Russian) Defense—
  2 . . . N-KB3
Greco Counter Gambit—
  2 . . . P-KB4

Queen's Pawn Counter Gambit—
  2 . . . P-Q4

Philidor's Defense—
  2 . . . P-Q3

KING'S LEAP

A special, privileged move made by a King which was somewhat similar to the move made by the modern Knight as described in early Sanskrit chess history. In France, the King exercised this privilege until about the year 1200. In Germany, traces of this privileged move can be found as late as 1400. Today, this special move is still in usage in the Malay Peninsula where His Majesty may "leap" like a Knight, to escape a checkmate. In our modern chess, the only time a King may make a limited "leap" is when during the castling process he may leap over one vacant square. See *Castling*.

KING'S PAWN OPENING

1. P-K4

This is one of the oldest and most analyzed of all chess openings. It gives White a maximum scope for a safe and quick development by going straight to the center, where he controls the all-important squares which hold the key to many future tactical operations. Furthermore, this move opens the lines for the development of two powerful pieces: the King's Bishop and the Queen. This opening exemplifies the practical application of how to control the center while promoting quick development. This is the main objective of the opening phase of the game.

KING'S SIDE

A general term applied to that entire area of the chessboard which embraces the King's file and the files of his Bishop, Knight and Rook. The other side of the board is referred to as the Queen's side. These two divisions of the chessboard are shown in the accompanying illustration.

KNIGHT

The Knight is a minor piece shaped like the head of a horse. At the opening of a game, each player has two Knights and they are placed immediately next to the Rooks on the same rank. The Knight on the Queen's side of the chessboard is known as the Queen's Knight and the one on the King's side of the board is the King's Knight. In chess notation, the Knight is symbolized as ♞, and is briefly recorded by the abbreviation of Kt. or the letter N. To avoid any possible confusion, this Dictionary is using the letter N in all references to the Knight.

The Knight has been characterized in chess literature as: the showman of the chessboard; the clown of the chessboard; the terror of the chessboard; the bugaboo of the beginner; the most capricious of all chessmen; the short-stepping piece; the jumper; the practical joker; and Peck's bad boy on the chessboard.

How the Knight Moves. The movement of the Knight on the chessboard symbolizes the horse's ability to prance along and jump over an obstacle. From where the Knight stands, it moves two squares along the same rank or file *and* then one square over to either the right or left, as shown in the accompanying diagram. This move may be made regardless of whether the squares over which the Knight passes are vacant or occupied by friendly or enemy chessmen, as long as the square on which the Knight lands, indicated by arrows in the diagram, is not already occupied by a friendly man. If there is a hostile man on the square, it may be captured.

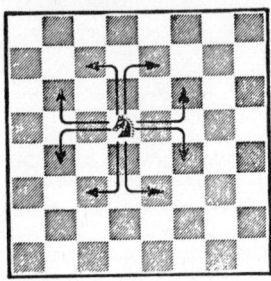

How a Knight Moves

From where the Knight stands, it can make an L-shaped move to a square of a different color.

The Knight's move is usually described as L-shaped. The long line of the "L" represents two squares (symbolic of the long neck of the horse) and the short line of the "L" represents one square (symbolic of the horse's head). Some writers explain the Knight's move as a combined one-square move of a Rook and a one-square move of a Bishop. In making a Knight move, chess writers sometimes use the expression that the Knight can "jump" over chessmen stationed on the squares along the path over which the Knight moves. In fact, in some countries the Knight is called the "Jumper" or "Springer."

Value of a Knight. Generally, the Knight is about equal in value to three Pawns and is slightly less in power than the Bishop. The effectiveness of the Knight decreases as the number of chessmen on the chessboard is diminished throughout the game. Experi-

enced players find that a Knight is more valuable than a Bishop in cramped positions but a Bishop is more effective than a Knight in the end-game Pillsbury and Tchigorin are said to have generally preferred Knights to Bishops. Today, however, leading chessmasters do not seem to share this preference. The International Master Larry Evans, speaking of the end-game, says: "Woe unto him who exchanges Bishop for Knight without just cause!"

Advantages and Disadvantages. The Knight and the Bishop are the "minor pieces" in a game of chess. Of these, the Knight is the short-range piece in contrast to the Bishop which is the long-range piece. The Bishop can cover only the squares of his own color whereas the Knight can cover the entire board in his movements (See *Cruising Range.*) A unique advantage of the Knight is his ability to attack any other piece without placing himself in immediate danger from that piece. Once a Knight makes an attack no piece can be interposed between the Knight and his objective. Only the Knight has this privilege. No other piece on the chessboard, not even the Queen, can emulate this singular prerogative of the Knight. Furthermore, the Knight is the only piece that can move before any of the Pawns have been moved at the opening of the game. See *Réti Opening;* and *Queen's Knight Game.*

Its History. Originally, the Knight was referred to as a horse. In medieval times, emphasis was placed on the horseman, the rider, or, as we call him now, the Knight. He is known as "Springer" by the Germans, and "Cavalier" by the French. The powers and movements of the Knight have not changed for the past twelve centuries. See "A Short History of Chess," Chapter 7, entitled: "Old Grey Mare," by Henry A. Davidson, M.D., in *Chess Review,* August, 1956, page 237.

KNIGHT ODDS

Removing the stronger player's Knight (usually the Queen's Knight) at the beginning of the game so as to equalize to a degree the playing strength of the two participants. The one giving the odds plays with the white pieces. It is generally recommended that when Knight odds are given, Black proceeds with the French Defense, the Sicilian, or the Caro-Kann opening. Black is usually warned not to sacrifice time or position to force exchanges; White, on the other hand, will strive for gambits and complications so as to exercise his superior combinative chessplaying power most effectively.

KNOCKOUT TOURNAMENT

A tournament consisting of several rounds in which the losers or low scorers are eliminated in each of the successive rounds. Hence, this type of tournament is sometime referred to as the "elimination type of tourney." This procedure is utilized when there are a large number of entries in a tournament. Drawn games must be replayed until a definite final winner is obtained.

KOCH'S NOTATION

A co-ordinate, nonverbal nomenclature which uses numerals to identify

The first number in each square represents the file; the second number represents the rank. The dash between the numbers is optional.

the squares on a chessboard. As shown in the accompanying diagram, the files are numbered 1 to 8. The ranks are also numbered 1 to 8 beginning with the square at White's left-hand corner. Thus, a notation of 51 would mean the fifth file and the first rank, or White's K1 in the Anglo-American system of notation. Likewise, 86 in this Koch's notation means the eighth file and the sixth rank, or White's KR6. This system of notation was used in central Europe in the 18th and 19th centuries.

KOLISCH

Baron Ignace von Kolisch (1837-1889), a Grandmaster chessplayer, was born in Pressbourg, Hungary. He was a writer, private secretary and banker. His chess career, which lasted only ten years, began at the Café de la Régence, in Paris. During his brief chess career, he played with Anderssen in 1858 and finished in a draw. At the 1861 Bristol Chess Congress, he finished in seventh place, but he finished first, ahead of Steinitz at the Emperor's Tournament held in Paris in 1867. The following year, he met one of the Rothschilds in Vienna who was so impressed with Kolisch's good manners and good chessplay that he started him in the banking business. The banking business in which Kolisch amassed a fortune, prevented him from being an active participant in any further chess tournaments.

KOLTANOWSKI

George Koltanowski, an International Chessmaster and International Wizard of Blindfold Chess, was born in Antwerp, Belgium, in 1903. Early in life, he demonstrated an extraordinary ability to memorize with the greatest of ease. He applied this talent to chess in which he became interested at the age of fourteen. This Belgian "quiz kid" has a knowledge of seven foreign languages. He has traveled the world over playing and teaching the game. He is now an American citizen living in San Francisco, California.

"Kolty," as he is affectionately known, has gained for himself a most remarkable record of successful accomplishments. He was the Champion Chessplayer of Belgium six times. In San Francisco, in 1949, he played 271 games simultaneously, winning 251 and losing only three games; the others were drawn games. On September 20, 1937, in Edinburgh, Scotland, he established a world's record for simultaneous blindfold chess, playing 34 games, winning twenty-four, and drawing ten. On December 2, 1951, in San Francisco, he played 50 games blindfolded in nine hours, at the rate of ten seconds a move, winning 43, drawing 5, and losing 2. On May 22, 1955, he established another record by playing 110 games simultaneously, starting all games at one time. After twelve hours and ten minutes of continuous play while taking his nourishment en route from table to table where his opponents sat, he finished by winning 89 games, drawing 17 and losing only 4 games.

He is chess editor of five west coast publications and conducts a chess column in many papers throughout the country. He has written several books of which *Adventures of a Chess Master* is, as one reviewer says: "the only book of its kind." It deals with blindfold chess in all its phases, such as the history of blindfold chess, an autobiography of Koltanowski, anecdotes, stories and many games.

KOSTAL, MIROSLAV

see *Havel.*

KOSTICH

Boris Kostich, a world champion contender, was born at Versecz, Hungary, on February 24, 1887. He learned the game of chess when he was a stu-

dent at Vienna. His first official match was in 1911, against Wiarde, a champion chessplayer of the city of Cologne, whom he beat by 5 wins and 2 draws. Between 1913 and 1915, Kostich played and defeated all the best players of South America, and between 1915 and 1918 he played with the best players in the United States and won the majority of the games. On June 4, 1916, he established the record at that time of playing twenty games in a simultaneous blindfold exhibition in New York City. Later, in five tournament games with Capablanca, Kostich secured a draw in every game. In a subsequent match between Capablanca and Kostich held in Havana in 1919, Kostich lost badly. He claimed that the climatic conditions were against him.

According to Reinfeld, Kostich "is a player of the old school who has learned to accomodate himself to the modern theories. His style is therefore an interesting blend of contrasting theories."

KRIEGSPIEL

A composite German word meaning, literally, "war game." Kriegspiel originated in Switzerland about 1811. Blocks and figures were used to represent various parts of armies and equipment. These were moved about on maps according to strategical plans and tactical maneuvers. This game was considered to be very instructive to military students because the basic principles of this game correlated favorably with actual military operations on the battlefield.

After the Franco-German War of 1870, this game was introduced into the English army with some modifications. A chess version of this Kriegspiel was claimed to have been developed by Michael Temple, a journalist on the *Globe* newspaper, who died

October 25, 1929, at the age of sixty-four. From time to time, other names have been applied to this game. The late English problemist H. D'O. Bernard (1878-1955) called it "Commando Chess," and the late R. C. Griffith (1872-1955) referred to it as "Screen Chess."

According to this English chess version of Kriegspiel, chessplay is conducted without the sight of the opponent's chessboard. Each player has his own board on which he maintains with each move the position of his own forces and disposes his adversary's men as he thinks them to be on his opponent's board. A referee keeps the actual position of both Black and White on a third board for his own use.

The referee announces when the next move is to be made by saying, for example, "White has moved." The next player then moves in accordance with the limited inferences which may be drawn from the limited remarks of the referee, if any are given. For example, 1) the referee must announce all captures and the square on which it takes place but not the piece making the capture. 2) The referee also announces every check and the direction from which it is made, as, "Black has moved, giving check on the file," (or, on the rank, on the long diagonal, on the short diagonal, or, by the Knight). 3) Any attempted move, if legal, stands as played. If an illegal move has been made the referee merely says "No" and the player must then seek a correct move. For a fuller discussion of Kriegspiel see the articles published by W. H. Stephens in the *British Year Book of Chess,* 1913 and 1914; and those by R. C. Griffith in the January, March, May and July, 1944 issues of the *British Chess Magazine.* See also *The Official Blue Book and Encyclopedia of Chess,* pp. 242-246.

L

LA BOURDONNAIS

Louis Charles Mahé de la Bourdonnais, a noteworthy chessplayer and chesswriter, was born in France in 1797. He was the grandson of Mahé de la Bourdonnais, who was Governor of Mauritius and the famous commander who won a great victory over the English fleet off Madras in 1746. Louis La Bourdonnais died in London on December 13, 1840.

La Bourdonnais was a compatriot of Philidor and was regarded as the strongest chessplayer of his day. Although he was the author of a textbook entitled: *Traité sur le Jeu des Echecs* and was associated with the first publication of *La Palamedé,* his reputation rests not so much on writing about chess as in playing chess. In 1834, La Bourdonnais went to London for a series of games with McDonnell which resulted in a final score of: La Bourdonnais 45, McDonnell 27 and 13 drawn games. Of this encounter, the celebrated English chessmaster George Walker says: "We cheerfully admit the superiority of La Bourdonnais. His blows are dealt with greater vigor; his stratagems better timed; his powers of counter-attack more forcible; his judgment of position sounder."

LADDER ARRANGEMENT OF CHESSPLAYERS

A device used by chess clubs whereby the names of its members are placed on movable cards, arranged in order of their playing strength and posted in the club vestibule and/or in the club bulletin. The name of the strongest player is placed on the top and is said to be at the top of the ladder. This ladder arrangement is revised periodically, usually once a week. Each club specifies its own rules as to the use that is to be made of this ladder type of arranging their members. For a detailed discussion of the uses made of this device see *The Official Blue Book and Encyclopedia of Chess,* pages 208-221.

LADY

The "Lady" of the chessboard is the Queen. About three hundred years ago, the term Lady was in common usage but the term Queen is more popular now, especially in English speaking countries. See *Queen.*

LANGE ATTACK

1. P-K4	P-K4
2. N-KB3	N-QB3
3. P-Q4	PxP
4. B-QB4	N-B3
5. 0-0	B-B4
6. P-K5	P-Q4

An attack credited to Dr. Max Lange, who was born in Magdeburg, Germany, in 1832. He was a strong chessplayer. He won first prizes in Germany as well as at the international tournaments at Aix la Chapelle in 1867, and at Hamburg in 1868. He

founded a local chess club in 1849 and organized the West German Chess Association about 1868. He contributed to the chess column in the *Leipzig Illustrated* and was the author of such books (written in German) as: *Collection of Chess Games; Paul Morphy, His Life and Labors; Textbook of Chess; Evaluation of Chess Openings; and a Handbook of Chess Problems.* He died in Leipzig on December 8, 1899.

In an obituary column, the *British Chess Magazine* stated that Lange is "remembered as a most ingenious combatant over the board and a fertile inventor of new modes of play in several openings and a valuable contributor to chess openings." One of the openings which he developed is now known as the Lange Attack, which is illustrated in the accompanying diagram. Freeborough and Ranken point out that "the Max Lange Attack is not so much a regular opening as a form of proceeding applicable to several openings. It produces some fine and critical positions, calculated to embarrass an inexperienced opponent, and is thus a formidable weapon in the hands of an expert." Horowitz and Reinfeld observe that the Lange Attack is "tricky and full of traps . . . and . . . has puzzled the experts for decades."

LANGUAGE, CHESS

Chess language is a body of words, symbols, phrases and expressions used by chessplayers. This chess terminology grew and developed throughout the centuries. These terms have been obtained from various sources. Some of them have been 1) borrowed from other languages (Zugswang, en passant, etc.); 2) developed by new schools of thought (modernism, hypermodernism, etc.); 3) labelled after the name of the originator of a unique chess procedure (Réti Opening, Philidor's Legacy, etc.); 4) named after the place where a particular line of play was first used or popularized (Sicilian Defense, the Scheveningen Variation, etc.); and, 5) coined by chess writers, analysts and commentators (skewer, chestnuts, organ-pipes, etc.)

Chess has developed an international language of its own which is expressed through internationally standardized movements of the chessmen operating on the chessboard. It is well known that chessplay, as is evidenced in international chess tournaments, can be reduced to an absolute minimum of linguistic terminology. Through the aid of the World Chess Federation (F.I.D.E.) which standardized chess procedures, chess could be played with the knowledge of but one spoken word: *mate,* which is understood wherever chess is played.

LASKER, EDWARD

Dr. Edward Lasker, one of the leading American chessmasters, a champion chessplayer and author, was born in Kempen, Poland (then Germany) in 1885. His mother was American, his father German. Although he had a penchant for medicine, he studied mathematics and engineering at the University of Berlin in 1904. After he was graduated in 1911, with a degree of Doctor of Engineering, he became Project Engineer with the German General Electric Company. In 1912, he was transferred to the firm's office in London. Three months after the outbreak of World War I, he came to the United States where the editor of the *American Chess Bulletin* arranged a chess exhibition tour for him. This brought him to Chicago where he met Julius Rosenwald and Albert Loeb, also chessplayers and heads of the Sears Roebuck Company. They offered Lasker an engineering job with the mail order firm. In 1921, Edward Lasker became a citizen of the United States. He is now a mechanical and electrical engineer in New York City.

In 1922, Edward Lasker gave an account of his own interest in the game of chess. At that time, he stated, "My father showed the game to me when I was not quite six years of age, because it happened that Emanuel Lasker, to whom I am only remotely related, at that time became the most prominent figure in the world of chess." During his college days, he devoted a good deal of his time to chess, and, shortly before being graduated, he published his first book on chess, entitled: *Schachstrategie,* which later was translated and published in London under the English title of *Chess Strategy.*

Edward Lasker's chessplaying ability is noteworthy. In 1910, he defeated the Champion of Berlin, Erich Cohn. Later he won the Championship of London. In the United States, he won the Championship title of New York in 1915, of Chicago in 1916, and he became the Champion chessplayer of the Western States in 1916, 1917, 1919, 1920 and 1921. In 1923, he played a brilliant match with Frank Marshall for the U.S. Championship in which he finished with a score of $8\frac{1}{2}$ to $9\frac{1}{2}$ in Marshall's favor. However, on the strength of his excellent performance, Lasker was invited in 1924 to participate in the World's Masters' Tournaments of New York. Since that time, due to his professional engineering activities, Edward Lasker has been unable to devote much time to chess. In the last number of years he accepted invitations to chess tournaments which interested him because of exceptionally strong competition or because the countries in which they were played promised some fascinating new experiences. Recently, he participated in tournaments held in Mar del Plata in 1949; in Vienna in 1951; in Hastings in 1952; in Havana in 1953; and in Mexico City in 1954.

Edward Lasker has written a number of stimulating books, such as *Chess and Checkers; The Adventure of Chess; Chess Strategy; Chess Secrets;* and many others. He is now interested in writing about his experiences with the great masters.

His chess stature is recognized by contemporary chessplayers throughout the chess fraternity. He has the honor of being the President of the famous Marshall Chess Club in New York City.

LASKER, EMANUEL

Dr. Emanuel Lasker, World Champion chessplayer from 1894 to 1921, was born in Berlinchen, near Berlin, Germany, on December 24, 1868. He studied at the universities of Berlin, Goettingen, Heidelberg and Erlangen where he received the degree of Doctor of Philosophy. By training he was a mathematician and philosopher. For a time, he taught mathematics and wrote a book in the field of algebra. Eventually he gave up his mathematical profession in favor of a chess career. The last few years of his life were spent in New York where he died on January 11, 1941.

At about the age of ten, Emanuel Lasker learned chess moves from his older brother, Dr. Berthold Lasker, who according to Bernstein "was an extraordinary gifted man and chessplayer." In 1890, Emanuel Lasker accepted an invitation to go to London as a chess professional. From then on, he participated in numerous chess tournaments and matches with the best chessplayers of his time. Over the years, from 1889 to 1936, he played 325 games in official chess tournaments. Of these, he won 59% of the games, lost 10.5% and drew 30.5%. In 1894, Dr. Lasker won the World Championship title by defeating Steinitz. He retained the championship crown for twenty-seven years. In 1921, Dr. Lasker lost his crown when he was defeated by Capablanca.

Dr. Lasker took a philosophical view of chess. He saw in chess a great similarity with life itself. Chess like life is, he says, "a constant struggle." To struggle means to overcome difficulties which stand in the way of reaching a desired goal. Since chess is an intellectual and straightforward struggle, with a definite objective in view, Dr. Lasker tried to discover general laws which might serve as general guides in a game of chess.

Dr. Lasker is usually referred to by chess writers as one of the greatest of all chess personalities. For example, Dr. Bernstein observed that Dr. Emanuel Lasker "was an inspiring companion. His foresight was uncanny; his strategy and precaution incredible; the courage which he manifested in battle, the independence of his judgment concerning openings and positions were remarkable." Chess writers assert that Dr. Lasker's style of chessplay was clear and precise. He seemed to have enjoyed defending precarious and complicated positions as was well demonstrated in the games he played against his namesake Edward Lasker, at the New York Tournament in 1924. Interestingly enough, Dr. Lasker founded no school of chess, but, as Dr. Fine points out, that "in reality all chessplayers are his pupils." This undoubtedly can be inferred from the fact that Dr. Lasker wrote several books, some of which have become classics in chess literature, such as *Common Sense in Chess* and *Manual of Chess.*

Browsing through the literature, the following complimentary epithets are associated with Dr. Emanuel Lasker, namely:

Chess Champion of the world.

The philosopher of chess.

The apostle of common sense.

The superman of the chess world.

The dramatist of the chessboard.

A cheerful pessimist and a
   moderate optimist.

Lasker, a piece of chess history.

Lasker the unique!

LATINIZATION OF CHESS TERMS

Translating chess terms into Latin —a language of scholars. When, in medieval times, chess terms were latinized, it was definitely assumed that the game of chess appealed to scholars. The principal latinized chess words are:

scacorum ludus: the game of chess.

scacum: (neuter noun) check.

scacco, scaccare: (verb) to put in check

scaccus: a chessman; plural: *scacci*: chessmen.

Rex: King.

Regina or *Fercia*: Queen.

Alphilus: Bishop.

Equus: Horse or Knight. Also *Miles*: soldier, most soldiers were mounted.

Roccus: Rook.

Pes, Pedis: Pawn—a foot soldier.

LATVIAN COUNTER GAMBIT

see *Greco Counter Gambit*.

LAUSANNE, TREATISE OF

A name given by some writers to an early treatise on the game of chess which was published in 1698 under the title of *"Traité du Jeu Royal des Echecs,* par B. A. D. R. G. S., a Lausanne, par David Gentil."* Staunton points out that "its contents seems to have been derived largely from Lopez and Greco."

LAWS, BENJAMIN

Benjamin Glover Laws, a noteworthy English chess problemist, was born at Barnsbury, on February 6, 1861. In his early days, he was a clerk in the Royal Italian Opera Company and subsequently worked for a shorthand writers' and solicitors' firm of Fooks, Chadwick, Arnold and Chadwick. He died on September 21, 1931.

Laws acquired the rudimentary knowledge of chess in 1877. Nine years later, he helped to produce the *Chess Problem Text Book*. For about ten years he served as the chess problem editor of the *Chess Monthly* magazine. He published several books, such as *Two-Move Chess Problems* in 1890, and *Chess Problems and How To Solve Them* in 1923. He became Problems Editor of *British Chess Magazine* in 1898. In 1918, he was elected to serve as President of the British Chess Problems Society. The *British Chess Magazine* referred to Benjamin G. Laws as "a rich, diversified and fruitful problemist."

LAWS OF CHESS

Our present Laws of Chess were adopted by the General Assembly of the World Chess Federation (Fédération International des Echecs) at the 23rd Congress of the Federation, meeting in Stockholm, 1952, and amended at the 24th Congress, Schaffhausen, Switzerland, 1953. The following copyrighted translation is reproduced here by permission of The United States Chess Federation.

Official American Translation
Copyright, 1954, by
The
UNITED STATES CHESS
FEDERATION
(American Unit of the F.I.D.E.)

Preface to the American Translation

Since the idiom of speech and the ideology of thought vary with race and language, it remains obvious that a literal translation of the wording of any document defeats the primal purpose of translating the basic ideas of that document. For that sufficient reason, in preparing an official American translation to the "Regles du Jeu des Echecs", the translators have given more attention to the expression in clear language of the basic ideas of the text than to an exact literal translation of the French original. This paraphrasing of the original text is not always indicated in the body of the translation, but certain notes, which have been added to lend clarity to the translation, are printed in italic type to indicate their explanatory nature.

It is also to be noted that certain modifications of a minor character have been made in translating the text of Supplement No. 1. These modifications are designed solely to create conformity between the standard practice in the United States and the official regulations in regard to chess notation, since traditional practice in this country has developed several slight variations from the system of notation as used in Europe.

This translation is the composite product of the work performed by:

Harold M. Phillips
A. Wyatt Jones
Frank R. Graves
William M. Byland
Montgomery Major
Kenneth Harkness

THE LAWS OF CHESS
PART ONE
General Laws

Article 1
Introduction

The game of chess is played between two opponents by moving men on a square board called a "chessboard."

Article 2
The Chessboard and its Arrangement

1. The chessboard is composed of 64 equal squares alternately light (the "white" squares) and dark (the "black" squares).

2. The chessboard is placed between the players in such a way that the corner square to the right of each player is white.

3. The eight rows of squares running from the edge of the chessboard nearest one of the players to that nearest the other player are called "files."

   (*In a chess diagram, the files are the vertical rows of squares.*)

4. The eight rows of squares running from one edge of the chessboard to the other at right angles to the files are called "ranks."

   (*In a chess diagram, the ranks are the horizontal rows of squares.*)

5. The straight rows of squares of one color, touching corner to corner, are called "diagonals."

Article 3
The Chessmen
and their Arrangement

At the beginning of the game, one player commands 16 light-colored men (the "white" men), the other 16 dark-colored men (the "black" men).

These men are as follows:

One White King
with the usual symbol in print of ♔

One white Queen
with the usual symbol in print of ♕

Two white Bishops
with the usual symbol in print of ♗

Two white Knights
with the usual symbol in print of ♘

Two white Rooks
with the usual symbol in print of ♖

Eight white Pawns
with the usual symbol in print of ♙

One black King
with the usual symbol in print of ♚

One black Queen
with the usual symbol in print of ♛

Two black Bishops
with the usual symbol in print of ♝

Two black Knights
with the usual symbol in print of ♞

Two black Rooks
with the usual symbol in print of ♜
Eight black Pawns
with the usual symbol in print of ♟
The initial position of the men on
the chessboard is as follows:

Article 4
Conduct of the Game

1. The two players must alternate in
making one move at a time. The
player with the white men com-
mences the game.

2. A player is said to "have the move"
when it is his turn to play.

Article 5
General Definition of the Move

1. With the exception of castling
(Article 6), a move is the transfer
of a man from one square to
another square which is either vacant or occupied by an enemy man
(*a man of opposite color*).

2. No man, except the Rook, in castling, and the Knight (Article 6)
may cross a square occupied by
another man.

3. A man played to a square occupied by an enemy man captures, in
the same move, this enemy man,
which must be immediately removed from the chessboard by the
player making the capture. See
Article 6 for capturing "en passant."

Article 6
Moves of the Individual Men
The King

Except in castling, the King moves
to any adjacent square that is not
attacked by an enemy man.
Castling is a move of the King and
either Rook, counting as a single move
(of the King), executed as follows:
The King is transferred from its original square to either of the nearest
squares of the same color in the same
rank; then that Rook toward which
the King has been moved is transferred over the King to the square
which the King has just crossed. Castling is permanently impossible (*illegal*) if the King or castling Rook
has previously moved. Castling is
momentarily prevented: a) if the
King's original square, or the square
which the King must cross, or that
which it will occupy, is attacked by
an enemy man; b) if there are any
men between the King and the Rook
toward which the King must move.

The Queen

The Queen moves to any square
(except as limited by Article 5, No.
2) on the file, rank, or diagonals on
which it stands.

The Rook

The Rook moves to any square (except
as limited by Article 5, No. 2) on
the file or rank on which it stands.

The Bishop

The Bishop moves to any square
(except as limited by Article 5, No.
2) on the diagonals on which it stands.

The Knight

The Knight's move is composed
of two different steps: first, to a contiguous square along the rank or file,
and then, still moving away from its
square of departure, to a contiguous
square on a diagonal.

The Pawn

The Pawn moves forward only.

a) Except when capturing, it advances from its original square one or two vacant squares along the file on which it is placed, and on subsequent moves only one vacant square along the file. When capturing, it advances to either square, contiguous to its own, on the diagonal.

b) A Pawn attacking a square crossed by an enemy Pawn, which has been advanced two squares in one move, from its original square, may capture, but only in the move immediately following, this enemy Pawn, as if the latter had been advanced only one square. This capture is called taking "en passant" (*or "in passing"*).

c) Any Pawn reaching the last (*eighth*) rank must be exchanged immediately, as part of the same move, for a Queen, Rook, Bishop, or Knight of the same color, at the choice of the player and without reference to the other men still remaining on the chessboard. This exchange of a Pawn is called "promotion", and the action of the promoted man is immediate.

Article 7
Completion of Move

A move is completed:

a) in the transfer of a man to a vacant square, when the player's hand has released the man;

b) in a capture, when the captured man has been removed from the chessboard and the player, having placed on its new square his own man, has released the latter from his hand;

c) in castling, when the player's hand has released the Rooks on the square crossed by the King; when the player has released the King from his hand, the move is not yet completed, but the player no longer has the right to make any other move than castling;

d) in the promotion of a Pawn, when the Pawn has been removed from the chessboard and the player's hand has released the new man after placing it on the promotion square; if the player has released from his hand the Pawn that has reached the promotion square, the move is not yet completed, but the player no longer has the right to play the Pawn to another square.

Article 8
The Touched Man

Provided that he firsts warns his opponent, the player having the move may adjust one or more men on their squares.

Except for the above case, if the player having the move touches one or more men, he must make his move by moving or capturing the first man touched which can be moved or captured.

No penalty is entailed if the opponent does not claim a violation of this rule before himself touching a man, or if none of the moves indicated above can be made legally.

Article 9
Illegal Positions

1. If, during a game, it is found that an illegal move has been made, the position shall be reinstated to what it was made before the illegal move made. The game shall then continue by applying the rules of Article 8 to the move replacing the illegal move. If the position cannot be reinstated, the game shall be annulled and a new game played.

2. If, during a game, one or more men have been accidentally displaced and incorrectly replaced, the position shall be reinstated to what it was before the displacement took place and the game shall be continued. If the position cannot be reinstated the game shall be annulled and a new game played.

3. If, after an adjournment, the position has been reinstated incorrectly, it shall be re-established to what it was at the adjournment and the game shall be continued.

4. If, during a game, it is found that the initial position of the men was incorrect, the game shall be annulled and a new game played.

5. If, during a game, it is found that the board has been wrongly placed, the position reached shall be transferred to a board correctly placed and the game shall be continued.

Article 10
Check

1. The King is in check when the square on which it stands is attacked by an enemy man; the latter is then said to give check to the King.

2. Check must be parried by the move immediately following. If check cannot be parried, it is said to be "mate". (See Article 11, No. 1).

3. A man intercepting a check to the King of its own color can itself give check to the enemy King.

Article 11
Won Game

1. The game is won by the player who has mated the enemy King. (See Article 10, No. 2).

2. The game is won by the player whose opponent resigns the game.

Article 12
Drawn Game

The game is drawn:

1. When the King of the player who has the move is not in check, but such player cannot make any legal move. The King is then said to be "stalemated."

2. By agreement between the two players.

3. Upon demand by one of the players when the same position appears three times, the same player having the move each time. The position is considered the same if men of the same kind and color occupy the same squares. The right to claim the draw belongs exclusively to the player:

    a) who is in a position to play a move leading to such repetition of the position, if he declares his intention of making such move;

    b) who is in a position to reply to a move which has produced the repeated position.

    If a player makes a move without claiming a draw in the manner prescribed in a) and b), he loses the right to claim a draw; this right is restored to him, however, if the same position appears again, the same player having the move.

4. When a player having the move demonstrates that at least fifty moves have been made by each side without the capture of any man, or the movement of any Pawns. This number of fifty moves may be increased for certain specific positions, provided that this increase in number and these positions have been clearly established prior to commencement of the game.

PART TWO

Supplementary Regulations for Tournaments and Matches

Article 13
Recording of Games

1. In the course of play, each player is required to record the game (his own moves and those of his opponent), move after move, as clearly and legibly as possible, on the score sheet prescribed for the contest.

2. If, extremely pressed for time, a player obviously is unable to meet the requirements of section No. 1 above, he should nevertheless endeavor to indicate on his score sheet the number of moves made. As soon as his time trouble is over, he must complete immediately his record of the game by recording the omitted moves. However, he will not have the right to claim a draw, on the basis of Article 12(3), if the moves in question were not recorded in conformity with the stipulations of section No. 1 above.

Article 14
Use of the Chess Clock

1. Each player must make a certain number of moves in a given period of time, these two factors being specified in advance.

2. Control of each player's time is effected by means of a clock equipped with special apparatus for this purpose.

3. At the time determined for the start of the game, the clock of the player who has the white men is set in motion. In the continuation of the game, each of the players, having made his move, stops his own clock and starts his opponent's clock.

4. Upon the execution of the prescribed number of moves, the last move is not considered as being completed until after the player has stopped his clock.

5. Every indication given by a clock or its apparatus (*the flag attached to some chess clocks*) is considered as conclusive in the absence of evident defects. The player who wishes to claim any such defect, is required to do so as soon as he himself has become aware of it.

6. If the game must be interrupted because of some situation for which neither player is responsible, the clocks shall be stopped until the situation has been adjusted. This should be done, for example, in the case of an illegal position to be corrected, in the case of a defective clock to be exchanged, or when the man which a player has announced he wishes to exchange for one of his Pawns that has reached the last rank, is not immediately available.

7. When in the case of Article 9, Nos. 1 and 2, it is not possible to establish the time used by each player up to the moment of irregularity, each player shall be allotted up to that moment an amount of time proportional to that indicated by the clocks when the irregularity is observed.

   Example: After Black's 30th move it is found that an irregularity took place at the 20th move. If, for these 30 moves, the clocks indicate 90 minutes for White and 60 minutes for Black, it shall be assumed that the times used by the two players for the first 20 moves were in proportion, thus:

   White $\dfrac{90 \times 20}{30} = 60$ minutes

   Black $\dfrac{60 \times 20}{30} = 40$ minutes

Article 15
Adjournment of the Game

1. If a game is not finished upon conclusion of the time prescribed for play, the player having the move shall write his next move in unambiguous notation on his score sheet, place his and his opponent's score sheets in an envelope, seal the envelope, and then stop the clocks. If the player has made the said move on the chessboard, he must seal this same move on his score sheet.

2. Upon the envelope shall be indicated:
   a) the names of the players;
   b) the position immediately before the sealed move;
   c) the time used by each player;
   d) the name of the player who has sealed the move, and the number of that move.

3. Custody of the envelope must be assured.

Article 16
Resumption of an Adjourned Game

1. When the game is resumed, the position immediately before the sealed move shall be set up on a chessboard, and the time used by each player at the time of adjournment shall be indicated by the clocks.

2. The envelope shall be opened only when the player having the move (the player who must reply to the sealed move) is present. That player's clock shall be started after the sealed move has been made on the chessboard.

3. If the player having the move is absent, his clock shall be started, but the envelope shall be opened only at the time of his arrival.

4. If the player who has sealed the move is absent, the player having the move is not obliged to reply to the sealed move on the chessboard. He has the right to record his move in reply upon his score sheet, to place the latter in an envelope, to stop his clock, and to start his opponent's clock. The envelope should be placed in security, and opened at the time of his opponent's arrival.

5. If the envelope containing the sealed move at the time of adjournment has disappeared, and it is not possible to re-establish, by agreement of the two players, the position and the times used for the adjourned game, or if, for any other reason, the said position and said times cannot be re-established, the game is annulled, and a new game must be played in place of the adjourned game. If the envelope containing the move recorded in accordance with Section 4 hereof has disappeared, the game must be resumed from the position at the time of adjournment, and with the clock times recorded at the time of adjournment.

6. If, upon resumption of the game, the time used has been incorrectly indicated on either clock, and if such mistake has been established by either player before making his first move, the error must be corrected. If the error is not then established, the game continues without correction.

Article 17
Loss of the Game

A game is lost by a player:

1. Who has not completed the prescribed number of moves in the time specified.

2. Who arrives at the chessboard more than one hour late.

3. Who has sealed an illegal move, or one so inaccurately or vaguely defined as to render impossible the establishment of its true meaning.

4. Who, during the game, refuses to comply with these laws of chess. If both players arrive at the chessboard more than one hour late, or refuse to comply with these laws of chess, the game shall be declared lost by both players.

Article 17A
The Drawn Game

1. An offer of a draw under the provisions of Article 12 (2) can be made by a player before or after he has made his move on the board, but in both cases only when his clock is running.

2. If a player claims a draw under the provisions of Article 12 (3), his clock must continue to run until the Director has verified the legitimacy of the claim.

If the claim is found to be correct, the game will be declared drawn, even if the claimant, in the interval, has overstepped the time limit.

If the claim is found to be incorrect, the game will continue, unless the claimant has, in the interval, overstepped the time limit in which case the game will be declared lost by the claimant.

Article 18
Conduct of the Players

1. a) During play the players are forbidden to make use of notes, manuscripts, or printed matter, or to analyze the game on another chessboard; they are likewise forbidden to receive the advice or opinion of a third party, whether solicited or not.

b) No analysis is permitted in the playing room during play or during adjournment.

c) Players are forbidden to distract or annoy their opponents in any manner whatsoever.

2. Infractions of the rules indicated in Section 1 hereof may incur penalties even to the extent of loss of the game.

Article 19
Tournament Director or Match Referee

To manage the competition, a tournament director or match referee must be designated.

His duties are:

a) to see that these laws of chess are strictly observed.

b) to supervise the progress of the competition; to establish that the prescribed time limit has not been exceeded by the players; to arrange the order of resumption of play in adjourned games; to supervise the arrangements set forth in Article 15, above all to see that the information on the envelope is correct; to assume custody of the sealed envelopes until such time as adjourned games are resumed; etc . . .

c) to enforce the decisions he has reached in disputes that have arisen during the course of the competition.

d) to impose penalties on the players for all infractions of these laws of chess.

Article 20
Interpretation of the Laws of Chess

In case of doubt as to the application or interpretation of these laws, the F.I.D.E. shall examine the evidence submitted and render official decision.

Decisions published in the "Revue de la F.I.D.E." are binding on all affiliated federations.

(In the United States, disputes as to the intention or interpretation of these laws should be forwarded in writing to the Secretary of the United States Chess Federation. The U.S.C.F. will render an interpretation of the law in clear cases, and in cases of doubt or ambiguity will forward the question to the F.I.D.E. for a final decision.)

SUPPLEMENT NO. 1
Chess Notation

F.I.D.E. Laws at present recognize only the two most generally known systems of notation: the algebraic system and the descriptive system.

Each affiliated unit is free to employ whichever of these two notations it prefers. *(The U.S.C.F. accepts both the algebraic and descriptive systems as valid.)*

THE ALGEBRAIC SYSTEM
General Notation

The chessmen, with the exception of the Pawns, are designated by their initials. The Pawns are not specifically indicated. *(In American usage, Knight is indicated by "Kt" or "N", as the initial "K" indicates the King.)*

The eight files (left to right from White's side of the chessboard) are designated by the letters a to h.

The eight ranks are numbered from 1 to 8, counting from White's first rank. (In the initial position, the White men are on ranks 1 and 2, and the Black men on ranks 7 and 8.)

Each square is thus invariably defined by the combination of a letter and a number. To the initial of the man moved (except the Pawn), the square of departure and the square of arrival is added; in abbreviated notation, the square of departure is omitted.

Thus Bc1-f4 means that the Bishop on square c1 is moved to square f4. In abbreviated notation: Bf4.

Or: e7-e5 means that the Pawn on square e7 is moved to square e5. In abridged notation: e5.

(Omission of the initial indicates that the move is made by a Pawn.)

When two similar men can be moved to the same square, abridged notation is expanded as follows:

For example, two Knights are at g1 and d2; the move Ktg1-f3 is written Ktg-f3 in abridged notation. If the Knights were at g1 and g5, the move Ktg1-f3 would be abridged to Kt1-f3.

Abbreviations

0-0	Castles with the Rook h1 or h8 (short castling)
0-0-0	Castles with the Rook a1 or a8 (long castling)
: or x	Captures
†	Check
‡	Mate

COMMON ABBREVIATIONS

!	Well played
?	Poorly played

THE DESCRIPTIVE SYSTEM

The chessmen, with the exception of the Pawns, are designated by their initials. The Pawns are not specifically indicated. *(In American usage and notation, the Pawns are also indicated by their initials; Knight is indicated by Kt or N, as the initial K is reserved to indicate the King.)*

The King-Rook, King-Knight, and King-Bishop are distinguished from the Queen-Rook, Queen-Knight, and Queen-Bishop, by the addition of the letters "K" and "Q".

(Thus, the King-side men are designated KR, KKt (or KN) and KB; the Queen-side men QR, QKt (or QN) and QB. A Pawn is identified by adding the initial, or initials, of the file on

which it stands. For example, KRP identifies a Pawn on the King-Rook file. See below.)

The eight files (from left to right for White, and inversely for Black) are designated as follows:

Queen-Rook file	(QR)
Queen-Knight file	(QKt or QN)
Queen-Bishop file	(QB)
Queen file	(Q)
King file	(K)
King-Bishop file	(KB)
King-Knight file	(KKt or KN)
King-Rook file	(KR)

The eight ranks are numbered from 1 to 8, counting from White's first rank for White, and from Black's first rank for Black.

A move is described by writing the designation of the man played, and the square to which it is played. Example: Q-KB4 means that the Queen is moved to the fourth square of the King-Bishop file (*counting from whichever side makes the move.*)

When two similar men can be moved to the same square, both the square of departure and the square of arrival are indicated. Thus R(KN4)-KN2 means that one of the two Rooks which is on KN4 square is moved to the second square of the same file. (*The abridged form of R(N) or R(4) is usually sufficient, i.e., if the two Rooks are not both on the N file or both on the 4th rank.*)

Abbreviations

0-0 or Castles KR	Castling with the King-Rook (K-side or short castling)
0-0-0 or Castles QR	Castling with the Queen-Rook (Q-side or long castling)
: or x	Captures
CH or †	Check

COMMON ABBREVIATIONS

!	Well played
?	Poorly played

SUPPLEMENT NO. 2
Expressions in General Use

1. Piece. A general term comprising all chessmen except the Pawn. (*In American usage, a Queen or Rook is a "major piece", a Bishop or Knight is a "minor piece"; the collective term "men" is used to designate both pieces and Pawns.*)

2. To Interpose. To place a man between one's own King and the enemy piece giving check. A check by a Knight cannot be parried by interposing.

3. Pinned Man. The man interposed to parry a check, whose freedom of movement is thereby destroyed, is said to be "pinned." (*This refers to an "absolute" pin. A man shielding an attack is also said to be pinned, if its movement would involve loss of material when the shielded man is captured.*)

4. Discovered Check. Check by a piece whose action has been unmasked by the moving of another man.

5. Double Check. Check simultaneously obtained by moving a man which itself gives check, and which at the same time uncovers the action of a piece which also gives check.

6. Long Castling (or Queen Castling). Castling with the Rook at a1 or a8 (Queen-Rook)

7. Short Castling (or King Castling). Castling with the Rook at h1 or h8 (King-Rook)

8. Winning the Exchange. To exchange a Knight or Bishop for a Rook.

9. Losing the Exchange. To exchange a Rook for a Knight or Bishop.

10. I Adjust (or "J'adoube"). Expression used when the player adjusts a man on its square (*in order to forewarn his opponent—See Article 8*).

LAZARD

Fred Lazard (1883-1949) the most all-around chessmaster of his time, was born in Paris, France. He was an excellent tournament chessplayer and won many prizes as a problem composer. His fame as an end-game composer was world-wide.

LEGAL'S LEGACY

A game developed by Legal, in which White sets a trap by offering his Queen as a bait which, if taken, results in Black's mate, as shown in the accompanying diagram.

White		Black
1. P-K4		P-K4
2. N-KB3		P-Q3
3. B-B4		B-N5
4. N-B3		P-KN3
5. NxP	If	BxQ
6. BxPch		K-K2
7. N-Q5 mate		

De Kermur, Sire de Legal (1710-1792) was considered a strong French player and champion of the Café de la Régence. He was finally beaten by one of his own pupils, the famous A. D. Philidor.

Legal's legacy consists of the accompanying moves, of which 5. NxP is the most brilliant.

LENGTH OF GAME

The number of moves that are needed to mate the opponent's King. This depends upon the skill of the players. The shortest game is the Fool's Mate which consists of two moves by each of the two players. (See *Fool's Mate.*) The longest officially recorded game, according to Chernev, consisted of 168 moves which occurred in a game played at the Carlsbad Tournament in 1907, between Duras and Wolf. The average game consists of about forty moves. Good chessplayers usually do not checkmate their opponents in much less than twenty-five moves, unless their opponents blunder badly.

Current rules indicate that a game may be stopped when identical positions are repeated three times or when fifty pairs of moves have been made without the advance of a Pawn or a capture. Donald McMurray is reported to have calculated that under the current rules, the *maximum* number of moves that can be made in any one game is 6,237. Allowing fifteen moves per hour, this would take 415.8 hours to play the longest possible game of chess.

LIGHTNING CHESS

A game of chess played with the speed of lightning. In lightning chess, both players are required to make one move after another without hesitation. Correct action performed with the greatest of speed is the essence of this method of chessplay. Many chessplayers and chesswriters use the German word "Blitz" instead of "Lightning Chess." See *Blitz Chessplay.*

LINE-PINNED

A piece which can move along, but not off, the rank, file or diagonal on which it is pinned. A Rook, for example, may when it is line-pinned, move from one square to another along the rank on which it is pinned but it can not leave the rank without exposing the protected chessman to immediate danger. See *Pin.*

LION

A figurine of a lion, representing the "King of the Beasts" was used by the chessplayers of Tibet as the equivalent of our King. See *Animals.*

LITTLE BARE KING

see *Bare King*

LITTLE GAME OF CHESS

see *Szen Problem*

LIVE CHESS

A picturesque and dramatic presentation of a game of chess enacted by living human beings. "Live Chess" or "Living Chess" as it is sometimes called has a long history. Its exact origin is unknown. However, it is known that as early as 1408, the Sultan Mohammed played live chess in Granada, Spain. One of the Dukes of Weimar, Germany, had a courtyard in his castle laid out in black and white marble squares, like a chessboard, for playing "live chess."

It is reported that in 1454, two eligible bachelors were about to fight a duel to decide who was to win the love of the daughter of the Governor of Marostica, Italy. The Governor, however, forbade the duel and proposed instead a game of chess, the winner of which was also to be the winner of his daughter. In order to keep the public immediately informed of the progress and outcome of the game, a group of citizens acted out every move on a specially prepared chessboard in the public square. This event developed into a sentimental tradition which consisted of playing an annual memorial "live chess" game in the public square for the amusement of its citizens and traveling visitors. (See *Selenus.*)

In the present century, live chess games are played from time to time in various places. A live chess game was staged at the Blanche Theatre, in Stockholm, Sweden. Here, living people appropriately dressed, moved about on a chessboard of 400 square meters, re-enacting the moves of two chess experts who were playing a game of chess in the foreground. Live chess games have also been played in other places, such as at the Polo Club in Mexico City. Live chess was also an attraction at a flower show in San Jose, California. In June, 1936, Capablanca played a live game in England against the British champion. In the same year, the Adult Recreation Project of the United States Works Project Administration (WPA) staged a live chess game in Boston.

LOCK

A piece is said to be locked when it is so confined that it has no mobility. The term was suggested by Horowitz and Kmoch, who applied it to a position in which "White has locked in his Queen Bishop" and consequently is temporarily immobilized. They believe that the term lock may well serve as a secondary name for all variations having this restricting characteristic. They indicate that "many an opening (or defense) has a lock variation." For a fuller justification for the use of this term see *World Chessmasters in Battle Royal,* by Horowitz and Kmoch, page 191.

LOLLI

Giovanni Baptiste Lolli, an eighteenth century first-rate chessplayer and author, was born at Modena, Italy. In 1763, he published at Bologna, a theoretical and practical treatise on the game of chess which utilized the Italian method of castling. See *Free Castling*.

LONE KING

A King standing by himself on the chessboard after having been stripped of all of his forces. To checkmate a lone King, it is necessary for the opponent to have at least any one of the following combinations of material forces: (a) King and Queen; (b) King and Rook; (c) King and two Bishops; (d) King, Bishop and Knight; or (e) at times it is possible to give mate with a King and Pawn. It is impossible to mate a lone King when the opponent has only his King and a Bishop or a Knight, or even two Knights. See *Checkmate Positions*.

LONG RANGE PIECE

Any one of the three pieces which can control an entire rank, file or diagonal. The "long range pieces" are: the Queen, the Bishop and the Rook.

LONG RANGE PROBLEM

An orthodox problem which usually requires more than three moves to produce a mate. Long range is a relative term. No precise number of moves has been established as to when a long range problem begins and a normal problem ends.

LOPEZ

Ruy Lopez de Seguri was one of the strongest and most influential sixteenth century chessplayers in Spain and Rome. He was a clergyman of Safra, in Estramadura, Spain. In 1559, he visited Rome and defeated all the notable Roman chessplayers. Philip II of Spain frequently invited Lopez to his court to play chess. Because of the extraordinary skill Lopez demonstrated in his chessplay, King Philip II became his patron and rewarded him handsomely. In 1561, Lopez published what is considered to have been the first textbook on chess. It contained a general discussion of chess openings and, among other things, it also contained a code of chess rules and regulations as well as some general advice to chessplayers. Lopez is credited for the use of the term "gambit" in chessplay. He also developed an opening which bears his name.

LOPEZ OPENING

1.	P-K4	P-K4
2.	N-KB3	N-QB3
3.	B-N5	

A classical opening developed by Ruy Lopez. White's third move; 3. B-N5 constitutes the characteristic Ruy Lopez opening move. This opening exerts pressure on Black from the very beginning of the game. Dr. Emanuel Lasker asserts that "this opening is dearest and nearest to the spirit of the old game—that spirit which dislikes rigid dogmas but loves motion and struggle." This opening has retained its popularity throughout the history of chessplay largely because, as Walter Korn points out, "it is an inexhaustible source of new ideas and gives rise to a variety of strategems from which players of different styles may choose." No wonder this opening is generally considered White's strongest opening and is one of the most favorite opening procedures so frequently utilized by so many chessplayers. It is sometimes referred to as "the Spanish Game."

Practically all chess books dealing with the opening phase of the game contain more or less lengthy treatments of the Ruy Lopez opening. See:

Modern Chess Openings, Ninth Edition, by Walter Korn.

Practical Chess Openings, by Reuben Fine, pages 325-399.

A Guide to Chess Openings by Leonard W. Barden.

Digest of Chess, by Mordecai Morgan, Part I.

Chess Openings—Ancient and Modern, by Freeborough and Ranken, pages 124-236.

Chess Openings, by James Morgan, pages 3-12.

LOSING A MOVE

Making a move which, relative to the immediate position on the chessboard, is of little importance. It is a wasted move. It usually consists of moving a piece twice to reach a position which, under similar circumstances, could be reached in one move. Losing a move or "losing a temp," as some writers prefer to call it, also occurs when any useless or indifferent move is made which permits the opponent to bring a piece into a playing position where it may make a direct or indirect attack.

LOSING CHESS

A frivolous method of playing chess according to the established rules of movement and in which the object of the game is to be the first to lose all of one's pieces, including the King. In this game, each player is obliged to make a capture whenever it is possible

to do so. A stalemate is regarded as a win for the player who is stalemated. For further information, see "Losing Chess" in *The Fairy Chess Review*, October, 1953.

LOSING THE EXCHANGE

An expression used whenever an exchange of chessmen results in material loss or a loss of an advantageous position. A player is said to have "lost the exchange" when an exchange of chessmen results in giving up a man of greater value for one of lesser value; for example, a player who is forced to give up his Queen in exchange for a Rook has "lost the exchange." See *Value of Chessmen*, and *Winning the Exchange*.

LOSS OF THE GAME

see *Laws of Chess*, Article 17

LOWENTHAL

Johann Jacob Lowenthal, a chess enthusiast, was born in July, 1810, in Budapest. In 1849, he left Hungary for a two year stay in the United States and then he settled in London where he became an English subject. He became a popular chessplayer in London chess circles and participated in the famous London Tournament of 1851. In 1858, he won the first prize in a chess tournament at Birmingham over Falkbeer, Staunton and others. He organized the St. James Chess Club and eventually became a chess analyst and editor of chess columns in the *Illustrated News of the World*. One of Lowenthal's famous q'iotations is: "The judicious violation of general principles marks the master-mind." He died at St. Leonards on July 20, 1876.

LOYDESQUE

A term applied to a chess problem in which the solution follows the style of play developed by the great American problemist Samuel Loyd (1841-1911). It was characteristic of Loyd to propose an unexpected key move or a continuation which was purposely designed to give the solver of the problem the idea that he was on the wrong trail. Hence, these problems were noted for their unique originality and brilliancy in execution. See *Sam Loyd and His Problems,* by Alain C. White, published in Leeds, 1913.

LUCENA'S MATE

Juan Ramirez Lucena, a Spaniard, was famous for a work on the game of chess which he published in 1497. It contained an account of games that later became known as Damiano's Gambit, the Ruy Lopez and other openings. It also contained many endgames or problems. One of his classical end-games which has become known as *The Mate of Lucena* consists of sacrificing the Queen so that the capturing piece blockades its own King who is immediately checkmated on the next move. The accompanying diagram illustrates the mate of Lucena.

1. Q-K6 ch	K-R1
2. N-B7 ch	K-N1
3. N-R6 dbl. ch.	K-R1
4. Q-N8 ch	RxQ
5. N-B7 mate.	

Staunton is of the opinion that "Lucena's work appears to mark the date of the transition from Persian chess to the modern form of play, for some of the problems are constructed on the principle of the old game and on that of the new." This is evidenced from the changing power of the Queen—La Dama.

M

MAGAZINES ON CHESS
see *Periodicals*

MAGEE THEME

A chess problem theme named in honor of J. F. Magee, Jr. (born in 1867), the founder of the Good Companion Club of Philadelphia. Magee was not a very noteworthy composer himself but was an enthusiastic chess problem devotee. The theme which was a complimentary dedication to him is illustrated in the accompanying diagram. In this theme, four black interferences are introduced by the four possible moves of two Black Pawns, without capture. White's key move is R-N8 which threatens RxN on the next move. Now, if Black replies P-B4ch, then White moves N-Q6; if Black replies P-B4ch, then White moves N-K5; if Black replies P-Q3, then White moves QxB; if Black replies P-Q4, then White moves NxN.

Key: R-N8

MAIDENS' GAME

A so-called game of chess which is believed to have been discovered by the maidens of Ultramar, in Morocco, prior to 1500. It is also called a "Forced Game." This game proceeds as usual, except that the players are obliged to capture a chessman whenever it is possible to do so. Players must avoid moving pieces on squares where they can be captured or exchanged by chessmen of lesser value.

MAJOR PIECES

Queens and Rooks. They are called "major" pieces because they are of greater value than the Bishops and Knights. See *Value of Chessmen* and *Cruising Range*.

MAN

A general term applied to any chess unit. It is a short word used in place of chessman.

MANDARINS OF THE YELLOW BUTTON

"The Order of Mandarins of the Yellow Button" was the title of an informal group of Bostonian chessplayers which adopted its name from one of the nine grades of public officials in the Chinese Empire who were entitled to wear a yellow button on the hat as a mark of their distinctive position. These chessplayers met on Saturday afternoons to play chess and to dine in the evenings. This coterie consisted of C. F. Burille, F. H. Harlow, Dr. E. M. Harris, C. F. Howard, Major O. E. Michaelis, Gen. W. C. Paine, Dr. H. Richardson, C. W. Snow, H. N. Stone, P. Ware, Jr., and F. K. Young. These men won considerable fame. Their social chess meetings served as the nucleus of the presentday famous Deschapelles Chess Club.

MANEUVERING

A method of handling one's chessmen so skillfully that the opponent will be obliged to take up uncomfortable positions for his own defense. It is a process of executing tactical movements so adroitly that when one method of attack is repulsed, another line of attack can be waged before the opponent can remobilize his forces for a new defensive position.

MANHATTAN CHESS CLUB

America's oldest, yet ever progressive club. It was organized in 1877. This Club is probably the leading chess Club in the country as far as the strength of the players is concerned. Among its membership will be found: Samuel Reshevesky, Arthur B. Bisguier, Robert Fischer, Arnold S. Denker and many other well known chess artists.

The Club sponsors many activities. At times important tournaments and matches have been held at the Club. For example, in 1885 Zukertort played Steinitz a series of games at this Club which resulted in Zukertort's favor 4 to 1. Exhibition affairs have taken place on numerous occasions. Capablanca and other famous chessmasters have lectured at the Club.

In 1952, under the capable leadership of Hans Kmoch, groups of Junior Chessplayers were organized. In order to provide a more adequate competitive opportunity for its members to participate in weekly rapid transit chessplay and other matches, all members are classified into A, B and C sections. Usually five, six or more club tournaments for players of every strength are continuously in progress. Since February 1955, this Club publishes its own mimeographed *Bulletin* in which club activities are reported.

The Secretary and Manager of the Manhattan Chess Club is Hans Kmoch. Its address is 39 West 64th Street, New York City.

MARGINAL PAWN

A term applied by some chessplayers to a Rook Pawn which moves along the border or edge of the chessboard.

MARKED PAWN

see *Capped Pawn*

MAROCZY

Geza Maroczy, Hungarian Chess-master and world champion contender, was born March 3, 1870 in Szeged, Hungary. He studied in Zurich and made engineering his profession. After holding a professorship at the Municipal Intermediate School for Mathematics, he finally accepted a position in a newly created Government Accident Insurance Department. He died May 28, 1951.

Maroczy played his first game of chess when he was fifteen years of age. Ten years later, he entered the international arena in Hastings and in the following year, 1896, he played in the International Chess Tournament in Nuremberg where he finished second to the famous Dr. Emanuel Lasker. Maroczy played in many important tournaments winning first, second, and third prizes.

As a chessplayer, Maroczy was energetic in his attacks, very careful in defensive play, and most accurate in the end-game. Chess writers acclaim his excellency as a chess artist. For example, Reinfeld points out that "Maroczy's unique combination of slickness and artistry was seen at its best in his fabulous mastery of queen and pawn endings, in which department he was supreme." Dr. Fine considers Maroczy "a solid master of the positional school." Edward Lasker writes that Maroczy "was perhaps the kindest of chess masters I have ever met." And, W. H. Watts of England says that Maroczy "invariably plays enterprising and interesting chess, and is a master of the first class."

MARSEILLAISE CHESS

A type of unorthodox chess which consists essentially in making two moves at a time. It was invented in 1925 and was in popular use for a number of years. The basic deviation from orthodox chess is that each player makes two moves, one after the other, either with two different pieces or two moves with the same piece. If, during the game, check is given with the first move, the second move is forfeited. In a losing game, a player may, instead of making two moves, make one move with his King and place his Majesty in a stalemated position.

MARSHALL

Frank J. Marshall, United States Chess Champion 1909-1936, was born in Brooklyn, New York, in 1877 and died in 1944. When he was eight years of age, his family moved to Montreal, Canada. Here he learned the game of chess from his father. It is reported that as soon as he knew the movements of the game, he played at least one game of chess every day. He became so enthusiastic over chess that he took a miniature chess outfit to bed so that he could work out plays that suddenly might occur to him. At the age of fourteen, he won first place in a tournament at the Montreal Chess Club.

His first appearance in international chess was in 1899 when he went to London and captured the first prize in the Tournament for Minor Masters. He reached his greatest success at Cambridge Springs in 1904, where he won the first prize. He was equally successful at Scheveningen in 1905. In fact, from 1899 to the time he retired from his chess career, Marshall was a successful participant in practically every important international tournament. In 1909, he won the United States Championship from Jackson W. Schowalter. This honor he maintained until 1936 when he retired undefeated from official chessplay.

Marshall established the world

record as a simultaneous chessplayer. On several occasions he encountered more than a hundred opponents at one time. At the invitation of the National Chess Club of Montreal, he visited that city in January, 1922, and played 156 games simultaneously, winning 129, drawing 21 and losing 6. This world record was established in seven hours and fifty minutes.

Marshall wrote several books, such as *Chess Step by Step,* and *Comparative Chess,* in which, among other items, he popularized the term "swindle." He received many prizes and trophies. The famous Marshall Chess Club was established in his honor.

Chess writers point out that Marshall was a tactician *par excellence* and that he disliked defensive play. Dr. Fine says that "the attack was (Marshall's) battle-cry, and given half a chance he plunged into it with unquenchable eagerness." Reinfeld states that Marshall "played by instinct rather than calculation;where others analyzed painstakingly, he intuitively sensed hidden possibilities." As a result, comments Dr. Fine, Marshall's "games are always full of zest."

MARSHALL CHESS CLUB

One of the most famous chess clubs in America, founded in 1914, in honor of Frank J. Marshall. It had its origin in the beginning of this century when a small group of chess enthusiasts met under the leadership of Frank J. Marshall, in Keen's Chop House located at 35th Street and Sixth Avenue, New York City. It was then known as the Marshall Chess Divan. Later, it became known as the Marshall Chess Club and was housed for nine years in temporary headquarters on West 12th Street in New York City. Eventually, a group of Marshall's admirers under the sponsorship of Gustavus Adolphus

Pfeiffer, Alrick H. Man and Charles Kelly purchased the building where the Club is now located on West 10th Street. Members of the Club have come to regard their present home "as permanent as the Statue of Liberty."

Its several hundred members include such leading American chessmasters as Edward Lasker, Larry Evans, Anthony E. Santasiere, Edmar Mednis and many others.

All forms of chess activities find expression in this Club which is open every day of the year from noon to midnight. Generally, the weekly program consists of the following events. Sundays, the days of greatest activities, are devoted to championship matches. Mondays and Thursdays are set aside for skittles (informal chess games). Tuesdays are reserved for Rapid Transit play, consisting of a move every ten seconds. Wednesdays are used for club tournaments. Fridays are days of special events. Saturdays are given to junior championship tournaments in the afternoons and, in the evenings several "pots" are usually in progress. (See *Pots.*)

The President of this Marshall Chess Club is Edward Lasker. The Secretary is Mrs. Caroline D. Marshall. The address of the Marshall Chess Club is 23 West 10th Street, New York 11, New York.

MASKED BATTERY

A problem situation in which there is not only a White piece shielding the black King from immediate attack but where there is also a black piece located between the long range attacking White piece and the black King. Obviously, the black King cannot be checked immediately. The black man must also be removed. If, however, the White "firing piece" moves first, the intervening black man is pinned. A

Masked battery is sometimes referred to as a "mixed battery." See *Battery*.

MASON

James Mason, chessmaster and chess writer, was born in New York on November 19, 1849. He spent his earlier years in New York but after participating in the International Masters Tournament at Paris in 1878, he made London his home. He died there on January 17, 1905.

He learned to play chess when he was about eighteen years of age. He quickly gained a good reputation as a strong chessplayer by winning several tournaments. He won the first prize at the American Chess Congress which met in Philadelphia in 1876. He also took the first prize in the New York Clipper Centennial Tournament. In 1878, his admirers sent him to the Paris International Masters Tournament. In this, as well as in other tournaments, Mason played excellently in the early stages of the tournaments but lost ground in the later stages.

In the last fifteen years of his life, Mason devoted himself to writing on the game of chess. He is the author of *Principles of Chess*, 1893; *The Art of Chess*, 1895; *Chess Openings*, 1897; and *Social Chess*, 1900. He was also an Annotator of Games for the *British Chess Magazine*. Commenting on his writings, the *British Chess Magazine* stated that Mason was a "fluent and imaginative writer," and that his "books are classics and thoroughly reliable."

MASTER

A term used by Japanese and Siamese chessplayers in place of our King.

MASTER CHESSPLAYER

A comprehensive term applied to a star chessplayer who by his training, experience and insight into any given chess situation has demonstrated superior skill and proficiency. "What makes a chessmaster," says Edward Lasker, "is not practice. It is thorough understanding of the principles of chess strategy. Once a player has this understanding, he is sure to reach the master class, and since understanding isn't something one loses after one attained it, a chessmaster always remains in his class."

In actual practice, chessplayers have come to recognize several grades of master chessplayers. The United States Chess Federation classifies masters into the following categories: Grandmasters (2600 points and up); Senior Masters (2400 to 2599 points); and Masters (2200 to 2399 points). Throughout continental Europe, there is a generally accepted yardstick that in order for a chessplayer to gain the master title officially, he must score at least one third (Meister-drittel) of the possible points in a master tourney. Today, the title of an International Master chessplayer is awarded officially by the Fédération Internationale des Echecs.

All chessmasters have their own characteristic virtues which serve as the distinctive hall-mark of their individuality in chessplay. For example, chess writers refer to the scintillating brilliancy of Alekhine; the unerring accuracy of Capablanca; the profound depth of Lasker; the uncanny originality of Nimzovitch and the scientific thoroughness of Steinitz. For a further discussion of this topic see *Championship Chess*, by Philip W. Sergeant, Chapter IV, entitled: "The Masters."

MATCH

A contest conducted between two chessplayers or two chess teams under more or less formal regulations. A match differs from a tournament in that a match is a contest between two players or teams, whereas a tournament consists of a larger number of contestants, all of whom in one way or another compete with each other. See *Tournament* and *Byes*.

MATE

A word borrowed from the old French, meaning: overcome or overpowered. The idea of the word probably originated from the Persian word *manad* meaning, trapped or dead. Hence, as used in the game of chess, the word "mate" signifies the King's doom—"The King is Dead!" The game is ended. See *Checkmate*.

MATERIAL

As used in chess, material is another name for chessmen. It may include some or all chessmen with the exception of the King. His Majesty, the King, is always in a class by himself. "Material" is a player's force. The more material a player has at his disposal, the more manpower he controls. All other things being equal, loss of material invariably leads to loss of position and loss of power.

MATHEMATICAL CALCULATIONS IN CHESS

Determining intricate chess processes which involve problematical difficulties. In chessplay, mathematical calculations demonstrate, among other things, the magnitude of the possible number of moves that may be made in a game. It also indicates the profundity of the study of chess and the existing opportunities for developing new openings and new combinations. It has been calculated that the number of possible ways of playing *the first ten moves* on each side of the board amounted to the astronomical figure of 169,518,829,-100,544,000,000,000,000,000. From this it has been estimated that if every man, woman and child on the face of the earth should play chess without cessation, at the rate of one move per minute, it would take about 217 billions of years to exhaust all possible combinations of chessplay.

F. V. Morley asks a good question in which he indicates the mathematical possibilities of making the first four moves. He asks, "How can I claim to know all about it, when I am aware that there are as many as 197,299 ways of playing the first four moves in chess, and nearly 72,000 different positions at the end of the first four moves of which 16,556 arise when the players move Pawns only?" For reference for these calculations see: *Mathematical Recreations and Essays,* by William Rouse Ball; *Mathematics and the Imagination,* by E. A. Kasner and James Newman, and *Mathematical Recreations,* by M. Kraitchik.

MATING FORCE

Any force sufficient to mate a King. A minor piece by itself is not considered a mating force.

MATING NET

A situation in which a King is caught but strives to stay alive by capturing a piece or by moving to a flight square. However, in so doing the King is inevitably checkmated. Such a situation is shown in the accompanying diagram.

Black to move.

MAXIM, CHESS

A chess proverb. Chess literature contains many words of caution which have been expressed tersely by master chessplayers. Their implications suggest strong warnings to hasty procedures in chessplay. Some of the maxims which are in common usage are:

Always check, it might be mate.

Be wary of the obvious move.

The threat is stronger than the execution.

Beware of gifts — Grecian or otherwise.

Help your pieces so that they can help you.

McCUTCHEON VARIATION

An adventurous play in the French Defense opening. Its characteristic move is 4 . . . , B-N5. It calls for cautious procedure for both Black and White. The development of the game leading to the McCutcheon Variation is given in the accompanying diagram

which is arrived at from the following moves:

1.	P-K4	P-K3
2.	P-Q4	P-Q4
3.	N-QB3	N-KB3
4.	B-KN5	B-N5

McCONNELL'S DOUBLE GAMBIT

see *King's Bishop Opening*

M. C. O.

see *Modern Chess Openings*

MEDIAN SYSTEM

As used in chess, the "median system" refers to a method of breaking ties in Swiss tournaments. It is most effective in tournaments having nine or more rounds. In this system, the final standing of each player who finishes in a tie score is determined by the sum of the scores of his opponents except the highest and lowest. Rule 74 of the official tournament rules of the United Chess Federation states that tied players are to be arranged in the order of the sums of the median scores with the following adjustments:

(a) In a tournament of 8 rounds or less, all the opponents' scores except the highest and lowest.

(b) In a tournament of 9, 10, 11 or 12 rounds, all the opponents' scores except the two highest and the two lowest.

(c) In a tournament of 13 rounds or more, all the opponents' scores except the three highest and the three lowest.

For a more detailed explanation and a comparison of this median system with other systems, see *The Official Blue Book and Encyclopedia of Chess*, pages 161 to 172.

MEDINESE VICTORY

A winning end-game situation adopted by some early Muslim chessplayers in which a solitary King was considered defeated the moment he was bared, i.e., deprived of his last man. Other Muslim chessplayers maintained that such a game should be considered a drawn game whenever the solitary King could capture the opponent's last man with the move following the one in which he was bared.

MEISTER-DRITTEL

A competitive goal whereby the winning of one third or more of one's games in a master tournament entitles one to a Master's title. This is the generally accepted method of being officially recognized as a master chessplayer throughout continental Europe.

MEMORIZATION OF GAMES

The process and ability to retain, recall and recognize games of chess and the specific and sequential moves in these games. This type of memorization has its merits. It can be fun and helpful in recognizing deviations from notable games played in the past. Memorization of moves is also a very important requisite in playing blindfold chess or mental chess as it is sometimes called. However, a complete and slavish reliance on memorized games can be a serious handicap to a player who does not understand the basic principles underlying the various movements of the game. Chessplayers have experienced and tested the success of various moves for over a thousand years. The study of chess strategy and tactics has been explored very scientifically. The results of these experiments and investigations have been recorded, especially in the past seventy-five years, for our edification and references. The great chessmasters are unanimous in pointing out that is is far more important to gain a thorough grasp of the philosophy and and principles of the game than to confine one's chess interests to the mere memorization of detailed moves.

Understanding the wisdom of the moves makes for resourcefulness. Relying on memorization alone may lead to bewilderment and loss of a game when an opponent tries out a newer approach to the game.

MEN

A shorter word for chessmen. See *Chessmen.*

MENCHIK

Vera Francevna Menchik, the first World Woman Champion chessplayer of modern times, was born in Moscow on February 16, 1906, of an English mother and a Czech father. In 1921, the family moved to Hastings, England, where Vera lived the rest of her life. In 1937, she married R. Stevenson, but among her chess friends, she continued to be known by her maiden name. On the night of June 27, 1944, an enemy bomb demolished her home, killing Vera, her mother and sister Olga.

Vera Menchik learned the game of chess from her father at the age of nine. In 1923, she joined the famous Hastings Chess Club where she displayed an extraordinary understanding of positional chessplay and a remarkable knowledge of chess openings and defences, especially the French Defense. In 1927, she won the first Women's World Championship by a score of 10½—½. She defended her title successfully on seven occasions. In these tournament events, she played 83 games, winning 78, drawing 4, and losing only one game. In her chessplay, she encountered such prominent chessplayers as her tutor Maroczy, Rubinstein, Capablanca, Flohr, Colle, Euwe and Reshevsky.

Miss Menchik's chessplaying ability was held in high repute by the great chessmasters and renowned chess writers. Commenting on the Carlsbad

Tournament of 1929, Alekhine observed: "Vera Menchik is without doubt an exceptional phenomenon among women. She possesses great aptitude for the game." On one occasion Salo Flohr remarked: "Vera Menchik was the first woman in the world who played chess strongly . . . like a man." Fred Reinfeld gives the following insight into the first queen of modern chessplayers: "Miss Menchik is undoubtedly the most placid of all the masters. She sits stolidly, surveying the scene and shunning the spectators. She is imperturbable, unless some unlucky onlooker whispers a bit too audibly. Then she will turn slowly around, regard the culprit, and emit a loud *Shhhhh*."

MENTAL CHESS

The art of playing chess without the aid of a chessboard or chessmen. The game is conducted without any kind of aid which will help in keeping the position of the chessmen visually present. For the sake of accuracy and reference, each move is recorded. This type of chessplay requires an infallible memory of the exact position of every chessman throughout the game, superhuman powers of concentration, and, a vivid imagination of simultaneous alternation of continuous chessplay. See *Blindfold Chess*.

MEPHISTO

The name of a chess automaton. It was invented by Charles Godfrey Gumpel, a manufacturer of artificial limbs. It was reported that a chessmaster of small stature by the name of Gunsberg was cunningly concealed within this mysterious chessplayer. It was first exhibited in the presence of Bird, Blackburne and other notables at Gumpel's house, 49 Leicester Square, London, on March 30, 1878. Du Mont states that "many brilliant games

by Mephisto have been preserved." For other automaton chessplayers see *Ajeeb* and *Turk*.

MERAN DEFENSE

1.	P-Q4	P-Q4
2.	N-KB3	N-KB3
3.	P-QB4	P-K3
4.	N-B3	P-B3
5.	P-K3	QN-Q2

One of the more important Queen's Gambit defenses in which many wild combinations can develop and in which Black can secure a relative degree of equality. The situation at the end of the first five moves is shown in the accompanying diagram. The exact order of moves may be somewhat varied but the general effect should unfold itself. This defense receives its name from Meran, Austria, the place where Rubinstein and Tartakower popularized this opening procedure.

"Throughout the years," says Arthur Bisguier, "the chameleon-like Meran Defense has been subjected to the vagaries of fashion. Periodically it is refuted and abandoned, only to be resuscitated time and again by a new move or idea. Currently, its stock is as high as it ever has been." For a presentation of this Meran Defense procedure and its variations, see *Modern Chess Openings,* Ninth Edition, by Walter Korn, or *Practical Chess Openings,* by Reuben Fine.

MEREDITH

A term applied to a chess problem containing eight to twelve men. This type of a problem was named after William Meredith (1835-1903) of Philadelphia, Pennsylvania, who was a respected member of the "Good Companions." See *Miniature*

MESSENGER

see *Runner*

MIDDLE GAME

That phase of the game which follows the opening development and then continues to the final struggle which is identified as the end-game. In the middle game, White unfolds his *plan de campagne* by vigorous, tactical maneuvers and attacks. Black offers an effective resistance and counter challenge. Co-ordination of one's pieces and their freedom of mobility are the essential characteristics of a successful middle game. Tartakower states that "castling frequently denotes the evolution from the opening to the middle game." There are, however, no definite lines of demarcation that can always be drawn between the various phases of the game. Chess writers indicate that a well-developed opening game points to successful tactical maneuvers in the middle game, and a well fought middle game will lead smoothly into a victorious end-game.

Authorities point out that a successful execution of the middle game is the result of a vivid imagination and practical experience. There are a number of good books available which might be helpful in gaining this practical experience, such as:

The Middle Game, by Eugene Znosko-Borovsky.
Strategy and Tactics in Chess, by Dr. Max Euwe.
Judgment and Planning in Chess, by Dr. Max Euwe.

Modern Ideas in Chess and *Masters of the Chessboard,* by Richard Réti.
My System and *Chess Praxis,* by Aron Nimzovitch.
The Middle Game, by Reuben Fine
How to Win in the Middle Game of Chess, by I. A. Horowitz.

"MIDSUMMER MADNESS"

An expression used by the editor of *The Field* when he referred to Steinitz's twentieth move (20 . . . P-KN4) as "midsummer madness." No further explanatory comment was given. The game was played between Blackburne and Steinitz in a Vienna tournament.

MIESES

Jacques Mieses, an international master, was born in Leipzig on February 27, 1865. He was christened Jakob but he preferred to be known by his adopted name Jacques. He came from a financially well-to-do family and was a cultured gentleman noted for his charm, manners and eloquence. He was educated at the universities of Leipzig and Berlin. He devoted more than fifty years to chess. He was known throughout Germany as one of the best chess columnists and author of *Chess Pilot, Manual of the End-Game,* and *Instructive Positions from Master Chess.* He died in London on February 23, 1954.

As a chessplayer, he was a master in the art of attack. He dared to rush original points of play which won for him many brilliancy prizes but never won for him first place honors. Mieses stands second only to Alekhine in winning so many brilliancy prizes. Reinfeld stated that "Jacques Mieses could always be relied upon for colorful games."

MINIATURE

A term applied to any chess problem containing not more than seven men. See *Meredith.*

MINIATURE GAME

The idea of a "miniature game" does not admit of exact definition. It is a relative concept. Mr. Du Mont, who probably knows more about miniature games than anyone, limits the length of such games to about twenty moves.

MINOR PIECES

Knights and Bishops. They are called "minor" pieces because they are of lesser value and importance than the Queens and Rooks. See *Value of Chessmen* and *Cruising Range.*

MIRROR MATE

A fanciful idea applied to a problem situation where a mated King finds himself surrounded by unoccupied squares, all of which, however, are guarded by his opponent's forces. The underlying idea is that the mated King is supposed to see his own reflection on all the vacant squares around him but on which he can not go for self protection. Some authorities insist that a mirror mate must also be a pure mate. (See *Pure Mate.*) For a fuller explanation see *Mate in Two Moves,* by Brian Harley; and *Enjoyment of Chess Problems,* by Kenneth S. Howard.

MISTAKE

An error resulting from an oversight, misapprehension or misunderstanding. Being human, chessplayers are not infallible. In fact, Rubinstein observed that "no game can be won without some mistake on our opponent's part." Dr. Euwe points out that "the experienced chessmaster knows that in every game won, no matter how well the winner played, there is always at least one point, generally in the middle game, where one can find the decisive mistake." All mistakes are costly. Even little errors may eventually snowball into a catastrophe. In general, the mistakes frequently made in a game of chess are 1) faulty and slow development; 2) neglecting to provide adequate protection for the King; 3) leaving a piece *en prise;* and 4) cramping pieces together so that their mobility is restricted. See *Blunder.*

MOBILITY

Freedom of action. The principle of mobility consists of giving the chessmen the greatest possible freedom of movement. This principle is of paramount importance in deciding where to place a piece. In general, the player who applies this principle is in a better position to muster reinforcements in case of attack or to take advantage of making an attack than the player who finds himself in a cramped position. According to Chernev and Harkness the principle of mobility, especially in the opening, "is often more important than the principle of superior force." Edward Lasker confirms the importance of this principle of mobility by stating that "the grasp of the far-reaching influence of the mobility of pieces in the opening upon the further development of the whole game is really what distinguishes the master from the average player."

MODEL MATE

A term suggested by the British chess composer H. D'O. Bernard (1878-1955) who applied this term to a mating situation which is both pure and economical. Kenneth S. Howard, the former Problem Editor of the *American Chess Bulletin,* describes the model mate as "a mate in which the square on which the black King stands and each adjoining square, constituting the black King's field, is guarded or blocked only once, and every white piece on the board takes part in the mate, with the possible exception of the white King, whose employment is optional." For a fuller explanation of the use of this term see *How to Solve Chess Problems,* by Kenneth S. Howard. See *Pure Mate* and *Economical Mate.*

MODENESE SCHOOL

A so-called school of chess thought which was named after the city of Modena, Italy, the home town of Ponziani and Lolli, famous chessplayers of the eighteenth century. These chessplayers and their followers developed ideas which were in direct contradiction to those of the great Frenchman, Philidor. Many of our modern chess theories can be traced to this Modenese School. For example, the Modenese players encouraged gambit chess procedures and they discouraged the early advancement of the Bishop to N5 thereby avoiding being caught in what is known as the Noah's Ark Trap. See *Noah's Ark Trap.*

MODERN CHESS

A term which is applied to the time and style of chessplay which originated with Wilhelm Steinitz and was further developed by Lasker, Tarrasch, Schlechter, Maroczy, Pillsbury, Marshall and many others. The characteristic features of this school of chessplay are safety, solidity and analytical correctness in the opening and middle game. Positional play is of pre-eminent importance. The center controlled position is regarded as an urgent and vital need for the modern chessplayer. Undoubtedly, this is the reason why Horowitz states that "in the modern school, the skirmish waxes openly and merrily for the domination of the mid-section of the playing field from the very first move." He insists that "the modernist will not give ground in the center" without strong resistance. See *Victorian Era,* and *Ultramodern Chessplay.*

MODERN CHESS OPENINGS

The title of an indispensable book in any chess library. This book contains a compilation of chess openings and their variations. Copious notes are appended. Each and every recorded play has been carefully checked and verified. All openings are indexed. It is released by the Pitman Publishing Corporation.

"*Modern Chess Openings,*" writes Walter Korn, "is the only English book of its kind which has regularly been kept fully up to date since its first publication almost half a century ago . . . The first edition was by R. C. Griffith and J. H. White. Although some co-editors changed with time, R. C. Griffith always remained the chief editor, till after the seventh edition which was revised by me and appeared in 1946." Editorial rights were then transferred to Mr. Korn. The Eighth Edition (1952) was edited and revised solely by Mr. Korn. The current Ninth Edition (1957) has been edited by Walter Korn and revised by John W. Collins.

This MCO has frequently been referred to as "the Bible of chess." Jack Straley Battell, the Executive Editor of *Chess Review,* recommends this book not only to all those chessplayers who would keep up on the openings, but suggests that "today MCO is *the good book* also for the masters." See *Griffith.*

MONKEYS

Figurines shaped as monkeys are used by Burma chessplayers as black Pawns. Their light colored Pawns are carved as images of men. See *History of Chess*, by H. J. R. Murray.

MONOCHROME ECHO MATE

A problem situation in which the black colored King is mated in an echo mate on a square of the same color. When the King is mated in an echo mate on a square of a different color, it is referred to as a chameleon echo mate. See *Echo Mate*.

"MORALITIES OF CHESS"

Using chess equipment and the manner of playing the game as instruments for demonstrating moral principles and good social relations. In the Middle Ages, a number of publications dealing with chess appeared under the name of "Moralities." Later, chess writers retained this title but they were interested not so much in strict moralities as in presenting edifying parallels between the game of chess and the prevailing organization of human life and social activities. Benjamin Franklin wrote an essay on *Morals of Chess* in which he set forth rules of conduct for chessplayers. For a historical discussion of how chess was used for moralizing purposes, see *A History of Chess*, by H. J. R. Murray, especially Part II, Chapter V, entitled "The Moralities." See *Symbolical Explanation of Chess* and *Etiquette, Chess*.

MORLEY'S DOUBLE CORRIDOR BOARD

A proposal made by F. V. Morley for an enlargement of the standard chessboard. He suggested that a corridor be added to each side of the board as shown in the accompanying illustration. The corridor running parallel to the Queen-Rook's file is to be known as the Queen-Rook-Corridor (QRC) and the one running parallel to the King-Rook's file is to be called the King - Rook - Corridor (KRC). Everything else remains the same.

The purpose of this proposal is to give the Rook Pawns the same opportunities which the other Pawns possess. Instead of limiting the Rook Pawns to scraping alongside a blank wall, they should also be permitted to strike out to the right or left, if the occasion should arise. Obviously, this type of board also offers the Knights and some of the other pieces another possible opening move. For a fuller explanation of the use of this so-called "improved chess board" read *My One Contribution to Chess*, by F. V. Morley.

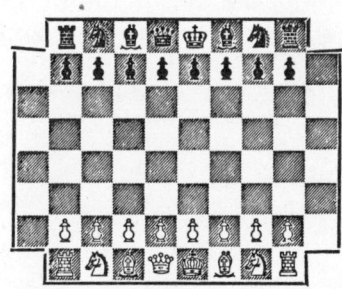

MORPHY

Paul Charles Morphy, the first U. S. Chess Champion, was born in New Orleans on June 22, 1837. His parents were cultured people, prominent in the social life of New Orleans. His father was a judge of the Supreme Court of Louisiana. Paul Morphy was educated at the Jefferson Academy and at St. Joseph's College near Mobile. He was prepared for the legal profession and was admitted to the bar at the age of nineteen on the condition that he would not practice law until he came of age.

He learned the game of chess when he was about ten years of age. From the very beginning, he gave remarkable signs of a budding chess genius. In 1850, he gave a good account of himself in the games he played with the famous chessmaster Johann Lowenthal. In 1857, Morphy was invited to be a contestant in the First Chess Congress held in New York City. The *Chess Monthly* magazine for January 1857, referred to him as "the most promising player of the day." It is said that Morphy became an unofficial world champion when he defeated Adolf Andersen of Germany in a match played in Paris in December, 1858. His rise to fame in the chess world was extraordinary. After playing victoriously in American and European chess centers, Morphy was most anxious to meet Howard Staunton, the British champion.However, Staunton seems to have used every possible excuse to avoid a match. While waiting for an encounter with Staunton, Morphy became a chess celebrity in Paris. It is reported that after a particularly brilliant exhibition, he was carried through the streets on the shoulders of a cheering crowd. Not obtaining an opportunity to play with the British champion, Morphy returned to New Orleans and offered to give the odds of a Pawn and a move to any noteworthy chessplayer in the world. Receiving no response, Morphy declared his career as a chessplayer closed. Delusions of persecution followed. He died July 10, 1884.

The most noteworthy features of Morphy's chess career, writes Willard Fiske, "are the strange rapidity of his combinations, his masterly knowledge of the openings and ends of games, and the wonderful faculty which he possesses of recalling games played months before. While engaged at the board he is quiet, courteous, and undemonstrative, and is neither depressed by defeat nor excited by victory." Dr. Fine points out that "Morphy remains one of the giants of chess history. His meteoric career together with the freshness and originality of his games

will always continue to inspire all who love chess." Many of Morphy's games are preserved and published in *Morphy's Games of Chess*. In this book, Philip W. Sergeant gives a biographical account of Morphy and states: "Above everything, Morphy was an artist; and the best way to enjoy an artist is not to dissect him." *See Paul Morphy—Seine Leben und Schaffen*, by Dr. Max Lange, Leipzig: Veit & Company, 1894.

MORPHY'S MATE

Sacrificing a major piece for a minor piece in order to obtain a mating position. In a New York tournament game between Morphy and L. Paulsen, Morphy sacrificed a Queen for a Knight so as to gain a winning attack which culminated in a checkmate. This Morphy mating situation is illustrated in the accompanying diagram. Its solution consists of the following moves:

1. QxN   PxQ
2. R-N1 ch   K-R1
3. BxP mate.

MOVE

The transference of a chessman from one square to another. A move is completed the moment the hand that moved a chess unit has been removed from it. On no account can a legally completed move be taken back. "To retract a move," says DuMont, "even with the consent or even at the invitation of your opponent is very bad for your chess generally, and not exactly sporting."

In chess, only one man is moved at one time, except when castling or capturing one of the opponent's men. There are three kinds of moves that can be made. They are developing moves, attacking moves or defensive moves. In theory, there is an ideal reply to every move. But chess is not played by formulated theories. In fact, every move depends upon the players' strategical plans and tactical maneuvers. Hence, chess is not played merely move by move, but in a well-considered series of moves, all of which have a definite and unified purpose. "If a move leads to nothing," says Znosko-Borovsky, "it is of no value; you must be thankful if it does not ruin the game." The best move is the one which hurts your opponent most is the suggestion of Chernev and Harkness. When making a move, James Mason admonishes: "Always make your move deliberately, unhesitatingly and with decision; without hurry, vacillation or regret." For the official regulations governing the manner of making moves in a game of chess, see *Laws of Chess*, Articles 5, 6 and 7.

MOVIE, CHESS

Chess movie or the "film method" as it is sometimes called, is a term applied to a chess game which is presented in a series of diagrams, that is, a new diagram with each move or after a few moves have been made. Such pictorial presentation keeps the development of the game in open view, places less strain on one's memory and facilitates greater concentration on the progress of the tactical and strategical development of the game. It is an adaptation of the Chinese proverb that one picture is worth a thousand words. This pictorial style of presenting chess games appeared as early as 1819, in a 500 page London publication entitled: *Chess Rendered Familiar by Tabular Demonstrations of the Various Positions and Movements as Described by Philidor*, by J. G. Pohlman. Some of the more recent books which utilize the idea of "Chess Movies" are: *An Invitation to Chess—A Pictorial Guide to the Royal Game*, by Chernev and Harkness; *How to Win in Chess Openings*, and *Modern Ideas in the Chess Openings*, by I. A. Horowitz.

MURRAY

Harold James Ruthven Murray, the famous historian of the game of chess, was born in Camberwell, England, on June 24, 1868. He was the oldest son of Sir A. H. Murray, the celebrated pioneer editor of the *Oxford English Dictionary*. After completing his studies at Balliol College, Oxford University, he became by profession an educator. He served as Headmaster of Ormskirk Grammar School from 1891 to 1900, and later accepted an appointment as a Board of Education Inspector of Schools. After his retirement from this post he took an active interest in local government work. He died in May, 1955.

Murray's interest in the history of the game of chess began in 1893 when he organized at Ormskirk a chess club. He subsequently published a number of articles on chess. His most notable work appeared in 1913 under the title of *History of Chess*. This 900 page volume, profusely illustrated and thoroughly documented throughout, was the result of Murray's own studies of original source material. It has received the universal acclaim of scholars and critics.

Three months after Murray's death, the *British Chess Magazine* paid him the following tribute: "Murray brought a fine scholarship to his immense task. He had, in addition, the true historian's gifts of meticulous research, of a grasp of detail, of the critical sifting of evidence; to this scientific technique was added the art of lucid exposition . . . Murray has left an enduring monument, the greatest book ever written on the game."

MUTATE

A word derived from the Latin word *mutare* meaning, to change. Mutate is a descriptive term, coined by Brian Harley (1883-1955), who applied it to "a cumbrous-looking situation of many variations, in which the Key alters one or two commonplace mates." For a fuller explanation see *Mate in Two Moves*, by Brian Harley; or, *The Enjoyment of Chess Problems*, by Kenneth S. Howard. See *Harley*.

MUZIO GAMBIT

1. P-K4	P-K4
2. P-KB4	PxP
3. N-KB3	P-KN4
4. B-B4	P-N5
5. 0-0	PxN
6. QxP	

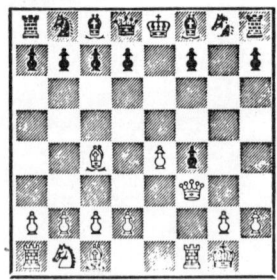

After White's 6th move.

This so-called Muzio Gambit was named after Don Muzio, a skillful amateur chessplayer of the seventeenth century. According to Fletcher, "This opening was alleged to have been invented by a man named Mutio and Sarratt more than two centuries later wrongly transcribed Mutio into Muzio."

With the fifth move, White sacrifices a Knight to gain time and to secure a formidable attack. As Reinfeld says: "White has a furious attack." However, James Mason points out that because of its recognized unsoundness, this opening is rarely adopted in important contests, for, in such, winning play and not brilliant play is the first object proposed." For a treatise on the Muzio Gambit see *The Laws and Practice of Chess*, by Howard Staunton, Chapter 15. For a brief presentation of the Muzio Gambit procedure see *Modern Chess Openings*, Ninth Edition by Walter Korn; or *Practical Chess Openings*, by Reuben Fine, page 115.

N

NAJDORF

Miguel (Moishe) Najdorf, an outstanding chessmaster of South America, was born in Warsaw on April 10, 1910. He distinguished himself in his native Poland as a strong chessplayer in Polish tournaments. In 1939, he went with a Polish team to the International Chess Tournament in Buenos Aires where he shared the first prize with Keres. Due to the outbreak of World War II, and the Nazi invasion of Poland, Najdorf decided to stay in Argentina. He changed his name from Moishe to Miguel and devoted himself more seriously to the game of chess. After the war, he participated in many European as well as South American tournaments. He won the first prize at the 1950 International Tournament at Amsterdam. Here he finished one full point ahead of Reshevsky.

The Swedish Grandmaster Stahlberg, who encountered Najdorf in tournament play, stated that Najdorf's "comprehension of everything that concerns chess is very great and his powers of accurate calculation are considerable."

Dr. Reuben Fine observes that Najdorf is superb in quick chess, and "in blindfold chess incredibly phenomenal; he holds the world's record of 45 games played in Brazil in 1947." For a fuller biographical sketch see *Chess and Chessmasters*, by G. Stahlberg, pages 91-93.

NATIONAL CHESS FEDERATION

A chess organization founded in 1926. It was an offshoot of the Western Chess Association. This Federation did not become prominent until United States Champion Chessplayer Frank Marshall resigned his title and entrusted it to the National Chess Federation to conduct biennial championship tournaments. Its first biennial championship tourney was held in 1936 and the title was won and bestowed upon Samuel Reshevsky. In 1939, the National Chess Federation united with the Western Chess Association and the American Chess Federation to form the present United States Chess Federation.

NIMZOINDIAN DEFENSE

1.	P-Q4	N-KB3
2.	P-QB4	P-K3
3.	N-QB3	B-N5

A development of the Queen's Indian Defense which has been modified and popularized by Nimzovitch. "This is the most complex and the most in-

teresting of all the so-called irregular replies to 1. P-Q4," says Dr. Emanuel Lasker. This defense, he continues,

"abounds in finesses and calls for strategical understanding of the highest order." Reinfeld states that this opening is most interesting, most enterprising and most successful in practice. After Black's third move, a number of variations have been proposed, such as, the Milner-Barry Variation or the Zurich Variation (4. Q-B2, N-K3); the Rubinstein Variation (4. P-K3); and the Saemisch Variation (4. P-QR3, BxN). For a discussion of this opening and its developmental procedures and variations see *Modern Chess Openings*, Ninth Edition, by Walter Korn, or, *Practical Chess Openings*, by Reuben Fine.

NIMZOVITCH

Aron Nimzovitch, an outstanding chessmaster and one of the most original thinkers in the realm of chess, was born in Riga, Latvia, November 7, 1886. His father was a wholesale merchant, a poet and an excellent chessplayer. Aron Nimzovitch studied philosophy at the University of Munich. After the first World War, he emigrated from Russia and went to Denmark where he lived until his death in 1935.

He learned chess from his father at the age of eight. By the time he was seventeen years of age he had developed a very serious and active interest in chess. Many delightful games which he played in various tournaments have been recorded and preserved. He developed an entirely original system of chessplay which he described in his book entitled: *My System—A Chess Treatise*. (English version by Philip Hereford. New York: Harcourt, Brace & Co., 1930.)

Nimzovitch was a forceful chessplayer. In his writings, he emphasized what he practiced on the chessboard, especially, the importance of having an objective for every move. Then, "do not shilly shally" was his repeated recommendation. He developed theories on over-protection, the blockade, the power of centralization and many others which gave the game of chess a new direction preparatory for the hypermodern school of chess. Chess writers are unanimous in paying tribute to "the uncanny originality of Nimzovitch."

Nimzovitch. was an extremely nervous individual. Smoking was a source of irritation to him. It is reported that when he played with Vidmar in the 1927 New York Tournament, Vidmar absent-mindedly took out his cigarette case. Nimzovitch quickly protested to Maroczy, the tournament director. "But," replied Maroczy, "he is not smoking." "You are a chessmaster," roared Nimzovitch, "and you must know that the threat is much stronger than the execution."

NIMZOVITCH DEFENSE

1.	P-K4	N-QB3
2.	P-Q4	P-Q4

A hypermodern defense which strives to control the center and at the same time seeks to induce White to move his Pawns forward in the hope of weakening them. Dr. Emanuel Lasker believes that "the Nimzovitch Defense is quite playable. It is an opening which suits that kind of temperament which can defend patiently and at times assail surprisingly and fiercely." Reinfeld, however, offers a word of caution by saying that "Black is apt to have a constricted game." For a presentation of this Nimzovitch Defense procedure and its variations see *Modern Chess Openings,* Ninth Edition, by Walter Korn, or *Practical Chess Openings,* by Reuben Fine.

NOAH'S ARK TRAP

A trap which proverbially is said to be as old as Noah's Ark. An example of this trap may occur when a Bishop is caught in a net of Pawns from which there is no escape. In the accompanying diagram, White's Bishop having moved earlier to N5 was forced back to R4 and then to N3 where he is now trapped by the onward push of Black's Pawns.

NORSE GAMBIT
see *Danish Gambit*

NOTATION

A "short-hand" method of describing positions and events on a chessboard; such as, P-K4, which means: Pawn moves to King's fourth rank; or PxB, which means: Pawn captures Bishop. Several systems of chess notation have been developed, such as, the Algebraic system, the Anglo-American system, the Forsyth system, the Koch's system, the Stamma system and the Uedemann code. These are defined in their respective alphabetical order. Chess recorders have also developed "short forms" for indicating various meanings given to chess moves. These have become standardized. For a list of these "short forms" or abbreviations, see *Symbols*.

NOWOTNY INTERFERENCE

A chess problem situation named after the Austrian problem composer Anton Nowotny (1829-1871) in which White sacrifices one of his pieces by giving Black a choice of making a capture with either one of two pieces. Regardless which piece makes the capture, the capturing piece will then interfere with the action of the other. In the accompanying illustration, it is Black's turn to move. He may capture White's Bishop with either the Rook or Bishop, with the result that either piece will, after making the capture, interfere with the controlling effect of the other.

NUMBERING THE MOVES

The orderly method of recording by number the consecutive moves made in a game of chess. See *Recording Moves*.

OBJECTIVE

The goal to be achieved. The major objective in a game of chess is to administer a checkmate to the opponent's King. Conversely, the major objective of the opponent is to defend his King from the attacks of the adversary and to wage a counterattack. With the mat-

ing or resignation of a King, the game is ended and the victorious King wins the game.

"It would be futile," says Znosko-Borovsky, "to think of a mate the whole time, when at first no attack can threaten the adverse King." Therefore, lesser or secondary objectives must be sought. Every phase of the game, every combination, every threat, and every attack has an objective, or at least, it should have a definite purpose. Nimzovitch emphasizes the importance of setting-up lesser objectives throughout the game. "Such objectives," he says, "may be a Pawn or a point." Securing one objective after another prevents drifting aimlessly and will eventually, except through bad play, result in the achievement of the major objective of the game. See *Accumulation of Advantage, Principle of*.

OBLONG CHESS

A modified form of chess played by some early Muslim chessplayers who used a chessboard which consisted of four by sixteen squares. The game was played with the use of dice. The chessmen were similar to those used in the regular game and had the same powers and functions. See *History of Chess*, by H. J. R. Murray. For other early Muslim chess varieties see *Decimal Chess, Round Chess*, and *Great Chess*.

OBSTRUCTION

A situation in which one chess unit is standing in another's path so as to deprive it from exercising effectively its ordinary function. Basically, it is a resistance to the movement of another chess unit. At the opening of the game, there is an absolute obstruction to the movement of all pieces except the Knights. As the game progresses, obstructions occur frequently, some of which are beneficial while others are detrimental. One chess piece may, while supporting another, necessarily suffer an obstruction because it cannot possibly move to the same square which is occupied by the supporting piece. This is generally regarded as a beneficial obstruction. However, when a piece of minor importance needlessly intercepts the line of action of other men, the obstruction may be disadvantageous.

ODDITIES

Chess oddities are usually occurrences which seem strange and bewildering. Irving Chernev, the "Believe It or Not" man of the chess fraternity, gathered a host of chess oddities which, though verified to be true, seem unbelievable. For example:

1. In 1850, Szechenyi was considered to be an insane character. After playing chess with a poor student for ten to twelve hours at a time, Szechenyi regained his sanity but the poor student went mad.
2. Steinitz was once arrested as a spy for playing chess with Tchigorin by correspondence. Police authorities thought that the strange chess code was a means of communicating war secrets.

See *The Fireside Book of Chess,* by Irving Chernev and Fred Reinfeld, published by Simon and Schuster, Part II, entitled: "Odd but True" for a listing of many chess oddities.

ODDS

The giving of "odds" is a method of adjusting the inequalities existing between players of various shades of playing strength so that they may compete with one another on a more equitable basis. To compensate for superior playing ability, the stronger contestant offers odds at the opening of the game by removing from the board at the very beginning of the game the one or more pieces offered as a handicap. The odds usually given, listed in order from the least to the greatest, are:

1. The Draw; that is, if the game ends in a draw, it shall be counted as a win for the weaker player.
2. Pawn and Move; usually, the King's Bishop Pawn is removed.
3. Pawn and Two Moves; the KBP and two moves are usually offered.
4. Knight odds; usually, the Queen's Knight is removed, but this is left entirely to the discretion of the one giving the odds.
5. Rook odds; usually, the Queen's Rook is removed.
6. Rook, Pawn and Move.
7. Two minor pieces; the pieces to be removed are usually left to the discretion of the odds giver.
8. Rook and Knight
9. Queen odds.
10. Capped Pawn. (See *Capped Pawn.*

Heinrich Fraenkel, whose pen-name is Assiac, states that many experienced chessplayers are opposed to the giving of odds because it tends "to spoil the inherent harmony of the game." Morley is more emphatic by stating that "to remove a piece at the beginning is obviously to commit mayhem. Such an initial mutilation is unsymmetrical and displeasing." He contends that giving odds is contrary to the philosophy of having fun and is not in conformity with the very nature of the game of chess. Not all chessplayers, however, accept this theory. Some chess writers state very positivly that "there should be no false shame about accepting odds." Frank Marshall suggested that inasmuch as club members are usually rated according to their playing strength, they might offer odds when playing with members of lower class ratings. See *Chess at Odds of Pawn and Move,* by Baxter-Wray.

OFFENSIVE

Waging an attack or taking aggressive action. Offensive and defensive are mutually related concepts. In waging an offensive chessplay, a positive goal is in view. Pressure must then be brought, says Chernev "to inflict our efforts on our opponent so that he must reply according to our will and desires." The enemy must be pressed unmercifully.

Chessmaster Larry Evans is of the opinion that "it is more agreeable to attack than to defend. "However once an offensive action is taken, warns Evans, the attacker "commits himself to such an extent that he is in no position to retreat or consolidate." See *Attack*.

OFFICIAL BLUE BOOK AND ENCYCLOPEDIA OF CHESS, THE

A book published for The United States Chess Federation by David McKay Company of New York, 1956, pp. 375. Its author, Kenneth Harkness, is the Membership Secretary and Rating Statistician of the U. S. Chess Federation. He also serves as the Federation's Business Manager.

This "Official Blue Book" contains and interprets the rules and regulations of organized chess; explains every phase in the organization of a chess club and indicates how it may function most effectively. It contains directories and tables of names, meeting places and addresses of chess organizations and clubs; chess tournaments held regularly in the United State; directories of chess periodicals, newspapers and magazine chess columns; official lists of International Grandmasters and Masters; the history of world championship competition; and the names of players who have won the national tournaments conducted by the USCF and its predecessors. It also contains the official American translation of the FIDE Laws of Chess and a detailed account of the author's numerical system of rating chessplayers which has been adopted by the U. S. Chess Federation, the British Chess Federation and the Chess Federation of Canada.

"ONE-KING MATE"

A term applied to a chess problem, credited to E. N. Frankenstein, in which the black King is purposely removed from the board. The solver of the problem must first replace the missing monarch on the correct square, and then proceed with the problem so that a subsequent mate or sui-mate will take place as the given directions indicate.

OPEN FILE

A file cleared of all Pawns. Such a file can be utilized as a supply highway for conveying major pieces needed for offensive or defensive purposes. Rooks are most effective when stationed on open files.

OPEN GAME

A term applied to a game in which both Black and White open with P-K4 as their first move. This single move provides an opening for the development of Queens and Bishops. (See *Closed Opening*) Some examples of the open game are: (after 1. P-K4, P-K4)

2. P-Q4   Center Game
2. P-KB4   King's Gambit
2. N-KB3   King's Knight Opening
2. N-QB3   Vienna Game
2. B-B4   King's Bishop Opening.

OPENING GAME

The first phase of the game, in which the major objective is to organize and to coordinate one's forces as quickly as possible so that they may exert their maximum power. The King's safety is, of course, of paramount importance in any phase of the game. There is no sharp line of demarcation between the opening phase of the game and the second phase, known as the middle game in which tactical maneuvers predominate. Chess writers indicate that the opening is usually accomplished within the first eight to twelve moves. Edward Lasker offers this general guide: "Strictly speaking the opening comprises only such moves as are *necessary* for the development of the pieces, and any move which a player—without being compelled—makes with a piece that is already developed, ought to be regarded as a Middle Game." The opening procedures have been studied extensively by the master chessplayers and are recorded in most modern chessbooks. See *Openings*.

OPENINGS

Well established patterns of opening moves. Such patterns are generally identifiable from the first, second and/ or third moves. Many openings are named after the chessmasters who originated or popularized them. Some are named after the place or tournament where they were introduced into official chessplay.

All intelligent moves in chess openings are based on ideas which chessplayers believe can be developed step by step to a favorable climax. These ideas should be guided by certain general strategic principles. (See *Principles*.) However, the various opening moves may necessarily have to be changed at any moment in an actual game to meet the challenging moves of the player on the opposite side of the chessboard. It is also noteworthy to indicate that some openings are suited better than others to meet the various temperaments and styles of players. For example, some openings (like the Ruy Lopez and Giuoco

Piano) are conservative, while others (like the Sicilian and the Nimzovitch) are more daring and risky.

It is humanly impossible to memorize all of the opening moves of the many games which have been recorded in the books. It has been calculated that the number of possible ways of playing the first ten moves amounts to the astronomical figure of 169,518,829,-100,544,000,000,000,000,000. (See *Mathematical Calculations in Chess.*)

For "The Relative Strengths of the Openings" see the *British Chess Magazine,* June, 1955, pages 177 to 180. For other references on opening procedures see:

1. *Modern Chess Openings,* Ninth Edition, by Walter Korn.
2. *Practical Chess Openings,* by Reuben Fine.
3. *Ideas Behind Chess Openings,* by Reuben Fine.
4. *Modern Ideas in Chess Openings,* by I. A. Horowitz.
5. *Chess Openings,* by James Mason.
6. *Guide to Chess Openings,* by Leonard W. Barden.

OPEN LINE

Any rank, file or diagonal which is freed of Pawns. This gives Rooks, Bishops and Queens an opportunity to get into action quickly and effectively. Znosko-Borovsky warns that "the weaker party must not open lines, especially where his weakness lies, as it would benefit his adversary." On the other hand, he points out that "opening a line is of advantage to the stronger player and it should be where the player's position is strongest." See *Open File.*

OPEN TOURNAMENT

A tournament in which chessplayers may compete without restrictions as to their class standing. Hence, a contestant is likely to meet players of all different levels of chessplaying ability. The first real "open" tournament was held in Chicago, in 1934, and was won jointly by Samuel Reshevsky and Reuben Fine, who finished with a tie score. It was sponsored by the newly formed American Chess Federation. For a list of the United States Open Chess Champions since the beginning of this century, see *The Official Blue Book and Encyclopedia of Chess,* pp. 282-283.

OPPONENT

The player on the other side of the chessboard.

OPPOSITION

A situation in which the two opposing Kings stand on the same rank, file or diagonal and are separated from each other by an odd number of squares. If there is only one square between the Kings, they are said to be in *direct opposition.* When there is an odd number of squares greater than one between the two Kings, they are said to be in *distant opposition.* The Kings are not in opposition to each other when they are separated by an even number of squares. The player who just moved and placed the Kings in opposition is said to "hold the opposition" or "he has the opposition." The advantage of holding the opposition is

Vertical Opposition or opposition on a file. It is Black's move, White therefore holds the opposition. If Black retires, White may follow him and retain the opposition.

that it gives the holder both defensive and offensive powers. See *Chess Fundamentals,* by José Capablanca, page 41.

Horizontal Opposition or Opposition on a rank. The player holding the opposition can prevent his opponent's King from moving to a closer file.

Diagonal Opposition. This is valuable as a means of obtaining direct opposition on a rank or file.

ORANG-UTAN OPENING

1.   P-QN4

Geza Maroczy states that the day before the New York tournament was held in 1924, Dr. Tartakower visited the New York Zoological Gardens and there mentally developed this opening. The following morning Tartakower utilized this opening successfully against Maroczy. Leonhard Schiffler cites Dr. O. Faber of Heidelberg as saying in 1932 that Bogoljubow gave this opening its present name, although records can be found that this opening was known earlier as "the Polish Opening."

This Orang-Utan opening can be developed by a large number of varia-

tions depending to some extent on Black's opening reply. By this opening, White has laid the ground work for fianchettoing his Queen's Bishop. For an interesting account of the history, theory and 93 games in which this Orang-Utan opening was utilized see *Orang-Utan Eroffnung* by Leonhard Schiffler, Berlin: Sportverlag, 1954, p. 159.

"ORGAN PIPES"

A descriptive term invented by Sam Loyd in 1857 and applied to a Grimshaw theme which, instead of merely having two black pieces interfere with each other, now has two distinct pairs of pieces interfering with each other. As shown in the accompanying diagram, the arrangement of Black's Rooks

Mate in Two Moves
Key: Q-Q4

and Bishops led Loyd to give it the fanciful name "Organ Pipes." When

the pairs of the mutually interfering pieces are separated, F. Janet speaks of them as "Split Organ Pipes."

ORIGIN OF CHESS

Historical evidence seems to indicate that the beginning of the game of chess as well as its later development was not the creation of any one single individual but the result of the cumulative experience of many individuals in many lands. The game as it is known today is a composite of material forces, their positions, and their movements in time and space. All of these elements blend symbolically into one composite struggle for survival. It is patent, then, that chess is the result of the pooled and cooperative experiences of hundreds of improvisers.

Many historians believe that the earliest game from which our modern game of chess originated and developed was *chaturanga*. This is a Sanscrit term meaning "four arms." As applied to chess, *chaturanga* was an old Indian army game which represented the King and his four fighting arms, namely, chariots, elephants, cavalry and infantry.

With the development of chess literature, which probably had its origin in the early days of Persia, many terms now in modern usage, came to life during the eighth century when early Sanscrit words were given Persian designation. The Indian word *rajah* became known as *shah*, its Persian equivalent. This Persian *shah* or King, was retained with slight modifications in other nations; thus, in Germany, it became known as *schach;* in Russia, *shak;* in Italy, *scacchi;* in Norway, *sjaak;* in the Latin language, *scac,* and in the French language *échecs,* from which our English word *chess* originated. See *History of Chess.*

ORTHODOX

This word comes from *orthos* meaning right or true; and *doxa,* meaning opinion. Hence, the word "orthodox" may be applied to anything which is sound and true and in conformity with recognized standards. In chess, we speak of orthodox chess, an orthodox problem, an orthodox opening, as distinguished from anything that is unorthodox or a deviation from that which is generally considered to be the correct standard or proper procedure. Orthodox chess may then be defined as that form of chessplay which utilizes the chessboard, chessmen and chess procedures as they are prescribed in the laws, rules and regulations of and enforced by the International Federation of Chess.

OUTPOST

A fortified position taken in enemy territory. Its purpose may be to exert increased pressure on the opponent as an offensive or defensive measure and to induce weaknesses in the opponent's forces.

OVEREXTENDED PAWN

A Pawn advanced into enemy territory without adequate support from its fellow Pawns. This is usually considered to be a weakness in a Pawn formation because the safety of the overextended Pawn requires the protection of a more valuable piece.

OVERPROTECTION

Supplying more protection than is necessary to safeguard a chess unit or position. "Only strategically valuable points should be overprotected," says Nimzovitch, "not a sickly Pawn, nor a King's wing which rests on a weak foundation."

OVERWORKED PIECE

A piece which must perform more than one important task at the same time. A piece which guards two pieces simultaneously, for example, is overworked and such a piece becomes especially vulnerable for attack. For a brief statement and fifty-four illustrations of different ways in which various pieces may be overworked, see Chapter 7 in *1001 Brilliant Chess Sacrifices and Combinations,* by Fred Reinfeld.

P

PAIRING

Matching partners in tournament games. Contestants may be matched by lot, selected by the Tournament Director, or according to some established and recognized ranking system. The fundamental pairing rules for a Swiss system tournament, as set forth by the United States Chess Federation, are first, that a contestant plays any other contestants once only; and second, that each player be paired in each round with another player whose score is equal to or most nearly equal to his score. For a discussion of the objectives, limitations and methods used in pairing players, see *The Official Blue Book and Encyclopedia of Chess,* pages 172 to 196.

PARTIE

A French word meaning a game, match or contest. Steinitz spoke of the "Immergrun Partie" meaning the "Evergreen game" played in Berlin in the eighteen fifties between Anderssen and Dufresne. See *Evergreen Partie.*

PASSED PAWN

A Pawn which has no adverse Pawn in front of it on its own file and at the same time has no opposing Pawns on its adjacent files. Such a Pawn may proceed to the queening square without any hindrance from opposing Pawns. The fact that a friendly or hostile *piece* is stationed in front of such a

Pawn which may hinder its progress towards the queening square does not deprive that Pawn from being called a "passed Pawn." Chess authorities stress the importance of passed Pawns and in general suggest that "passed Pawns must be pushed!" Nimzovitch considers an opponent's passed Pawn as "a criminal, who should be kept under lock and key." The following descriptive terms are sometimes applied to passed Pawns, namely:

a *half-passed Pawn* is a Pawn that is not blocked by a hostile Pawn on its own file but is prevented from advancing to the queening square by a hostile Pawn on *one* (but not both) of the adjacent files.

a *supported passed Pawn* is one that is defended by one or two of its adjacent Pawns. The defending Pawn does not necessarily have to be a passed Pawn.

united passed Pawns are two or more adjacent Pawns which are also passed Pawns. They may stand side by side or support one another.

For a discussion of the importance of passed Pawns and when they should be advanced see *My System,* by Aron Nimzovitch. See *Queening.*

PATRON OF CHESS

An influential individual who is sufficiently interested in the game of chess to give his moral and financial support to a worth-while program which is designed to promote a greater interest in and enthusiasm for the game of chess. Just as famous painters and musicians had their patrons in the Middle Ages, so likewise many strong chessplayers had their patrons. In the sixteenth century, chess flourished in Spain under the patronage of Philip II. Ruy Lopez, Leonardo da Cutri and Paolo Boi were invited to

Philip's court and given lucrative appointments to play chess. Greco was invited to play chess at the court of the Duke of Lorraine in Nancy and later received a remunerative appointment at the court of Philip IV in Madrid. In like manner, the famous Medici family, Henry IV of England and other wealthy noblemen patronized famous chessplayers. Patrons of chess may be found in every age and in every country. Recently, Lourens Hammond, the chairman of the board of the Hammond Organ Company offered the city of Chicago a large sum of money for the construction of a Chess Pavilion for the promotion of chess on a much larger scale than that developed in Washington Square Park in New York City.

PATZER

A term applied to an informal chessplayer who lacks ordinary skill. At times he is also called a "pfuscher."

PAULSEN

Louis Paulsen, a respected chessplayer of the nineteenth century, was born in Germany, on June 15, 1833. In 1854, he emigrated to America but six years later, he returned to Germany where he once more established residence. He was a fearless but cautious chessplayer. He encountered many of the chess notables in tournament and match games. His playing strength is indicated in his record against the great Anderssen, which shows Paulsen won 15 and lost 10 games. Paulsen was also an excellent blindfold chessplayer. In the 1883 Nuremberg tournament, Paulsen played against Mason by utilizing the Saragossa Opening and then transformed it into a French defense. Likewise, in 1892, Paulsen and Mason played at Dresden and repeated their Nuremberg opening performance. Paulsen's name and fame are still referred to by some modern chesswriters.

PAWN

The smallest and least valuable of all chessmen. The word Pawn originated from the Latin word *pes* meaning foot, hence a foot-soldier or infantryman. Each player has eight Pawns stationed at the opening of the game along the second rank. Each Pawn assumes the name of the piece before which it stands at the opening, as the King's Pawn, the Queen's Pawn, the King's Bishop Pawn, etc. In chess notation, a Pawn is symbolized as ♟ and is briefly recorded by the letter P.

How a Pawn Moves and Captures. The Pawn moves forward only, never backwards. It moves forward one square at a time provided the square is unoccupied. To hasten the forward movement of Pawns, it became the practice ever since the sixteenth century to allow *each and every* Pawn, if the player wishes, to move two squares on the first move, provided that both squares are unoccupied. The Pawn captures obliquely (diagonally), reminiscent of a soldier who slays his enemy by a sideward thrust of his sword. A special and unique method of capturing a Pawn is known as "capturing *en passant*" or "capturing in passing." (See *en passant.*) Generally, when there is a choice of capturing one of two Pawns on the adjacent files, it is desirable to capture towards the center, provided all other things are equal.

White's move. Position before making capture.

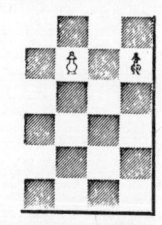

Position after White captured Black's Pawn.

Functions of a Pawn are 1) to control the third and fourth ranks so as to ward off opposing forces and to shield the King; 2) to defend and be the first to be sacrificed; 3) to engage the enemy in combat; 4) to prepare the way for more important chessmen to follow for offensive and defensive purposes; and 5) to struggle forward to the eighth rank for a promotion.

Advantages and Disadvantages. The Pawn is the only chess unit with a future. When a Pawn reaches the eighth rank it may be transformed into a Queen, Rook, Bishop or Knight depending upon the choice of the player. This Pawn promotion is mandatory. (See *Queening.*) The Pawn is also a very advantageous chess unit for offensive and defensive action. Nimzovitch says, "the Pawn is a born defender." Znosko-Borovsky points out that inasmuch "as it is an advantage to exchange a Pawn for a piece, the piece must retreat before an attack by Pawns." He also observes that "the Queen may be as strong as eight Pawns, but she must normally retreat when attacked by one of them."

Once a Pawn starts on its journey, it can never retreat. Once it makes a move, it can not retract. A wrong, foolish or unwise Pawn move is an irremedial mistake. Small disadvantages occurring in a Pawn structure are not easily corrected. The greatest of all Pawn weaknesses is for a Pawn to become isolated from its fellow Pawns. This becomes more serious when isolated Pawns are doubled or trebled. Such Pawns are an easy prey for enemy attacks. Their safety requires the protective services of more important chess units. Doctor Fine states it very succinctly when he says: "Pawns live by the motto: United we stand, divided we fall!"

Value of Pawns. Regarding the value of a Pawn in the opening phase of the game, Spielmann offers the following rule of thumb: "Three developing moves are approximately worth a Pawn." In general, a Pawn is strongest in home territory, less strong when advanced, and weaker when it enters enemy territory unless it is adequately supported. A mobile Pawn is strong and valuable; an immobile Pawn is weak and useless unless it serves as a desirable blockader. For comparative values of a Pawn with other chess pieces, see *Value of Chessmen*.

Importance of the Pawn. Although the Pawn is sometimes referred to as the "humble Pawn" or the "measly Pawn," nevertheless, chess authorities hold the Pawn in high esteem. Many chessplayers consider it a high achievement when they can inflict a checkmate with a Pawn. The Pawn may seem expendable in the opening of the game but as the game progresses, the Pawn becomes increasingly more valuable. "The Pawns are the soul of the game," wrote the great Philidor. Tarrasch said: "Nothing so easily ruins a position as Pawn moves," and, he facetiously remarked: "Never move a Pawn and you will never lose a game." Tartakower admonished: "In order to handle Pawns well, it is important to learn not to handle them too much."

Every book dealing with the game of chess contains a more or less adequate treatment of the Pawn. There is no paucity of obtainable information on this topic.

PAWN CENTER

The King Pawn and Queen Pawn squares on the fourth and fifth ranks for Black and White are usually referred to as the Pawn center. However, Steinitz's idea of a strong Pawn center included also the squares on KB3 and QB3 from where Pawns may fortify the King and Queen Pawns. Having established a fortified center, Steinitz would then take the offensive on the flank.

PAWN CHAIN

A series of Pawns stationed on a diagonal which are blocked by a similar series of the opponent's Pawns. The Pawn farthest back in the series is referred to as being at the base of the chain. Nimzovitch established the principle that to destroy a Pawn chain one must attack the base of the chain. Hence, the strength of a Pawn chain depends on the degree of protection the base of the chain receives from a major or minor piece.

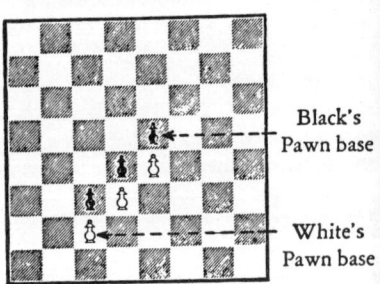

Black's Pawn base

White's Pawn base

PAWN DEFENSE OF CASTLED KING

Pawns stationed in front of a castled King to protect him from enemy attack. When castling on the King's side, the Pawns can assume any of the following positions.

Excellent; especially when opponent castled on the opposite side. With a Knight on KB3, this is a difficult position to attack.

Very good; especially when both players castled on the same side. It is not so strong if opponent castled on the opposite side.

Good, the fianchetto-ed Bishop occupies the weak square, making then a good defensive position.

Weak; the squares on KB3 and KR3 are very weak and the long diagonal KR1-QR8 is open for action of opponent's Bishop.

Weak. All Black squares are open. The square on N3 is a bad hole.

Very weak. The King is exposed for immediate attack.

PAWN-GRABBER

see *Pawn-Snatcher*

PAWN MAJORITY

Having more Pawns on the chessboard than the opponent. Generally, more material means more power. Moreover, a majority of Pawns is advantageous because it may have, or potentially can have, one or more passed Pawns which may be converted into major pieces when they reach the eighth rank. However, a mere numerical majority of Pawns can be impotent if the opponent's Pawn minority can keep them in check. This frequently occurs when there are double or treble Pawns.

PAWN ODDS AND MOVE

The stronger player gives odds of a Pawn and a move by usually removing from the board, at the beginning of the game, his KBP and allowing his opponent to play with the white pieces. By playing with the black pieces, the stronger player is said to have given his opponent the advantage of a move. See *Odds*.

PAWN ODDS AND TWO MOVES

This is the same as "Pawn Odds and Move" except that the player using the white pieces moves twice before the player of the black pieces makes his first move. In this case, White's first two moves usually are P-K4 and P-Q4. See *Odds*.

PAWN-SNATCHER

One who grabs Pawns without sufficient forethought. Capturing material is always desirable if it can be done with safety because in most games, material advantage is a very deciding factor. A Pawn-snatcher, however, usually seizes the opponent's Pawns before having developed an adequate reserve force and before having provided adequate protection for his King. By comparison, the advantage gained in snatching Pawns is small, whereas the risk involved is great. Sometimes the word "Pawn-grabber" is used in place of "Pawn-snatcher."

P. C. O.

see *Practical Chess Opening*

PEASANT

A term frequently used by some European chessplayers in place of the Pawn.

PERFECT GAME

A game in which neither player makes a mistake. This implies that all moves are made in compliance with *all* of the established principles, laws, regulations and rules of chess. Theoretically, such a flawless game should end in a draw. In practical application, however, individual judgment as to which principle or rule is best applied to a given situation may be in error.

Tartakower once remarked that "the winner of a game of chess is the man who makes the next-to-the-last mistake." Reinfeld interpreted this to mean that "chess is a contest in which there are often blemishes and imperfections on both sides." Many chess writers indicate by implication that the perfect game of chess has not yet been played. See *Mistake*.

PERIODICALS

Chess periodicals. are specialized publications containing feature articles, annotated games, challenging problems, current news items of what is going on in the chess fraternity, and announcements and reviews of new books in the field of chess. Some publishing organizations of these periodicals sponsor Correspondence Chess Clubs and devote a section of their periodicals to report on the progress of their members. Many individual chess clubs and chess associations publish a bulletin or mimeographed newspaper as a means of keeping their members and other interested parties informed of the club's activities. Some of the leading chess periodicals published in the English language are:

1. *American Chess Bulletin*. Issued bimonthly. Price $3.00 a year. Address: 150 Nassau Street, New York 38, New York.

2. *British Chess Magazine*. Issued monthly. Price $4.00 a year. Address: 20 Chestnut Road, West Norwood, London S.E. 27, England. (May be ordered through: *Chess Life*, Editorial Office.)

3. *Canadian Chess Chat*. Official Organ of the Chess Federation of Canada. Issued monthly (10 issues per year). Price $3.00 a year. Address: 2084 Decarie Blvd., Montreal 28, Quebec, Canada. (May be ordered through: *Chess Life*, Editorial Office.)

4. *Chess Correspondent*. Official Organ of the Correspondence Chess League of America. Issued monthly except May through August, when it is issued bimonthly. Price including annual membership in the CCLA is $4.50 a year. Address: 816 South Cecelia Street, Sioux City 6, Iowa.

5. *Chess Life*. Official Organ of the United States Chess Federation. Issued twice a month. Price including annual membership in the USCF is $5.00 a year. Subscription to non-members, $3.00 a year. Address: United States Chess Federation, Business Manager, 80 East 11th Street, New York

6. *Chess Reader*. Issued quarterly plus extra issues. Price 3/6 a year (55¢ a year). Address: K. Whyld, Editor and Publisher. 39 Charnwood Avenue, New Sawley, Long Eaton, Nottingham, England.

7. *Chess Review*—"the picture chess magazine." Issued monthly. Price $5.50 a year, two years $10.50, three years $15.00. Address: Chess Review, 134 West 72nd Street, New York 23, New York.

8. *Chess World*. A comprehensive Australian chess magazine. Issued monthly. Price $3.00 a year. Address: *Chess World*, 1 Bond Street, Sydney, Australia. (May be ordered through Chess Life, Editorial Office.

PERPETUAL CHECK

An endless series of checks. A player who has little hope of winning may avoid complete loss of the game by giving check to his opponent's King in such a manner that he can escape only by exposing himself to another check. According to the Laws of Chess a three-fold repetition of the same position ends the game and constitutes a drawn game. The slang expression "perp" is sometimes used in place of "perpetual check."

PETROFF'S DEFENSE

| 1. | P-K4 | P-K4 |
| 2. | N-KB3 | N-KB3 |

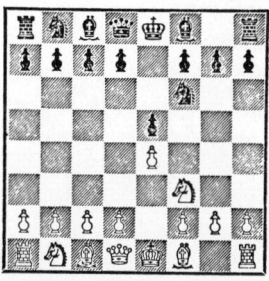

This is one of the oldest defenses to the King's Knight opening which dates from the Gottingen Manuscripts of 1490. It was described by the English master Walker in 1841, carefully analyzed by M. Jaenisch in the *Palamède* in 1842, and popularized about the same time by the distinguished Russian player von Petroff. Hence, this defense is sometimes known as the Russian Defense.

Black's second move is the characteristic move which identifies this opening as one of perfect symmetry thus far in the game. "At best," says Tarrasch, "this so far leads to equality and White retains a minimum of advantage—that of the first move." Reinfeld believes that "Black can generally hold his own with this enterprising counterattack, despite the fact that his second move is attacking at a very early stage." If White should play 3. N-B3, then Black can respond with 3 . . . B-N5 and bring about a Ruy Lopez opening with colors reversed. For a presentation of procedural development of the Pet-

roff Defense and some of its modern variations see *Modern Chess Openings*, Ninth Edition, by Walter Korn, or, *Practical Chess Openings*, by Reuben Fine.

PFUSCHER

see *Patzer*

PHASES OF THE GAME

The three parts of the game of chess known as: the Opening Game, the Middle Game, and the End-game. These three divisions of the game blend into one another and have no sharp line of demarcation. Each does, however, serve a distinct purpose. The Opening Game consists of the strategical development of the forces so that they will be readily available for the ensuing skirmishes and battle. The Middle Game consists of carrying out the tactical maneuvers of the *plan de campagne* for attack as well as defense. The End-game is concerned with the final stage of victory or defeat. Once the game is in progress, the success of each phase of the game depends to a large extent upon the success of previous performances. Capablanca urged very strongly that "whether you are a strong player or a weak player, you should try to be of equal strength in the three parts" of the game. See *Opening Game; Middle Game*, and *End Game*.

PHILIDOR

François André Danican Philidor, the greatest chess genius of the eighteenth century, was born in 1726, at Dreux, near Paris, France. He was a choir boy in Louis XIV's chapel and eventually became a French musical composer and musician. His last opera, *Thémistocle*, was performed at Fontainebleau in 1785. He learned to play chess when he was less than ten years of age. In time, he became the strongest chess player at the Café de la Régence. In 1749, he published his *Analyse du Jeu des Echecs*. During the political upheaval in France, Philidor fled to Holland and then to England where he made his living by playing and writing on the scientific aspects of the game of chess. He became the top ranking chessplayer at the Slaughter Coffee House in London and soon developed a reputation for himself as a chess genius of his time. He died in London, in 1795.

Philidor made several note-worthy contributions to chess. His classical French publication, already mentioned, was translated into English and published as *Analysis of the Game of Chess*, by A. D. Philidor. London: Printed for T. & J. Allman, Princess Street, Hanover Square, 1819. In this book, Philidor defined the principles of chess strategy and tactics. He also developed the thesis that "Pawns are the very soul of the game," and he pointed out the importance of "never to make a Pawn move without good reason." The book also contained "Rules of the Game of Chess" which were adopted by the Society of Chess in London. Philidor popularized not only an opening which bears his name (see *Philidor's Defense*) but also an end-game play which is known as Philidor's Legacy. (See *Philidor's Legacy*).

Murray, the famous chess historian, considers Philidor as "the leading personality in the chess circles of Paris and London" for more than forty years. Tartakower lists Philidor as the champion chessplayer of the world from 1745 to 1795. Gossip states very positively that "Philidor was unquestionably one of the greatest chess geniuses that ever lived."

For a more detailed account of Philidor's life and activities see *History of Chess*, by H. J. R. Murray; and,

The Life of Philidor, Musician and Chess-Player, by George Allen, Greek Professor in the University of Pennsylvania, Philadelphia; published in 1858.

PHILIDOR'S DEFENSE

1.	P-K4	P-K4
2.	N-KB3	P-Q3

This defense, popularized by Philidor, was believed to have been a safer means of defending the King Pawn than 2 . . . N-QB3. Tarrasch pointed out that 2 . . . P-Q3 is a voluntary shutting in of a Bishop. This, he claimed, is an unsound play. Walter Korn is of the opinion that this defense "has solidity but lacks mobility." Fred Reinfeld indicates that "Black's pieces have little scope and the defense is therefore rarely played."

PHILIDOR'S LEGACY

This so-called "Philidor's Legacy" is more generally defined and better known as the "smothered mate." It is an end-game play which can be traced to the time of Lucena in 1497 although Philidor is given the credit for having popularized it. The startling feature of this Philidor's Legacy is, as illustrated in the acompanying diagram, White maneuvers his pieces and even sacrifices his Queen so that Black's King is smothered in a corner from which he can not escape when the Knight administers the mate. See *Smothered Mate*.

Solution

1. N-R6 dbl. ch.	K-R1
2. Q-N8 ch	RxQ
3. N-B7 mate.	

or

1. N-R6 dbl. ch	K-B1
2. Q-B7 mate.	

PHILLIPS

Harold M. Phillips, President of the United States Chess Federation 1951-1954, a Vice-President of the Fédération Internationale des Echecs, and a chess organizer *par excellence,* was born in Lithuania, on December 15, 1874. He came to the United States in 1887. After attending the College of the City of New York, he entered in 1896, the Law School of Columbia University. By profession, he is an Attorney and Counselor at Law.

His chess career began in 1891. When he was a freshman at the College of the City of New York, he won every game from senior and junior students. He became the champion chessplayer of City College on five different occasions. While studying at Columbia University, he became the champion chessplayer of the Labourdonnais Chess Club on three different occasions. He was known to be a chessplayer who conceded odds to his opponents, ranging from a Pawn move and draw to a Rook. In 1901, having received the odds of a draw in a handicap tournament, he won a prize by defeating Dr. Berthold Lasker—the brother of the former world champion. The very following year, he won the championship of the famous Manhattan Chess Club. He also won first place honors in a knockout tournament, sponsored by The New York Sun newspaper, which was open to all chessplayers in Greater New York. From time to time, Phillips played in match and tournament games with such outstanding chessmasters as Alekhine, Capablanca, Duras, Mieses, Maroczy and Rubinstein. On several occasions he also served as a member of various chess teams that played over-the-board by telegraph or cablegram.

As a chess organizer and administrator, Mr. Phillips was and still is an active member of the Marshall Chess Club, the Manhattan Chess Club and the London Terrace Chess Club—all in New York City. He served as the Chairman of almost all the committees that sent American teams abroad that were so victorious in the International Chess Tournaments in the 1920's and 1930's. He also organized and served as Chairman of practically all tournaments for the United States Championship from 1936 to 1951. He served on the Board of Governors of the Marshall Chess Club; and as President of the Manhattan Chess Club, 1933-1941; Treasurer of the New York State Chess Association; President of the United States Chess Federation from January, 1951 to August, 1954; and is now one of the eight Vice-Presidents of the International Federation of Chess. In January, 1955, the Manhattan Chess Club elected Mr. Phillips as an Honorary Member for Life—the highest honor at the disposal of that Chess Club.

PIANO OPENING

A term used by some writers as an abbreviated name of the Giuoco Piano Opening. See *Giuoco Piano.*

PIECE CONTROL

An expression used by a problem composer when he refers to a chess piece which can not be omitted from a problem but must be kept subservient to the composer's wishes.

PIECES

Specifically, the term "pieces" refers to the Queens, Rooks, Bishops and Knights. These are usually classified into major and minor pieces. The major pieces, sometimes called the heavy pieces, consist of the Queens and Rooks. The minor pieces, sometimes called the light pieces, consist of the Bishops and Knights. More generally, the term "pieces" is often used when reference is made to all of the chessmen under consideration. This latter usage of the term occurs frequently in composed problems.

Major Pieces	Minor Pieces
	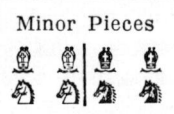

PILLSBURY

Harry Nelson Pillsbury, United States Champion Chessplayer from 1897 to 1906, was born in Somerville, near Boston, Massachusetts, on December 5, 1872. He made chess his profession but was also regarded as one of the twenty best checker experts in the United States. By the time he was twenty years of age, he was considered the best chessplayer in New England. In 1895, he won the first prize at the Hastings chess tournament and in 1900 he was again the first prize winner at the Munich tournament. Pillsbury was also famous as a blindfold chessplayer. Dr. Fine observes that Pillsbury's "blindfold powers and miraculous memory were a delight to behold." It is recorded that on one occasion, Pillsbury was given thirty unrelated words

and then proceeded to play chess and checker games blindfolded and at the same time played a game of whist, after which he repeated the thirty words in their exact order. He died on June 17, 1906, in Philadelphia, Pennsylvania.

Pillsbury was regarded as one of the most attractive and romantic figures in American chessplay. He had a dramatic style of play. In his tactical maneuvers he displayed, as Reinfeld observes, "a knack of springing surprises and creating tension in even the most simple and harmless positions.'

PIN

To pin a chess piece is to prevent it from moving away because it is needed on its location to shield one of the more valuable pieces or the King himself from an immediate attack. In the accompanying diagram, White succeeded in pinning Black's Bishop

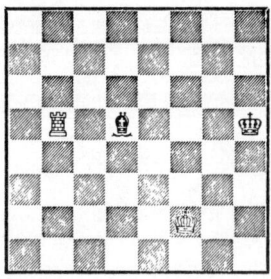

This Bishop cannot move because, if he did so, his King would be exposed to check—which is illegal. Hence, Black's Bishop will be captured on White's next move. Pinning a piece is the most frequently used tactical device in a game of chess. It is a powerful scheme of restricting the action of an opponent's piece because a pinned piece is rendered immobile, helpless, paralyzed. Reinfeld says that "the pin is mightier than the sword!" However, a pinned piece can be released by some violent counter move, such as, giving check, causing a mating threat, making a counterpin or counterattack, or undermining the piece which is causing the pin.

The term *absolute pin* or *wholly pinned* is used by some writers to indicate that the piece behind the pinned piece is the King. If any other chess unit is stationed behind the pinned piece, they would use the simple word *pin*. Mr. C. Mansfield of England used the term *half-pin* when the pinned piece has one or more squares along the line of pin to which the pinned piece may move. For a brief statement and 108 illustrations of this pinning process see *1001 Brilliant Chess Sacrifices and Combinations*, by Fred Reinfeld, Chapter 1, entitled, "Pinning."

PION COIFFÉ

Two French words: *pion,* meaning Pawn; and *coiffé,* meaning cap or hood. The expression is used in giving odds in a game of chess by designating at the beginning of a game that checkmate will be given by the "Pion Coiffé" or "Capped Pawn." Usually the King's Knight Pawn is selected for this purpose. This Pawn is identified by placing a ring upon it or tying a ribbon or string around it. The players agree at the outset that this marked Pawn will administer the final checkmate. It is further understood that this Pawn is not allowed to be queened, and that if this Pawn is captured or if the opponent's King is checkmated by any other piece, the player giving this extreme type of odds will forfeit the game. This type of odds is rarely given and only when there is very wide disparity between the skill of the players.

PITFALL

An apparently superficially sound situation in which a player is led to make a move which has more or less dire consequences. It actually amounts to a blunder which usually grows out of an unsuspected weakness in a player's position. See: *Chess Traps, Pitfalls, and Swindles* by I. A. Horowitz and Fred Reinfeld. As a special form of a pitfall see *Swindle.*

PLACHUTTA INTERFERENCE

An interference theme developed by the German problemist J. Plachutta (born 1883), in which two black pieces of similar motion, mutually interfere with each other on a critical square where a white piece is sacrificed for the sake of mating Black's King. If no sacrifice is made, it is known as a Wurzburg-Plachutta interference. For a fuller explanation see *The Enjoyment of Chess Problems* by Kenneth Howard, pages 117 and 151-2.

PLAN

A mental outline or scheme of procedure which is based on sound, basic principles. A plan may be viewed as a mental prescription for successful action on the chessboard. Its essential ingredients are: first, to have a definite objective clearly in view; second, to move forward wisely so that the desired goal may be reached as quickly as possible; and third, to be cautious, alert and flexible in meeting complications which may arise from an opponent's oversight, mistake, weakened position or threatening action.

A plan may be of a long-range or short-range nature. A long-range plan is made to wage a major attack or important skirmishes. A short-range plan consists of a few forward looking moves which are needed to overcome an interfering obstacle which may inhibit the progress of a larger plan of action. Since in chess we are called upon only to make every alternate move, the best and most pressing plan is to find the best move on the board. Cecil Purdy, World Correspondence Chess Champion admonishes that with the "Next move, plan afresh".

The importance of planning is stressed by all chess writers. They indicate that with planning, a game is no longer "fought in the dark" and that it gives "a satisfied feeling that chessmen are truly under your control." Dr. Emanuel Lasker pointed out that "an intelligent plan makes heroes of us, and absence of a plan cowards and dullards." See *Judgment and Planning in Chess* by Max Euwe.

PLAYER IN GAME OF CHESS

Technically, the player in a game of chess is defined as the one whose turn it is to make a move. The player on the other side of the chessboard is called the opponent. Every player in the chess fraternity can be classified according to his playing strength. In organized chess, a player can be identified as a World Champion, National Champion, Grandmaster, Master, Expert, Class A, B, or C player. An amateur chessplayer is sometimes referred to as a beginner, a dub, a duffer, a tyro or a woodpusher. See *Classification of Chessplayers*, and *Master Chessplayer.*

POLERIO

Giulio Cesare Polerio was a noted Italian chessplayer and writer in the late sixteenth and early seventeenth centuries. In his published manuscript on chess, one finds the first mention of a large number of the King's gambits which are now in common usage. Some of these gambit plays, however, have been renamed in honor of the chessplayers who popularized them in official chess tournaments.

POLISH OPENING

1. P-QN4

This opening is rarely seen in modern chessplay. Du Mont says "the

Polish opening has little to recommend it." See *Orang-Utan* Opening.

POLITICIAN, CHESS

A "chess politician" is one who promotes and popularizes chess interests. He talks, writes, sits on committees and makes himself important through his display of energy as a chess enthusiast. He is quick to offer criticism but generally has little to contribute towards the masterly progress and refinement of the game.

PONZIANI

Domenico Lorenzo Ponziani was born in Modena, Italy, on November 9, 1719. He was noteworthy as a Modenese patrician, an enthusiastic chess devotee, a sage jurist, an ordained priest, an Apostolic Prothonotary and a university Professor of Civil Law. He died on July 15, 1796.

Chess was for Ponziani a relaxation from his many cares and duties. He enjoyed the game, studied it, and endeavored to develop and to improve its theory. As early as 1749, he recorded his early experiences concerning methods of attack and defense. In his *Giuoco Incomparabile,* which was published in 1782 and reprinted in 1829, he developed his studies of chess. In it he revealed the powers of his analytical mind. Shortly after his death, a critic pointed out that "Ponziani's work is written on an excellent plan; he never suffers the player of the black pieces, to whom he addresses himself, to make any bad moves, and he shows him how to take advantage of those committed by his adversary."

PONZIANI OPENING

1. P-K4   P-K4
2. N-KB3   N-QB3
3. P-B3

An opening credited to Ponziani in which White strives to control the center by playing 3. P-B3. Obviously, this is a preparatory move for 4. P-Q4. However, since White's third move

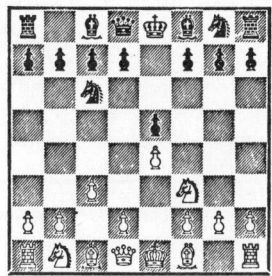

lacks a direct threat, Black can counteract by playing 3 . . . , P-Q4, or P-B3, or N-B3 and thereby upset White's plan. Dr. Emanuel Lasker does not recommend this opening. Dr. Tarrasch states very positively that "the move 3. P-B3 is to be condemned. Instead of making use of the tempo for his development, White misuses it in that he deprives his Queen's Knight of its best square, QB3."

POSITION

The arrangement of Pawns and pieces on the chessboard at any time at any stage of the game. The location of these chess units at any given moment is important to the extent of their mobility and the amount of pressure they can exert upon the opponent's forces. The ideal position at any given moment is one which 1) provides for the safety of the King; 2) exposes no piece for capture without adequate compensation; 3) maintains an adequate Pawn structure—being mindful of Philidor's admonition: "The Pawns are the very soul of the game;" 4) offers mobility to one's pieces to a greater extent than that of the opponent; and 5) is prepared to meet any threat. A positional analysis is always interpreted in terms of the entire scene on the chessboard which in actual practice usually contains some advantages and some disadvantages for each player. Frequently, one advantage offsets a disadvantage. One player may be ahead in material, or be more vulnerable, or have greater terrain in which to operate, but what good does it avail a chessplayer to be ahead in material for example, when his King is in a mating position?

POSTAL CHESS

Games played between players living in separated communities who transmit their moves by means of postal service. For convenience to the chessplayers, special post cards have been designed for sending chess moves. For a fuller explanation see *The Macmillan Handbook of Chess*, by I. A. Horowitz and Fred Reinfeld, pages 142-146. See *Correspondence Chess.*

POTS

A term applied to a jovial method of rapid chessplay whereby three or four contestants ante a small stake into a pot. Play proceeds at the rate of ten seconds per move. The first two opponents are chosen by lot. The winner is said to have a "leg" on the pot. The loser is replaced by the third (or fourth) contestant. The final winner takes the pot. Kibitzing is permitted and when a player can talk his opponent out of the game, he is considered to be a good pot player. (See *Marshall Chess Club*.) For a brief discussion of "Pots" see *The Official Blue Book* and *Encyclopedia of Chess*, page 239.

POWER OF CHESSMEN

The inherent ability or capacity given by a player to his chessmen so that they may be able to produce a desired effect. Power on the chessboard is generally represented by a player's available material or forces in time of need. When all other factors are equal, the more material a player has, the greater is his power. However, a large number of Pawns and pieces alone does not necessarily represent power. Chess units may be so cramped that they are powerless to act. The total power, then, of a player's force depends upon its quality as well as its quantity; that is, its number of available Pawns and pieces, their position and range of their movements.

PRACTICAL CHESS OPENINGS

A practical reference book of chess openings and their variations which has been compiled from the knowledge and experiences of the eminent author and Grandmaster, Reuben Fine and his contemporaries. In the preface of this book, which was published in 1948, Dr. Fine states: "It has been my purpose in this book to present a compact guide to the chess openings. I have attempted on the one hand to include everything that is important for current play, and on the other to exclude material which is too specialized to be of practical value."

This handbook of chess information about the opening phase of the game contains 1,240 columns of chessplay which are accompanied by numerous footnotes; a schematic overview of the openings; and critical appraisals of the various openings and variations which are given in a clear and forthright manner. Many modern chess writers frequently use the three letters P. C. O. when they refer to *Practical Chess Openings*.

PREMATURE ATTACK

A hasty attack. It is an attack made without sufficient preparation. Such an attack usually dies out quickly because it is not supported by a reserve force powerful enough to repel the enemy's counter-action.

PRINCIPLES

Words of wisdom expressing fundamental truths or doctrines which, when observed, will serve as guideposts for a player to reach his desired goal effectively and efficiently.

Such principles are the outcome of a sound philosophy and the tried and tested experiences of master chessplayers. To be of practical value, chess principles must be translated into action on the chessboard. The importance of observing these principles has been pointed out by Edward Lasker when he says: "In formulating general strategic principles it is assumed that both players will follow them, and it is taken for granted that if one player deviates from these principles and thereby weakens himself at some point, the other player is expected to exact full penalty for this deviation with any means at his disposal."

Dr. Fine stresses three basic principles which should be observed throughout a game of chess. They are:

1. The Principle of Safety. The safety of the King is of primary importance at all times.
2. The Principle of Mobility. The player who has more room for his pieces to move about has an important advantage.
3. The Principle of Force. The player who is ahead in material should win.

Some of the more specific principles which are frequently stated by various chessmasters are:

1. In the opening phase of the game, develop your pieces rapidly and efficiently by placing them in the most effective positions. Avoid moving a piece twice during the opening.
2. Develop your pieces where they will have the greatest scope, mobility and freedom of movement.

3. Develop Knights before Bishops.
4. Avoid exchanging Bishops for Knights, especially in the opening phases of the game.
5. Castle early. It brings a Rook into more active play.
6. Make moves which contain a threat.
7. Avoid premature attacks.
8. Strive to control the center.
9. Avoid making exchanges which develop another piece of your opponent's.
10. Do not bring your Queen out too early.

How these and other principles can be utilized, is shown in *Chess the Easy Way*, by Reuben Fine. In this book, Dr. Fine proceeds by first stating in bold type the basic principle pertaining to the topic under discussion and then develops its meaning and application.

PRIORITY RULE

The rule which requires that when a King is placed in check he must be freed from the check at the next move. This is the only case in the entire game of chess where a player is not free to make any move he pleases. The King's safety comes first at all times. There is no exception to this rule.

PROBLEM

A perplexing chess situation presented according to a planned idea or combination of ideas for the purpose of finding the most efficient manner of mating the black King. The problem composer usually indicates the number of moves needed by stipulating "Mate in Two" or "Mate in Three" or more moves.

Chess problems provide opportunities for learning the science of the end-game. These practical exercises can help in the development of those skills needed in exploiting the powers of various pieces, contriving effective combinations and producing mates without making unnecessary moves. According to James Rayner, "A problem should be strong all around. It should have an elegant key, brilliant strategy and pretty mates." He also points out that the construction of a problem "should be artistic, the variations natural and pleasing, whilst the difficulty should be just sufficient to make the solution more interesting when discovered." These and other basic principles which guide the modern chess problemist in constructing his problems have been developed over the years. They serve as present-day standards by which the merits of problems are determined. For a brief summary of these principles, see *Problemist*. For a better understanding and appreciation of the nature of chess problems see:

Chess Problems, by James Rayner.
How to Solve Chess Problems, by Kenneth S. Howard.
Enjoyment of Chess Problems, by Kenneth S. Howard.
Mate in Two Moves, by Brian Harley.
Mate in Three Moves, by Brian Harley.

PROBLEM BISHOP

An impotent Bishop. The expression is used when reference is made to a Bishop who is blocked-in and has no possible freedom of action. The confinement of a "problem Bishop" can be seen in the accompanying illustra-

tion where Black's Queen's Bishop is immobilized by his own men.

PROBLEMIST

A specialist in the science and art of constructing chess problems. The noted chess historian Murray points out that problem construction is a branch of chess activity for which we are indebted to the Muslim world. However it is only within the last seventy-five years that this branch of chess activity developed into a specialized science which is now governed by a body of well-established, conventional basic principles. Briefly summarized, a chess problemist constructs a problem by observing the following principles. A problem should

1. Represent a possible position in a game of chess.

2. Utilize only those pieces in the initial position of the problem which would be present on the board at the beginning of a game of chess. For example, it is not permissible to have at the beginning of a problem two Queens, or three Rooks, or three Knights or two Bishops on the same colored squares.

3. Have no chess unit on the board which is not necessary to the composer's theme. Unrelated or unimportant pieces are sometimes utilized to create temptations which might mislead the player who is seeking a solution to the problem.

4. For the sake of uniformity let White have the first move, which is known as the key move; and let the black King be mated.

5. Have only one key move which will lead to the black King's mate in the stipulated number of moves.

6. Offer the black King as wide a latitude as possible to make several moves, but White must mate as stipulated. For example many problems provide the black

King with a flight square to which he may go on the first move. To give a mate with White's first move makes the solution too obvious or too brutal.

7. Permit castling only if it can be shown that neither the King nor the Rook have moved. Castling is avoided in most problems.

8. Never have the King in check at the beginning of a problem.

9. Have only one possible solution.

10. Give aesthetic pleasure by 1) the surprising nature of the key; 2) the economy of force needed to mate the black King; 3) unpinning an important piece; or 4) some other subtle maneuver. As Edward Lasker said: "The main point at issue in a problem is not the *number* of moves in which the mate is accomplished, but the *method* in which it is accomplished."

PRODIGY

A chess prodigy is an individual who has exhibited an extraordinary ability as a successful chessplayer. Given the opportunity, this unusual faculty generally reveals itself at an early age and develops rapidly. For instance, Samuel Reshevsky, a chess prodigy of the first magnitude, learned to play chess when he was three or four years of age. At the age of six, he gave several small exhibitions, and by the time he was eight years of age he had the playing strength of a master. Brian Harley stated that "all the world champions, from Morphy to Alekhine, have been youthful prodigies."

In 1957, Bobby Fischer of Brooklyn, New York, emerged as a fourteen-year-old chess prodigy by winning in Cleveland, the U. S. (Open) Chess Championship. A few months later, he won in New York City the title of United States Chess Champion.

PROFESSIONAL CHESSPLAYER

One who makes chessplaying his major occupation and the source of his livelihood. It is a "commercial profession" as distinguished from a "learned profession" such as the academic, legal, medical or theological professions. Several famous chessplayers have attempted to earn their livelihood by playing chess but, unfortunately, most of them died in poverty. Professional chessplayers may be found in public or private places, cafes or clubs where anyone may challenge them to a game of chess with the understanding that if the professional wins the game, the loser will pay a stipulated fee.

PROHIBITION CHESS

A form of chessplay in which no check is allowed except the giving of a checkmate.

PROMOTED PAWN

A Pawn that has reached the eighth rank must, according to the rules of the game, be transformed or "promoted" to a major or minor piece. It cannot remain a Pawn. The player of the promoted Pawn has the privilege of choosing the piece which will replace the Pawn. It may be a Queen, a Rook, a Bishop or a Knight. Hence, a player may have sometime during a game more than two Rooks, Bishops or Knights or more than one Queen. See *Laws of Chess,* Article 6. See *Queening.*

PROTECTION

The guarding or supporting of one chessman with another so as to ward off a threatening attack. The term protection may also be applied to the safeguarding of one's interest by seeking adequate compensation in case of loss which might be sustained in an attack. Protection may also be offered by interposing a piece between the threatened piece or King and the long range attacking chess piece.

PSYCHOLOGY IN CHESS

The study of the mental operations of the personalities engaged in a mental struggle during a game of chess. The players are always conditioned by the rules and regulations of the game and all of the accompanying social and physical environmental influences. Réti pointed out that Dr. Emanuel Lasker's "most original contribution to the game of chess is not a purely technical but psychological element, the psychological play." Lasker uses the medium of the game of chess, continues Réti, "to fight above all the opponent's psyche," that is, to fight the opponent's nerves, his preferences, his peculiarities, his fears, his vanities and all other personality traits. Lasker was always interested in making moves which were most disagreeable to his opponent rather than in always making the objectively best moves. In his *Manual of Chess,* Lasker indicates his reliance on psychology as a winning factor in a game of chess by saying, "If logic fails me, psychology will aid me."

PURDY

Cecil John S. Purdy, World Correspondence Chess Champion, four times champion chessplayer of Australia, founder and editor of *Chess World* magazine, was born of English parentage, in Port Said, Egypt, on March 27, 1907. At that time his father, the late Dr. J. S. Purdy, was England's representative on the International Quarantine Board for the Suez Canal. Later, he moved with his family to Sydney, Australia, where he served as the Chief Public Health Officer.

Cecil J. S. Purdy was graduated from Sydney University. In 1934, he married Anne Crakanthorp, daughter of a former chess champion of Australia. Their son John Purdy, at the age of nineteen, became the Australian chess champion. As far as is known, this is the only family in which the wife of a champion is also the daughter of a champion and a mother of a champion—a family of champions.

Cecil J. S. Purdy learned chess at the age of fourteen. At seventeen he went to New Zealand and won the Dominion chess championship. In 1929, he won the New South Wales championship, and in 1934, he won the Australian championship title. He is the only chessplayer who has won the Australian chess championship title four times (1934, 1936, 1948, and 1951). In 1951, he was made an International Chessmaster by F.I.D.E. He played in a number of Correspondence Chess Tournaments and has won the World Correspondence Chess Championship title which he now holds.

By profession, Cecil J. S. Purdy is a chess writer. He began dabbling in chess journalism at the age of fifteen. In 1929, when he was a senior student at the University, he founded the *Australasian Chess Review*, a monthly magazine which is still in existence, except that in 1946, its name was changed to *Chess World*. He is also the author of a number of books, such as: *Guide to Good Chess*, of which three editions appeared so far; and in collaboration with G. Koshnitsky he published *Chess Made Easy*, of which more than eighty thousand copies have been sold.

Chess critics hold the literary contributions of Cecil J. S. Purdy in high repute. DuMont states in the *British Chess Magazine* that when Purdy writes, "it is the work of a genius." Krishnamachariar comments in *The Hindu* that in Purdy's accounts of games and notes "one sees the painstaking thoroughness which is the characteristic of all Purdy's efforts." Another critic writing in *Chess Correspondent* says that Purdy has "a genius for stating things with absolute basic simplicity." This may all be summa-

rized in the words of Fred Reinfeld, who says that Purdy "is an able analyst, an entertaining writer and a first-rate player."

PURE MATE

A mating problem situation in which every square next to the black King is guarded by a single white man or occupied by a black man. See *Impure Mate*.

Q

QUEEN

The Queen is the coroneted major piece, symbolized as ♛, and briefly recorded by the letter Q. In the opening position, each player has one Queen, placed next to the King on a square of its own color; that is Black's Queen is on a black square and White's Queen is stationed on a light colored square.

How the Queen Moves. The Queen may move like a Bishop or a Rook. She may move along a rank, file or diagonal in any direction and over as many unoccupied squares as may be desired. If an opponent's man is in her immediate path, she may capture him by removing him and taking his place.

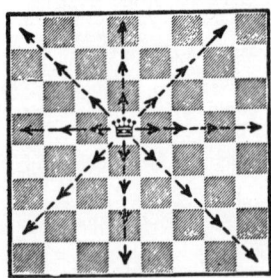

HOW QUEEN MOVES
The Queen may move from her present position to any square indicated by arrows.

Advantages and Disadvantages. The Queen is the most powerful piece on the chessboard. She has the combined power of a Rook and a Bishop. To be most effective, the Queen needs open spaces. Her full power of control can be seen in the diagram where she is pictured as being able to exercise from her centrally located position, a control over 27 additional squares. The Queen is least effective in cramped or restricted passageways.

Value of Queen. The exchange value of a Queen is roughly two Rooks plus or minus a Pawn depending upon the situation at hand. Her Majesty can also be valued as the equivalent of three pieces plus a Pawn. In an end-game, some writers claim that two Rooks may be more valuable than a Queen. It is conceded by all writers and authorities that the Queen is the most valuable piece on the board and consequently should not, as Horowitz and Reinfeld say, be sent lightly "on trifling expeditions to some remote spot on the board."

The Queen's History. Originally, there was no Queen on the chessboard. The early chessplayers used a piece known as *mantri,* a Sanscrit word meaning "Counsellor." (See *Counsellor.*) There are two theories which attempt to explain how the Queen came on the chessboard. One theory claims that in places and times when women had no social status, there was no Queen on the chessboard. In her place was the Counsellor or Prime Minister. As women were given some social recognition in civilization, the Queen made her appearance. At first, the Queen was given very limited powers but as her social status increased in society, so the Queen on the chessboard was given powers which were commensurate with the dignity of Her Majesty. Another theory claims that in medieval times, chess was viewed as a battle royal between two opposing kingdoms which were represented in the game of chess by their Majesties, the King and Queen, the noblemen and the foot-soldiers or Pawns. For a more complete treatise on the history of the Queen and her powers, see "A Short History of Chess," Chapter 3 entitled "The Female of the Species," by Henry A. Davidson, M.D., in *Chess Review,* March, 1956, page 77.

QUEENING

Promoting a Pawn that has reached the eighth rank to a Queen. The Laws of Chess state very explicitly that the moment a Pawn reaches the eighth rank it must be replaced immediately, as part of the move, by a Queen or some other piece of the same color. When a Pawn is transformed into a Queen, it assumes the powers of the Queen immediately. The same assumption of powers applies to all other pieces which may replace the promoted Pawn. In theory, it is possible for a player to have a maximum of nine Queens.

"Originally," says Davidson, "the idea was that the infantry private who had survived all the hazards of the battlefield, has earned a promotion to an officer's rank, but as with most battlefield promotions, it was to the lowest grade. And the weakest piece was the Queen." The question then arose whether it was proper to permit a player to have more than one Queen on the board, which would make the King a polygamist. For centuries, the Italian chessplayers adopted the rule that a Pawn could be promoted only to a piece which had been lost previously. By 1850, unlimited Pawn promotion had been generally accepted and is now the universal practice. Since the Queen is now in modern times the strongest piece on the board, most players promote the Pawn to a Queen and this process of transformation is known as "Queening." For a brief statement and forty-two illustrations of "Queening Combinations" see Chapter 11, in

1001 Brilliant Chess Sacrifices and Combinations, by Fred Reinfeld.

QUEENING SQUARE

The square on which a Pawn is promoted to a piece of greater value. When a Pawn reaches a square on the eighth rank it is said to have reached the queening square. Here a Pawn is transformed immediately into a major or minor piece, depending upon the wishes of the player. Since the piece of the highest value to which a Pawn may be promoted is a Queen and since most players decide upon a Queen, the square on which the Pawn can be coroneted is referred to as the queening square.

QUEEN ODDS

The giving of odds by removing the Queen from the board before making the first move of the game. This is one of the most serious odds given by a very strong chessplayer when playing with an opponent who is of a much lower playing strength. Usually the one removing his Queen plays with the white pieces and strives to establish a single or double fianchetto. For various types of odds and their relative importance see *Odds.*

QUEEN PAWN OPENING
1. P-Q4

This P-Q4 move opens the way for both the Queen and her Bishop and at the same time immediately defends the advanced Pawn which is not the case with 1. P-K4. Hence this opening is considered by some chessplayers to be better than 1. P-K4. The Queen Pawn opening can be transposed quite readily into any one of several other opening games. Horowitz and Reinfeld point out that "1. P-Q4 is irreproachable on theoretical grounds."

This opening was first mentioned in the Gottingen Manuscripts of 1490.

However it did not come into prominence until the time of the Vienna Tournament of 1873. Dr. Emanuel Lasker stated that "since the turn of the century, openings beginning with 1. P-Q4 have played an ever more dominating role in master chess and consequently in the games of all classes of players." C. H. O'D. Alexander and E. T. O. Slater writing in the June, 1955 issue of the *British Chess Magazine* state that "the Queen's Pawn is stronger than the King's Pawn opening for White. Whereas after 1. P-Q4 White scores about 56.4 per cent between equal players, after 1. P-K4 he only scores 54.3 per cent." For procedural development and variations of this opening see *Modern Chess Openings,* Ninth Edition, by Walter Korn, or *Practical Chess Openings,* by Reuben Fine.

QUEEN'S GAMBIT ACCEPTED
1.	P-Q4	P-Q4
2.	P-QB4	PxP

An old gambit play which was once called the "Gambit of Aleppo," after the name of a town in Syria where it was in early usage. Although this has been called a gambit, Fletcher states that "in reality it is nothing of the sort." Be that as it may, the fact remains that in accepting the proffered Pawn, Black's Queen Pawn is removed from the center. This gives White a stronger position in the center. Hence, says Reinfeld, "Black generally declines the gambit." Nevertheless, leading masters like Janowski, Reshevsky, Rubinstein, Schlechter, Steinitz and Tartakower have accepted this Queen's Gambit. For a procedural development and variations of this gambit play, see *Modern Chess Openings*, Ninth Edition, by Walter Korn, or, *Practical Chess Openings* by Reuben Fine.

QUEEN'S GAMBIT DECLINED

1.	P-Q4	P-Q4
2.	P-QB4	P-K3

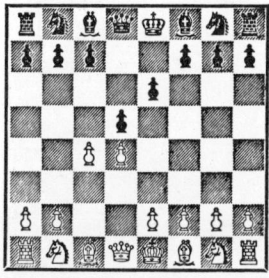

In order to maintain a Pawn in the center, Black may decline the gambit Pawn and play P-K3 or P-QB3. Tarrasch reasons that "since the gambit Pawn can not be maintained it is pointless to accept the gambit by playing 2 . . . PxP, for by that move Black merely gives up the center and loses a move." The Queen's Gambit Declined offers many opportunities to embark upon a lively game. The *plan de campagne* of declining the gambit may take the shape of the Albin Counter Gambit, the Cambridge Springs Defense, the Meran Defense, or the Tarrasch Defense. For a procedural development of this Queen's Gambit Declined see *Modern Chess Openings*, Ninth Edition, by Walter Korn, or *Practical Chess Openings*, by Reuben Fine.

QUEEN'S INDIAN DEFENSE

1. P-Q4, N-KB3

This opening is also known as the Indian Defense. It is one of the modern defenses in which Black endeavors to control the center not by occupation but by the action of his pieces. After the first opening moves, the game may proceed as shown in the accompanying diagram. Black controls K5 by fianchettoing his Queen's Bishop. White fianchettoes his Bishop at KN2 whereby he aims at the Queen's side. Although White does not always secure a strong Pawn center in this Defense, nevertheless, observes Reinfeld, "White usually obtains a slight but persistent initiative." Walter Korn indicates that "while the plan may rarely be carried out in its entirety, Black's defense remains aggressive in character." For a procedural development of this defense and its variations, see *Modern Chess Openings*, Ninth Edition, by Walter Korn, or, *Practical Chess Openings*, by Reuben Fine.

After Black's sixth move.

1.	P-Q4	N-KB3
2.	P-QB4	P-K3
3.	N-KB3	P-QN3
4.	P-KN3	B-N2
5.	B-N2	B-K2
6.	0-0	0-0

QUEEN'S KNIGHT GAME

1. N-QB3

This opening is also known as the Vienna Game. It is also referred to as the "Hamppe's Opening." See *Vienna Opening*.

QUEEN'S SIDE

A general term applied to that entire area of the chessboard which embraces the Queen's file and the files of her Bishop, Knight and Rook. The other side of the board is referred to as the King's side. These two divisions of the chessboard are shown in the accompanying illustration.

QUIET MOVE

A term applied by chess problem composers to White's moves which are neither checks nor captures. It is a correlative term of a "threatening move."

R

RADIO CHESSPLAY

The first international chess match conducted via radio was that played September 1-4, 1945, between the United States of America and the Union of Soviet Socialist Republics. Out of a total of 20 games played, the U.S.S.R. team won by a score of 15½ to 4½.

In 1954, the University of Buffalo Chess Club invited any university or private team to play chess via short wave radio.

RANDOM MOVE

A move which has no definite objective. One that serves no offensive or defensive purpose.

RANGE OF CHESSMEN

see *Cruising Range*

RANK

Any one of the eight rows of squares running straight across the chessboard in a horizontal manner. Each player calls the rank, or row, of squares nearest to himself the "first rank," the next in front is his "second rank," and so on across the board until he reaches his last rank which is his "eighth rank." Thus, White's first rank is Black's eighth rank, and in like manner what is Black's first rank is White's eighth rank. White's second rank is also Black's seventh rank, and so on as is shown in the accompanying illustration.

WHITE'S		BLACK'S
8th rank		1st rank
7th rank		2nd rank
6th rank		3rd rank
5th rank		4th rank
4th rank		5th rank
3rd rank		6th rank
2nd rank		7th rank
1st rank		8th rank

RAPID TRANSIT CHESSPLAY

A method of playing chess in which a player is required to make a move in not more than ten seconds. This differs from the more general practice which requires a player to make a move in not more than three minutes. Rapid chessplay does not necessarily cause an impairment in the quality of chess performance. Davidson indicates that "actual analysis of recorded games by good players shows surprisingly little loss of brilliancy in rapid chess." See *Blitz* and *Time Limits of Play*.

RATING CHESSPLAYERS

Assigning to chessplayers a class status and/or a significant number of an established and recognized system which presumably is indicative of their chessplaying ability. (See *Classification of Chessplayers*.) The United States Chess Federation and the Correspondence Chess League of America assign a class status to their members as well as a number which has a relative significance to all their members.

A new member may begin official chessplay by joining a chess club. He indicates his own estimate of his chessplaying strength. He is then assigned a number which is the midpoint of his chosen classification. He is now officially rated and begins official chessplay. With each official game played, his rating is adjusted as is indicated in the following tables.

For a detailed discussion of rating chessplayers and the USCF national rating regulations, see *The Official Blue Book of Chess*, Chapter VII, pages 331-360.

RATING ADJUSTMENT TABLE (U.S. Chess Federation)

Difference between Last Ratings	If High Wins Add to Winner and Deduct from Loser	If Low Wins Add to Winner and Deduct from Loser	If a Draw Add to Low and Deduct from High
0 to 9	50	50	0
10 to 19	48	52	2
20 to 29	46	54	4
30 to 39	44	56	6
40 to 49	42	58	8
50 to 59	40	60	10
60 to 69	38	62	12
70 to 79	36	64	14
80 to 89	34	66	16
90 to 99	32	68	18
100 to 109	30	70	20
110 to 119	28	72	22
120 to 129	26	74	24
130 to 139	24	76	26
140 to 149	22	78	28
150 to 159	20	80	30
160 to 169	18	82	32
170 to 179	16	84	34
180 to 189	14	86	36
190 to 199	12	88	38
200 to 209	10	90	40
210 to 219	8	92	42
220 to 229	6	94	44
230 to 239	4	96	46
240 to 249	2	98	48
250 or more	0	100	50

RATING CHART
(Chess Correspondence League of America)

Range between Players	High wins	Low wins	Draw
0 to 19	16	16	0
20 to 39	15	17	1
40 to 59	14	18	2
60 to 79	13	19	3
80 to 99	12	20	4
100 to 119	11	21	5
120 to 139	10	22	6
140 to 159	9	23	7
160 to 179	8	24	8
180 to 199	7	25	9
200 to 219	6	26	10
220 to 239	5	27	11
240 to 259	4	28	12
260 to 279	3	29	13
280 to 299	2	30	14
300 to 319	2	32	15
320 to 339	2	34	16
340 to 359	2	36	17
360 to 379	2	38	18
380 to 399	2	40	19
400 and up	2	44	21

RAT OPENING

1. P-N3

This so-called "Rat Opening" was used by the British chessplayer Mr. Manley as preparatory to the fianchetto move: B-N2. This opening has not received favorable recognition.

RECORDING MOVES

Writing down chess moves accurately, briefly and systematically. Some commentators and other writers use the linear style of recording moves whereby they write down several moves in one or more lines across the page. This is done by first writing the number of the move, then White's move followed by a comma; and then Black's move followed by a semicolon. For example, the so-called Fool's Mate is written as: 1. P-KB4, P-K3; 2. P-KN4, Q-R5 mate. Sometimes, only one player's move is written, such as: 1. P-K4 for White's move or 1 . . . P-K4 for Black. Moves may also be recorded in columnar style as shown in the following illustration:

The Fool's Mate

White	Black
1. P-KB4	P-K3
2. P-KN4	Q-R5 mate.

REFLEX MATE

A form of chessplay originated by the English problemist Benjamin G.

Laws. In this method of chessplay both players agree at the beginning of the game that each player will strive to *compel* the opponent to give mate. Whenever a player having the move can give mate, it must be given. The player who is mated wins the game. A reflex mate is a variety of "Suicidal Mate" with this difference. In a reflex mate each player is required to mate whenever it is possible to do so, whereas, in a suicidal mate, or sui-mate as it is frequently called, White struggles to force Black into a position where he has no other alternative but to inflict a mate upon White. Sometimes the term Reflex Chess is used in place of Reflex Mate. See *Sui-Mate.*

REINFELD

Fred Reinfeld, the world's most prolific chess writer, was born in 1910. He was the Intercollegiate Chess Champion in his undergraduate days. He won the New York State Championship on two different occasions and subsequently won the championship title of both the Marshall and Manhattan Chess Clubs.

Reinfeld is one of the best known of all chess expositors. He has written anywhere between fifty and one hundred books. Some of his more recent books are:

1001 Brilliant Chess Sacrifices and Combinations.
1001 Ways to Checkmate
Why You Lose At Chess
How to Win When You Are Ahead
How to Fight Back
How to Play the White Pieces
How to Play the Black Pieces
How to Play Like a Champion

Fred Reinfeld also co-authored such well-known books as *The Fireside Book of Chess,* and *Winning Chess,* both written with Irving Chernev. Likewise, *How to Think Ahead in Chess, Chess Traps, Pitfalls and Swindles* and *Handbook of Chess* were co-authored with

I. A. Horowitz. Furthermore, Free Reinfeld is also a Contributing Editor of *Chess Review*—the picture chess magazine.

Book reviews indicate that Mr. Reinfeld "explains general principles in clear, sharp, hard, practical exemplification." (*San Francisco Chronicle*) Again, in the *New York Times,* we read: "Mr. Reinfeld crams into a small space a large amount of chess wisdom, together with well-chosen examples of how that wisdom should be applied over the board."

REMISMONDE

A term coined by Dr. Tarrasch (1862-1934) which he applied to Karl Schlechter of Vienna. Schlechter was known to have terminated many of his games as drawn games. Hence, Dr. Tarrasch referred to him as the "Master of the Vienna Remismonde."

Literally, "Remismonde" is a compound French word. *Remis* in chess terminology means a draw. (See *Dictionnaire de la Langue Francaise,* by E. Littré, Paris, 1883.) *Monde* means world. There is no completely satisfactory or precise explanation of this compounded word. Dr. Felix Pollak of Northwestern University, a passionate chessplayer from Vienna, offered the following explanation. He wrote: "I believe it is simply a play on words, coining a parallel expression to 'demimonde' (denoting a lady of the 'half-world' i.e., of easy virtue). Hence, calling Schlechter the Master of the Remismonde denotes Schlechter to be king of the drawing world, the Master of the Vienna 'Grand-Master-Drawers." Mr. Hans Kmoch, the renowned Secretary and Manager of the famous Manhattan Chess Club concurs with this explanation.

REPETITION OF MOVES

An expression which refers to the established rule that when the same positional play occurs three times in a game, the player having the move may claim the game to be terminated as a drawn game. See *Laws of Chess,* Article 12, section 3.

RESHEVSKY

Samuel Herman Reshevsky, a one time child prodigy and now a Grandmaster extraordinary and four times United States Champion chessplayer, was born in Ozorkov, Russian Poland, on November 26, 1911. He learned to play chess when he was three or four years of age. At the age of six, he gave chessplaying exhibitions. When he was eight or nine years of age, his playing strength was that of a master. In fact, in 1919, he played a serious game of chess with Grandmaster Vidmar in Vienna. Vidmar won. In 1920, Reshevsky came to the United States and stirred American chessplayers by giving exhibitions of simultaneous chessplay in clubs, theaters, college, department stores, armories and public halls in Chicago, Milwaukee, New York and many other cities. He became affectionately known among American chessplayers as "our Sammy." After completing his high school and college education, which was sponsored by Julius Rosenwald, Reshevsky received his degree in 1933 from the University of Chicago where he specialized as an accountant.

In 1935, Reshevsky resumed international chessplay. He participated that year in a tournament at Margate, England, where he finished ahead of Capablanca, the former World Champion Chessplayer. The following year, Reshevsky won his first United States Chess Championship title. This feat he has repeated four times thus far.

It has been said that Reshevsky lives his life on the chessboard. As a chessplayer, he is known for his analytical ability, resourcefulness, patience and superb fighting qualities. Dr. Fine says,

"Technically, Reshevsky is characterized above all by his superb tactical skill." Sammy's supporters claim him to be the best match player in the world. In the 1955 Moscow match, which was not played for the world championship title but merely as a match between the teams from the United States and the Soviet Union, Reshevsky beat the World Champion Chessplayer Botvinnik. The *Manhattan Chess Club Bulletin* pointed out that Reshevsky "gives no indication of any slackening of his powers and should be a factor on the international chess scene for many years to come." For an autobiographical account of Reshevsky's amazing career and style of chessplay as revealed in 110 of his best games, see his book entitled: *Reshevsky on Chess.* For a beginner's book on chess which contains everything a beginner needs to know in order to play chess, see *Learn Chess Fast,* by Sammy Reshevsky and Fred Reinfeld.

RESIGN

A formal acknowledgement of defeat. A player may resign or "give up" any time he wishes to do so, although Tartakower warned against resigning too hastily by saying: "Nobody ever won a game by resigning." The game in which a player resigns is always counted as a lost game for the one who resigns and a won game for his opponent. As part of the definition, it is important to know *when* and *how* to resign.

When to resign.

1. When a player has no other alternative move. This is a forced resignation. It exists whenever a player faces a checkmate.

2. When a player resigns voluntarily. W. H. Watts of England observed that a "first-class player seldom waits for the execution of his King, but resigns to save

further bloodshed."

This may be done

(a) when a player experiences a serious loss of material, especially when the opponent is a good player.

(b) when a player considers his position to be completely indefensible.

How to resign.

Resign with grace. The late C. H. O'D. Alexander of England pointed out that chessplayers are peculiarly adept at finding excuses for defeat. He suggested that when resigning never explain "to your opponent how lucky he was or how unlucky you were." He observed that "everyone loses a great many games and it is absurd not to take defeat with a good grace."

RESISTANCE

A counter reply to offensive action. Resistance may be offered by improving one's position, or rallying one's forces so that they can exert obstructive influences or challenge the offensive action of the opponent.

RÉTI

Richard Réti, Hungarian chessmaster and the Founder of the Hypermodern School of Chess, was born in Pezinok, Czechoslovakia, on May 28, 1889. He was a student of mathematics and physics at the University of Vienna but as he himself said, he soon devoted himself to chess because "I discovered I had more talent for it." And then he adds, "Whatever success I may have attained is chiefly due to a faculty of hard work and the determination to do well." He won a number of important chess tournaments, such as, Kaschau in 1918, Goteborg in 1920, Teplitz-Schonau in 1922, Maehrisch-Ostrau in 1923 and Bruenn in 1928. "His greatest moment had come in

1924," says Cecil Purdy, "when he won a game from Capablanca." Réti died at Prague of scarlet fever on June 6, 1929.

Réti viewed chess as a struggle between two personalities and as his biographer, Horace R. Bigelow, stated, Réti "often deliberately made bad moves, or inferior moves, if in his judgment these tended to lure his opponent to destruction." Of his many writings on chess, the late C. H. O'D. Alexander says that Réti's *Masters of the Chessboard* is "one of the best written and most interesting of all books on chess." In his *Modern Ideas in Chess,* Réti developed his ideas of the Hypermodern School of Chess with the cooperation of Aron Nimzovitch. In this Hypermodern School of thought, Réti emphasized that *control* and not *occupation* of the center was most essential. Réti was known to allow his opponent to occupy the center while he would build up long range striking forces in the wings which would ruin the opponent's centralized position.

Chess authorities are agreed that Réti was a great chessplayer and a source of inspiration to other chessplayers. Dr. Fine states that Réti was above all an artist of the chessboard. He was a problem and end-game composer of the first rank, and in his games this love for beauty crops up again and again.

RÉTI OPENING

1. N-KB3

Although this first move does not disclose White's intention concerning the future disposition of his center Pawns, experience has shown that the basic objective in this hypermodern opening is to let Black develop a Pawn structure in the center while White holds back his center Pawns and builds up his forces at a distance which will enable him to cripple

Black's chain of Pawns. White usually accomplishes this by attempting to engage Black's staunch Queen Pawn by playing 2. P-QB3 (which is generally named the Réti Gambit) and eventually fianchettoing his King Bishop and sometimes his Queen Bishop as well. Dr. Fine cleverly characterizes this opening as a "come-hither-my-darling-and-let-me-snare-your-game."

The developmental procedure of this opening may be seen in the 1924 New York Tournament between Réti and Dr. Emanuel Lasker. This game opened with the following moves and is diagrammed in the accompanying illustration as the positions appear after Black's sixth move.

	Réti	Lasker
1.	N-KB3	P-Q4
2.	P-B4	P-QB3
3.	P-QN3	B-B4
4.	P-N3	N-B3
5.	B-KN2	QN-Q2
6.	B-N2	P-K3

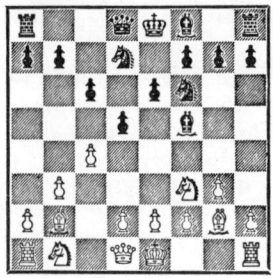

REVERSED OPENINGS

see *Inverted Opening*

RICE GAMBIT

1.	P-K4	P-K4
2.	P-KB4	PxP
3.	N-KB3	P-KN4
4.	P-KR4	P-N5
5.	N-K5	N-KB3
6.	B-B4	P-Q4
7.	PxP	B-Q3

This Gambit play was popularized in 1896 by Professor Isaac L. Rice of

the United States. Actually, this Rice Gambit is what L. Elliott Fletcher calls "a sub-sub-variation of the Kieseritzky Gambit." At one time, Rice went to Ostend, Belgium, where he organized a Rice Gambit Tourney to test, as the *British Chess Magazine* pointed out, "the pregnability of what is supposed to be the last stronghold of White in this much analyzed opening." In 1904, a master tournament was held at Monte Carlo which was organized exclusively to promote the Rice Gambit. Since that time, this Gambit has declined into obscurity.

ROBADO

A term used by chessplayers prior to the middle ages by which they meant the winning of a game of chess by "annihilation." See *Annihilation*.

ROBOT CHESSPLAYER

Any mechanical device shaped in human form which gives the external appearance of playing chess with a contestant. There were several well-known robot chessplayers, which were known as *Ajeeb, Mephisto* and the *Turk.* They are defined in their proper alphabetical order.

ROMAN THEME

A term used by the chess problemist H. G. M. Weenink (1892-1931) in a situation in which Black tries desperately to lure White away from an impending mate by offering a piece as sacrificial bait. Some writers call this theme "the Roman Decoy." In the accompanying illustration, White might capture the black Rook but this merely cripples Black's forces. White may also play 1. R(B8)xP, threatening to move next to B4 and mate; but, Black can prevent this last move by playing 1 ... R-Q3 pinning White's Rook. Therefore, White has a more forceful solution by proceeding as given in the accompanying illustration.

Solution

1. R-B7	R-K1
2. RxP(B3)	R-K3
3. RxR mate.	

ROOK

The Rook is a major piece, symbolized in chess notation as ♜, and is briefly recorded by the letter R. In the opening position, White has two Rooks and Black has two Rooks. These are placed at the beginning of the game in the four corners of the chessboard as is shown in the illustration appearing in the definition of *Chessmen.* Sometimes the Rook has been called a "Castle" but in modern chess literature this term is rarely, if ever, used.

How the Rook Moves. The Rook moves parallel to the sides of the chessboard across any number of unoccupied squares, in any file or rank. It may move forwards, backwards or side-

wards, but not diagonally. If an opponent's man is in its immediate path, the Rook may capture him by removing him and taking his place.

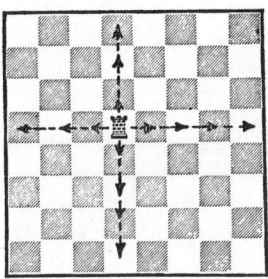

The Rook may move horizontally or vertically to any square as indicated by the arrows.

Advantages and Disadvantages. When placed in the middle of an otherwise unoccupied board, a Rook can control from its position a total of fourteen squares. Because of its great mobile power, the Rook is called a major piece. A Rook is very effective in open lines and almost valueless in closed lines. When placed on open lines, the Rook forms an impassable barrier for the opponent's King. A player's two Rooks should, as far as possible, work as a team, one supporting the other. Since the Rook and King are both involved in the process of castling, it is wise not to move the Rook until it is certain on which side of the board castling is to take place. Due to the original position, the Rook is hemmed in by its own pieces and consequently is seldom brought into active play in the early stages of the game. Tartakower pointed out that "the entrance into the fray of the Queen's Rook denotes frequently that the opening stage has been completed and that the more lively contest of the middle game has begun."

Value. After the Queen, the Rook is the next important piece on the chessboard. In general, a Rook's normal market value is a Bishop and two Pawns, or a Knight and two Pawns. Comparatively, two Rooks are slightly stronger than a Queen. Likewise, two Rooks are a little stronger than two Bishops and a Knight. The value of one Rook is said to be equal to five Pawns.

Historically, it has been claimed that the modern Rook originally represented a ship among maritime nations; a chariot in the early Indian army; and a mythical two-headed bird among the Arabs which could capture an elephant and carry it away in its powerful claws. The Italians viewed the Rook as a fortress or tower in which the King could flee for safety when danger threatened—an idea which developed into our present system of "castling." Etymologically, it seems that the Bengal Indians erroneously associated the Arab term *rukh* with the Sanscrit *roca,* meaning boat. (See *Boat.*) However, due to a similarity of sound in pronouncing these words, the use of the Arab word *rukh* seems to have developed into our modern use of the word Rook. For an historical account of the Rook see "A Short History of Chess," Chapter 4 entitled: "Castles With Wheels," by Henry A. Davidson, M.D. in *Chess Review,* the picture chess magazine, June 1956, pages 174-175.

ROOK AND KNIGHT ODDS

Very important odds given by a strong player to a very weak opponent so as to equalize to a degree their playing strength. The stronger player who gives these heavy odds usually plays with the white pieces. Before the game begins, White generally removes his Queen's Rook and his King's Knight from the board. As the game progresses, White seeks complications and is on the constant alert to take advan-

tage of his opponent's blunders. With conservative play, Black can play a good game. See *Odds.*

ROOK ODDS

Removing the stronger player's Rook so as to equalize to a degree the playing strength of the two participants. Usually it is the Queen's Rook that is removed at the beginning of the game, although this is left entirely to the discretion of the one giving the odds. The one giving the Rook odds plays with the white pieces. The player giving this particular type of odds may move his King as in castling in the same manner as though the Rook is present on the board. See *Odds.*

ROOK, PAWN AND MOVE ODDS

Important odds given by a strong player to his weaker opponent as a means of equalizing to a degree their playing strength. The one giving odds usually plays with the black pieces and removes, before the game begins, his Queen's Rook and his King Bishop's Pawn. By playing with the black pieces, the stronger player is said to have given his weaker opponent the advantage of a move.

ROUND CHESS

A modified form of the game of chess which was played upon a circular board of sixty-four squares arranged in four concentric rings each containing sixteen squares. The ordinary chessmen were employed. This game can be traced to the early Muslim and Byzantine chessplayers but in the past century several attempts have been made in London and Calcutta to revive this form of chessplay. See *History of Chess,* by H. J. R. Murray, page 342.

ROUND ROBIN

An administrative arrangement whereby every player in tournament games is given an opportunity to play with every other participant. After all games are concluded the one having accumulated the highest number of points is declared the winner. One point is scored for each game won and a half point is given to each contestant in a drawn game. Each round may consist of two games in which a player takes the white pieces in one game and the black pieces in the other game. This round robin type of tournament is generally used when there are not more than eight participants.

ROUTINIER

A chess routinier is an individual who proceeds mechanically to play chess according to some established pattern. Usually, this is a chessplayer who, as far as possible, slavishly follows the moves of a game as they are given in a book. Such a player lacks originality, fears variations, and is completely lost when deviations occur.

ROYAL GAME

A term which by long usage has been identified as the game of chess. Several reasons can be found in chess literature for the use of this term.

1. The game of chess is essentially a battle between two royal kingdoms; namely, White's kingdom versus Black's kingdom. The object of the game being to safeguard one's own King and to annihilate (mate) the opponent's King.

2. The game was originally played by the nobility. In early days only the aristocracy had the know-how and the time to devote to playing chess.

3. Kings and princes were patrons of the game and gave public approval to indulge in the science and art of chessplay.

4. Writers have identified the game of chess as the Royal Game in their writings and titles of their publications, such as, *The Royal Game of* *Chessplay,* by Biochimo; or, *The Royal Game,* by Edith L. Weart.

RUBINSTEIN

Alika Rubinstein, chess champion of Poland, international chessmaster and the 1914 contender for the world championship title, was born in Stawiski, a small town in a province of Russian Poland, on December 12, 1882. He came from a family of rabbis and scholars of the Hebrew classics. He learned the game of chess at the age of sixteen while studying at the Yeshiva, a higher academy of religious instruction. At nineteen, he went to Lodz and associated himself with chessmaster George Salwe. His subsequent rise to chess fame was rapid. He made his debut in international chess at the Ostend tournament in 1906, where he shared first prize honors with Bernstein. In 1909, at St. Petersburg, he tied with Dr. Emanuel Lasker for the first prize. His most successful year was 1912, when he gained a number of first prizes in several international tournaments. A match was scheduled in 1914 for the world championship title between Dr. Lasker and Rubinstein. Then World War I started. The match was never played. Finally, Rubinstein retired to Antwerp.

His biographer, Barnie Winkelman, states that Rubinstein "is indeed the Spinoza of chess. More geometrico, with crystal-clear, mathematical detachment, he builds up his position with grace, ease and restraint." W. H. Watts observes that Rubinstein was extremely studious, possessed an uncommon memory and that he knew "by heart almost every game that has ever been played." Dr. Fine indicated that "the tragedy of Rubinstein arose because he played too much beautiful chess and too little winning chess." Dr. Fine is also of the opinion that "by and large, for accuracy, profundity and sheer beauty, Rubinstein's end-games have never been equalled." See *Rubinstein's Chess Masterpieces—100 Selected Games Annotated,* by Hans Kmoch and translated by Barnie F. Winkelman.

RULES OF CHESS

A body of most desirable chess practices and procedures formulated by influential chessmasters and/or other recognized chess authorities. Rules are always based on the assumption that everything else is equal except the point or topic under discussion. Hence, every rule has its theoretical exception. It is also noteworthy that rules differ from laws in that laws must be observed but rules may or may not be followed. For example, it is a basic law of chess that White always moves first, unless otherwise stated. Likewise, it is a basic law in chessplay that a player must make a move when it is his turn to play. He can not waive the right or obligation to move. But, as Lasker stated, it is a good general rule not to exchange in the early stages of the game the long reaching Bishop for the Knight. "The rules of chess technique," says Réti, "are for our game what the rules of grammar are for speech." See *Laws of Chess* and *Principles.*

RUNNER

A term used in some European countries in place of our Bishop. Chessplayers in Croatia, Denmark, Germany, Holland, Norway, Poland and other countries have used the word Runner, Courier or Messenger in place of what we call Bishop.

RUSSIAN DEFENSE

see *Petroff's Defense*

S

SACRIFICE

Allowing one or more chess units to be captured in the hope of gaining some advantage which, however, can not be immediately determined with accuracy and assurance. "If the consequences of the sacrifices were foreseen from the first," says Spielmann, then "properly speaking, there is no sacrifice, only an advantageous business deal." Edward Lasker points out that "the less evident the way is in which a player recovers the material sacrificed or realizes an equivalent advantage, the more beautiful the sacrifice is considered."

A sacrifice in chess is always a means toward an end. For example, a clearance sacrifice may provide greater mobility to pieces which were in a cramped position. Some sacrifices will eventually result in material gain; others may improve an offensive or defensive position, or hasten a checkmate. Sacrifices are frequently made in the opening phase of the game to hasten development of one's pieces; to gain a move or material; to prevent the opponent's King from castling; or, to immobilize the opponent's forces. "A sacrifice is *sound* or correct," says Tartakower, "if the compensations expected from it are realized so that victory or, at least, equality is obtained. Otherwise, the sacrifice is said to be *unsound.*"

For a discussion of positional sacrifices, mating sacrifices, sacrifices for gain and sacrificial values, see *The Art of Sacrifice in Chess,* by Rudolf Spielmann, Edited and Revised by Fred Reinfeld and I. A. Horowitz. For a well-diagrammed book which illustrates how to be victorious in aggressive situations see *1001 Brilliant Sacrifices and Combinations,* by Fred Reinfeld.

SAEMISCH ATTACK

1. P-Q4	N-KB3
2. P-QB4	P-K3
3. N-QB3	B-N5
4. P-QR3	

An aggressive procedure in the Nimzoindian Defense which involves

a relatively slow building up of an attack on the King's side. This attack, or variation as it is sometimes called, is identified by the move 4. P-QR3. It was named after Friederich Saemisch, who was born in Charlottenburg, Germany, on September 20, 1896. After World War I, Saemisch took up chess seriously and played successfully in several Berlin tournaments. As a result of his success in the 1920 Berlin Haupturnier, he was credited as a master chessplayer.

Saemisch possesses a profound knowledge of chess theory and is a strong defensive chessplayer. "His style of play," says W. H. Watts, "is sound but versatile." When played by a strong aggressive player, the Saemisch procedure can produce some profitable attacking possibilities and, as some chess writers indicate, if this style of play is not counteracted immediately, it can become an irresistible blow.

SALVIO-COCHRANE GAMBIT

A continuation or variation of the Salvio Gambit. Although many chessplayers prefer to continue the Salvio Gambit by playing 6 . . . , N-QB3, Mr. Cochrane played 6 . . . P-KB6, which became the characteristic move of the so-called Salvio-Cochrane Gambit. "With all due deference to this celebrated player," says Gossip, "he (Cochrane) cannot be said to have made an important or even an original

discovery of this opening." For a treatise on the Salvio-Cochrane Gambit see Chapter 14, in *The Laws and Practice of Chess,* by Howard Staunton. See *Salvio Gambit* and *Cochrane Gambit.*

SALVIO GAMBIT

1.	P-K4	P-K4
2.	P-KB4	PxP
3.	N-KB3	P-KN4
4.	B-B4	P-N5
5.	N-K5	Q-R5ch.
6.	K-B1	

One of the oldest developments of the King's Gambit which had been brought into vogue in 1634, by Alessandro Salvio, a Doctor of Laws at Naples. This gambit opening was first mentioned by Salvio in his book which was published in 1604, although many later writers were of the opinion that the Salvio Gambit was "derived from some Portuguese writer now unknown." Howard Staunton states that although this opening has always been called a gambit, "it is in reality an *offensive-defensive* or a counter attack to a gambit." He believes "it is a good line of play for the second player, as it transfers the attack into his hands very early in the game. At the same time," continues Staunton, "it is rich in interesting combinations and hair-breadth escapes on both sides." Julius du Mont points out that the "Salvio Gambit which modern analysis condemns, . . . has, however, scored many successes for White, notably in the Steinitz-Anderssen match, after which Steinitz became the first official world champion." For reference to some of Salvio's chess games see *The Works of Damiano, Ruy Lopez, and Salvio on The Game of Chess,* by J. H. Sarratt.

SANDGLASS

A device used in chess for indicating the time remaining for completing the number of moves which players agreed to make by the time the sand would flow from one compartment to another. In 1861, Anderssen won a match from Kolisch in which sandglasses were used for the first time in organized chessplay. The sandglass, or hour-glass, had replaced "sitzfleisch." In 1876, in a match between Steinitz and Blackburne, it was planned to use the sandglasses, however, when the match began, alarm time-clocks were substituted for the first time in the history of chess. See *Sitzfleisch.*

SAN SEBASTIAN TOURNAMENT

An important chess tournament restricted to chessmasters held in 1911, in San Sebastian, Spain. According to Julius du Mont it "was the first contest which could be rightly called a grandmasters' tournament." Entries were limited to those who had won at least two third prizes in previous master tournaments. An exception was made in the case of Capablanca, who up to that time had not participated in any master's tournament but was admitted to play because of his "sensational victory of Marshall." Among the contestants were such noteworthy players as Bernstein, Capablanca, Janowski, Maroczy, Marshall, Nimzovitch, Rubinstein, Schlechter, Spielmann, Tarrasch and Vidmar.

SANTASIERE

Anthony E. Santasiere, United States Open Championship chess winner of 1945, six times Champion of the famous Marshall Chess Club, a chess writer and a Life-time Director of the United States Chess Federation, was born of Italian and French parents in New York City, on December 4, 1904. He worked his way through the College of the City of New York and became a public school teacher. He studied also at the Juilliard Foundation and developed his talents as a musician, artist and poet. He is also an author, a chess critic and analyst for the *American Chess Bulletin.*

His chess interests developed during his early teen age. His chess idols were Alekhine, Marshall, Nimzovitch, Spielmann and Tchigorin. He was the leader of his college chess team and for more than thirty-five years has been an active and respected member of the Marshall Chess Club of New York City.

As a chessplayer, he won the Marshall Chess Club championship title in 1922, 1926, 1936, 1943, 1946 and 1953. He also won the United States Open Tournament Championship in 1945. He won top honors as the Champion chessplayer of New York state in 1928, 1930 and 1946; of New England in 1943; and of New Jersey (Open) in 1946. In 1945, Santasiere served as a member of the United States chess team playing a radio match with a Russian team. Likewise, in 1953, he participated in the Milano International Tourney, where he won the first prize. As a chessplayer, Santasiere is not very sympathetic with scientific chessplay. He prefers to rely on his own good judgment.

As an individual, Tony Santasiere is deeply religious. On one occasion he stated: "My talents and my successes I owe to God; my failures to my imperfections." His philosophy of chess, as well as life in general, was stated in his own words, namely: "Trust in God and in love; fight and

LOVE your opponent; try to be fearless, no matter what the cost; trust the heart, distrust the mind."

SANTASIERE'S FOLLY
1. N-KB3, P-Q4; 2. P-QN4

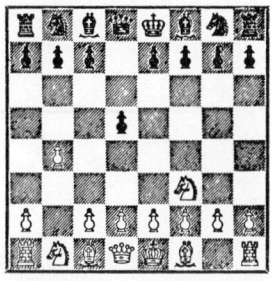

An irregular opening developed by Anthony Santasiere, who named it the "Santasiere's Folly." Alekhine played these opening moves in a game played against Drewitt in Portsmouth, in 1923. However, Santasiere is the only player who has developed this opening procedure and adopted it consistently in many tournaments. Santasiere has a book, in manuscript form, entitled: "The Santasiere's Folly," which appeared serially in *The Chess Correspondent* in the mid 1940's.

The motivation behind this hypermodern opening is somewhat mischievous or playful but mostly psychological. Black, who is traditionally committed to an early P-QB4 move, is involved in an immediate frustration, for if he exchanges his QBP for White's QNP, White is left with a Pawn majority in the center—a matter of strategical importance.

SARAGOSSA OPENING
1. P-QB3

A semi-inverted Caro-Kann opening which can be traced back to Ercole del Rio's book of 1750. Louis Paulsen used this opening at the 1883 Nuremberg tournament and again at the 1892 Dresden tournament. However, this Opening was really popularized in Saragossa, Spain, where the Saragossa Chess Club conducted several tourna-

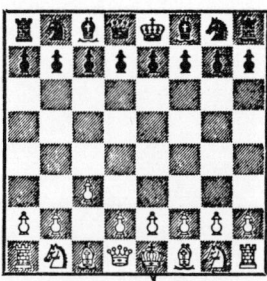

ments based on this opening. It was first fully analyzed in an article entitled "Apertura Saragozana" (Saragossan Opening) written by Señor José Juncosa of Saragossa, in the *Revista del Club Argentino de Ajedrez*, Buenos Aires, 1920. In it, Señor Juncosa stated that "P-QB3 constituting the Saragossa Opening which supports a 2. P-Q4 will, in our opinion, achieve better than any other opening the establishment of a center."

SARAJEVO MANUSCRIPT

A fifteenth century Arabic manuscript discovered in the 1950's by the Oriental Institute of Sarajevo, Yugoslavia. It was found in a Moslem household in that city and is believed to be a copy of an earlier manuscript of 897. If this manuscript is found to be accurate, the history of chess will be somewhat modified. The manuscript quotes Aristotle as advising his disciple, Alexander the Great, "I see that you constantly travel. When you are lonely, when you feel yourself an alien in the world, play chess. This game will raise your spirits and will be your counselor in war."

The Sarajevo manuscript gives diagrams and instructions on how to set and solve chess problems with the aid of mathematics and astronomy. It also recounts legends and theories concerning the origin of chess and offers advice to chessplayers. It claims that the sages of olden days did not consider chess a worthless game to pass away the time, but one that taught man orderliness in his life, to see the end of things at the beginning, not to take action before he foresaw the outcome of his action and to approach the realization of his goal with caution. Chessplayers are admonished that one who plays chess must wear clean clothes and have a sweet breath, be polished and cheerful, never lose his temper, speak the truth, be ready for pleasant conversation and be responsive to good advice. Above all, it emphasizes, one must not play chess when he is angry.

SARRATT

J. H. Sarratt was one of the strongest English chessplayers of the late eighteenth and early nineteenth centuries. He was also a professor of chess and the author of two treatises on the game of chess. He also collected and translated some of *The Works of Damiano, Ruy Lopez and Salvio* which were published in London, in 1813. Sarratt is given credit for having introduced into England in 1808, the Italian rule that a game ending with a stalemate is to be considered a drawn game, and by 1820, all leading chess clubs coming under his influence adopted this same rule.

SCACCIC DIALOGUE

A chess conversation or a literary exchange of ideas pertaining to chess matters. See *Latinization of Chess Terms.*

SCANDINAVIAN GAMBIT

see *Danish Gambit*

SCHACH

German name for chess.

SCHADENFREUDE

A German word meaning, gloating over someone's misfortunes. The term is sometimes applied to chessplayers who gloat over the mistakes or failures of other chessplayers.

SCHEVENINGEN VARIATION

1. P-K4	P-QB4
2. N-KB3	N-QB3
3. P-Q4	PxP
4. NxP	N-B3
5. N-QB3	P-Q3
6. B-K2	P-K3

After Black's sixth move.

This Scheveningen Variation was named after a small Dutch seaside resort where in 1923, a chess tournament was held in which the players of the black pieces utilized this procedural variation of the Sicilian Defense. The exact order of play is not essential as long as the general positional pattern is achieved. Although Black's play is rather passive, "yet, despite its apparently defensive character," says Dr. Euwe, "it has the underlying purpose of opening up the position when a favorable opportunity arises. It is therefore White's most important task to see to it that such a favorable opportunity does not arise." For a presentation of the so-called "classical" Scheveningen Variation of the Sicilian Defense procedure with several deviations and notes, see *Modern Chess Openings*, Ninth Edition, by Walter Korn.

SCHLECHTER

Karl Schlechter, a Viennese chessmaster and a contender for the world championship title, was born in Vienna on March 2, 1874. He intended to become a business man but soon changed his mind and became a professional chessplayer and chess writer. He died in Budapest on December 27, 1919.

Schlechter developed a passionate liking for chess in his youth. When he was twenty years of age, he was admitted to the International Tournament at Leipzig. From 1894 to 1918, he participated in practically all international tournaments. He is probably best remembered as the "Drawing Master." This title was conferred upon him by Dr. Tarrasch. It was quickly adopted by other chessplayers, not only because it was the irony of fate that many of his games resulted in a draw, but also because Schlechter was quick to accept an offer of a draw. Being good-natured and modest, he was easily influenced to accept such an offer even when he had the advantage. A striking and noteworthy incident occurred in 1910 when at the Hamburg tournament, Schlechter, the famous Drawing Master, needed a draw in his final game to become the World Champion Chessplayer. Contrary to his established reputation that he could draw at will with anyone, Schlechter decided to play the last game to win, but unfortunately, he lost.

During the last twenty years of his life, 1899-1919, Karl Schlechter was editor of the *Deutsche Schachzeitung.* The 1916 revision of Bilguer's *Handbuch* has been called Schlechter's literary memorial. It took Schlechter several years to complete this gigantic work and, as was stated by J. Mieses in the *British Chess Magazine,* this new edition was "greatly benefited by his (Schlechter's) extreme theoretical

knowledge, his thoroughness and sense of responsibility."

SCHOLAR'S MATE

1. P-K4	P-K4
2. B-B4	B-B4
3. Q-R5	N-KB3
4. QxBP mate	

This so-called mate is a short game which is sometimes played by an experienced player who takes advantage of a beginner's failure to see a one-move checkmate immediately before him. This entire procedure, according to Tartakower, is "a purely psychological calculation which could just as easily miscarry."

SCHOOLS OF CHESS

Schools of Chess are "schools of thought" composed of groups of chessplayers who generally adhere to the basic theories of renowned chessmasters and consequently produce a general similarity in their chessplaying procedures. L. Elliott Fletcher indicates that "for a long time there were two opposing schools of chess thought: the French, British and German on one side and the Italian on the other." The modern school of chess, he adds, "is the welding of these two, plus a strong Slavonic influence." See *Modern Chess* and *Hypermodern Chess.*

SCIENCE OF CHESS

A knowledge of the underlying principles, laws and rules of the game of chess. This science is derived from the observed and organized experiences of past and present chessmasters. This vast pool of organized experiences has been tested and retested under various circumstances by generations of experts in the knowledge and art of chessplay. It is only after these observed, classified and tested experiences have been thoroughly analyzed and systematized that the final outcome is termed a science. The opening moves in games of chess may be given names which will identify them with great chessmasters who used them with great satisfaction but the mere memorization of these opening moves does not necessarily imply an understanding of the science of the game. The acquisition of a scientific knowledge of chess may be obtained through study but how this science of chess is translated into the art of chess is always a matter of individual experience. Wilhelm Steinitz is generally considered the greatest of all chess scientists.

SCORE PAD

Sheets of paper, blocked together, which are designed for keeping records of the moves in games of chess. These pads are used by individual chessplayers and chess clubs as convenient devices for preserving their records of games played or being played.

SCOTCH OPENING

1.	P-K4	P-K4
2.	N-KB3	N-QB3
3.	P-Q4	

An old fashioned opening which can be traced back to the Italian chessplayers of 1750. It received its present name from its popular use made by the Scotch players in their celebrated 1824-1826 correspondence match between the players from Edinburgh and London.

This opening leads to an open type of game which opens the way for

White's Queen and Bishop and at the same time prevents Black from organizing a strong center. This opening has

been exploited by experts at various times as to its possibilities for attack and defense purposes. At present, it has lost its former popularity. Fred Reinfeld points out that "by moving his King Knight twice, White wastes time and gives Black an opportunity to fight for the initiative." Walter Korn observes that this "opening proves that an early center push, without massed preparation, tends to dissipate rather than generate White's initiative in this type of game." For a procedural development of this opening and its variations see *Modern Chess Openings* Ninth Edition by Walter Korn, or *Practical Chess Openings* by Reuben Fine.

SCREEN CHESS
see *Kriegspiel*

SEALED MOVE

A move which has been recorded and placed in a sealed envelope with other identifiable data and given to the Tournament Director at the time of adjournment of a game for safekeeping until the game is resumed. Article 27 of the official USCF tournament rules, pertaining to "Adjournment Procedure" requires that each player who has been instructed to seal his move must write his next move in unambiguous notation on his score sheet, place his and his opponent's score sheets in the envelope furnished by the Director, and seal the envelope. Upon the envelope must be indicated:

1) The names of the players;
2) The position recorded in Forsythe notation immediately before the sealed move. (If preferred, the adjourned position may be recorded on a diagram blank by writing the initials of the chessmen on the squares they occupy, encircling the initials of the black men.
3) The time used by each player.
4) The name of the player who has sealed the move and the number of that move.
5) The date and time of resumption of play.
6) The Director may require both players to sign the envelope.

See: *The Official Blue Book and Encyclopedia of Chess*, Page 84 "Adjournment Procedure," and "Recording Adjourned Positions," pages 133-4.

SEEDED PLAYERS

A recognized superior chess contestant who is permitted to participate in the finals of a chess tournament without first playing in the earlier elimination rounds. It is assumed that such a player's reputation is so well established that his qualifying ordeal is considered unnecessary.

"SEESAW" MOVES

A descriptive term applied to a situation in which the moves made by a player swing from side to side like the motions of a seesaw thereby causing the opponent's King to move into a checkmate position. Some writers prefer to use the term "Windmill" to describe such a situation.

SELENUS

Gustavus Selenus is a fictitious name. It is the pen-name of Augustus, the Duke of Brunswick, who in 1616 pub-

lished his *Bucher von Schach und Konigs Spiel*. In it, he gives the earliest detailed account of "Living Chess" as it was played in the village of Stroebeck, Germany, where chess was taught in the schools as part of the regular curriculum. See *Live Chess*.

SEMI-OPEN GAME

A game in which White opens the game with 1. P-K4 but Black, instead of playing . . . P-K4, replies with another move such as P-QB4, P-K3, P-QB3, etc. The more well known semi-open chess games are:

1 . . . P-K3; French Defense.
1 . . . P-Q4; Center Counter Defense.
1 . . . P-QB3; Caro-Kann.
1 . . . P-QB4; Sicilian Defense
1 . . . P-KN3; King's Fianchetto.
1 . . . P-QN3; Queen's Fianchetto.
1 . . . N-KB3; Alekhine's Defense.
1 . . . N-QB3; Nimzovitch Defense.

SEQUENCES

Series of consecutive moves which occur in established opening moves or in their variations. More generally, a sequence is an extension of moves in a theme.

SERVANT

A term sometimes used in English translations of Danish games of chess. When referring to a Pawn, the Danish chessplayers use the word "knegt" which when translated literally means "servant."

SET MATE

A term used by chess problemists which as Brian Harley explains, refers to a "mate prepared in answer to a particular Black move, before the key is made." See *Key*.

SHAKING CHESS

One of the varieties of chess mentioned by the famous chess historian

Murray, which was played by the children of Japan where it was known as Furi-shogi or "Shaking chess." Murray says that in this game "the chessmen are used as dice. If the chessman falls face upwards it counts 1; if face is downwards, 0; if it stands on its end, 10; and if it stands on its side, 5." See *History of Chess* by Murray, page 147.

SHAME-MATE

A mate which is inflicted by a humble Pawn. The chessplayers of Iceland consider such a mate to be very humiliating and disgraceful; hence, they refer to such a mate as a shameful mate, or briefly, a "shame-mate". For a player to have his King mated on his own square, especially when the King has never moved, is considered by them to be most shameful.

SHIP

A figurine of a ship is used in place of our Rook by the chessplayers of Java, Siam and parts of Russia.

SHOGI

see *Japanese Chess*

SHORT MATE

A term used by chess problemists and applied to a mate which is executed in less than the stipulated number of moves.

SHORT RANGE PIECE

A term sometimes applied to the Knight in contrast to the other pieces which are regarded as "long range pieces." See *Long Range Pieces.*

SHOWALTER

Jackson Showalter of Kentucky (1860-1935) was United States Champion chessplayer from 1906 to 1909. He was popularly known as the "Kentucky Chess Lion" because of his attractive mane of hair which made him a conspicuous figure especially during the tournament sessions of the Western Chess Association.

SICILIAN DEFENSE
1. P-K4, P-QB4

The characteristic move of the Sicilian Defense is 1 . . . P-QB4. It is the "English Opening" in reverse. In some European countries the Sicilian Defense is called the Sicilian Attack. It is an aggressive opening which leads to a fighting game. As Edward Lasker says: "Every move is a hammer blow." Tarrasch claims that with the Sicilian opening "White has better play for his pieces but Black has the better Pawn position." Two popular variations of this defense are the Dragon variation and the Scheveningen variation.

The Sicilian Opening can be traced back to Polerio in 1590. It was used in the MacDonnell-laBourdonnais match in 1834; in the Staunton-St. Amant match in 1843; and in the great London tournament of 1851. Recently, there has been a tendency on the part of leading chessplayers to shy away from the Sicilian opening. Dr. Fine points out that "Botvinnik, who used to play it consistently, now rarely adopts it; and the same is true of Reshevsky, Flohr, Fine, and others."

For a presentation of the Sicilian Defense procedure and numerous variations, illustrations and notes see *Modern Chess Openings,* Ninth Edition, by Walter Korn, or *Practical Chess Openings,* by Reuben Fine.

SIDEBOARD MATE

A descriptive term which has reference to the mating position of the black King. As illustrated, the black King is mated along the side or edge of the chessboard.

"SIGN OF THE CROSS" PROBLEM

A problem which appeared in Charles Godfrey Gumpel's *How the Devil Was Caught—A Chess Legend,* written in 1878. It also appeared in the April, 1878 issue of *La Stratégie.* According to the story, Satan played several games of chess in which he used the black pieces. When the position shown in the accompanying illustration was

reached, he was warned that he would be mated in seven moves. On the seventh move, Satan fled with a despairing cry when he saw himself mated with the men in the position of "the sign of the cross." The cross is completed with the following moves:

1. RxN ch	K-B3
2. QxR ch	RxQ
3. RxR ch	Q-Q3
4. RxQ ch	PxR
5. N-B7	P-Q4
6. NxP ch	K-K3
7. R-K7 mate.	

SIGNS

see *Symbols*

SIMPSON'S DIVAN

A famous English chess resort originally located at 101 Strand, London, where, among other notable events, the Constitution of the British Chess Association was adopted by the Governing Council meeting there on January 20, 1885. It was also here that the first chess tournament sponsored by the British Chess Association was held in June 1885. This famous Simpson's Chess Divan disappeared in 1904 when the old building was demolished in a street extension scheme.

SIMULTANEOUS ALTERNATION

The ability to shift from one chess situation to another within the same period of time. It is a term applied to a chessplayer's mind which operates like a searchlight that can be turned at will from one to another chess move, game or problem. This mental power is needed in playing "mental chess." See *Mental Chess*

SIMULTANEOUS CHESS

A method of playing chess whereby one player is challenged to play within the same relative period of time a number of games, each of which is played with a different contestant. Some of the more notable events in simultaneous chessplay occurred when Stahlberg played 400 games in Buenos Aires in 36 hours. Lillienthal played 202 games at Madrid. Capablanca played in 1903 at Cleveland, 103 games with a score of 102 wins and one draw. In January, 1922, Frank J. Marshall played 156 games simultaneously in the National Club of Montreal and finished with a score of 129 wins, 21 drawn, and 6 losses. On May 22, 1955, George Koltanowski played simultaneously in Los Angeles against 110 opponents ending with a score of 89 wins, 17 draws and 4 losses.

Dr. Fine indicates that for simultaneous chessplay, "the main requirements for the exhibitor are a pair of sturdy legs and a quick grasp of the board." The Los Angeles Times reported that in the exhibition of May 22, 1955, Koltanowski had moved up and down the long row of tables at which the 110 opponent's sat "for 12 hours and 10 minutes, without a break" before the last King was checkmated.

SITZFLEISCH

A German word meaning "sitting flesh." The word was used in chess when the glutei muscles were used as a winning factor. Kreymborg reported that his friend Dr. Siff used to say: "What you need for chess isn't brains, but buttocks." Kreymborg goes on to say that "during the classical era, a man with a lost position could wear down his opponent by sitting like Buddha and refusing to move—except once every hour or two." The British champion, Howard Staunton, is said to have won many a lost game in this fashion. In one of his games with St. Amant in 1843, only sixty-six moves were made, but it required the use of fourteen and one half hours of sitzfleisch.

SKEWER

A term applied to an attacking position in which a piece is held in a position so that it can be captured as soon as a more valuable chess unit moves out of the line of attack. Hence the real target is not the piece immediately attacked but the second piece stationed on the same line behind it. A *skewer* is the opposite of a *pin*. In a pin, the first piece under attack cannot move because it shields the second more valuable piece behind it. In a skewer, the first piece is more valuable and

must move out of the way for self-protection and thereby expose the second piece for capture.

In the accompanying illustration, Black's King and Queen are on the same rank. White's Rook has placed the black King in check. Black's King must move and thereby expose the Queen. She will then be captured. Some chess writers have used such terms as "hurdle" or "X-ray attack" in place of "skewer." See *Hurdle Check* and *X-ray Attack*.

SKILL

Skill in chessplay is the ability to apply one's knowledge of general principles effectively and with relative ease and precision. It is a knack of making fresh and most interesting combinations which result in particularly satisfying results. Hence, a skillful chessplayer is an artistic or creative player insofar as he develops masterful strategic plans which are executed with well timed maneuvers.

SKITTLES

An informal chess game played leisurely for pure enjoyment. Friendly comments and discussions concerning the moves made throughout the game are not out of order.

SLAV DEFENSE

1.	P-Q4	P-Q4
2.	P-QB4	P-QB3

The characteristic move of this defense which is also known as the Czech

Defense, is 2 . . . P-QB3. It was named after the Czechoslovakian chessplayers,

like Alapin and other masters, who made good use of this defense. Here the struggle is focused on the maintenance of a Pawn equilibrium in the center and the early development of the Queen's Bishop. Tarrasch affirms that "in actual practice, the defense can quite well be played and generally leads to equality." For a presentation of the Slav Defense procedure and several variations see *Modern Chess Openings,* Ninth Edition, by Walter Korn, or *Practical Chess Openings,* by Reuben Fine.

SMOTHERED MATE

A descriptive mating situation in which a shut-in King is so hemmed in that, when attacked, he has no place to go. As shown in the accompanying illustration, the Knight has checked the black King. Since the Knight can not be captured, and since the black King is completely surrounded by his own men and has no avenue of escape, he is said to be smothered. The Fool's Mate is a good practical example of

a smothered mate. The smothered mate is also known as "Philidor's Legacy" after the French master André Philidor,

who popularized this mating position. See *Philidor's Legacy* and *Fool's Mate.*

SMYSLOV

Vassily Smyslov, a former world champion chessplayer, was born in Moscow on March 23, 1921. He learned the rudiments of chess when he was six years of age. His tutor was his father, who was one of Russia's well-known chess strategists. At the age of sixteen, Vassily gained the Master chess title and four years later became a recognized Grandmaster chessplayer. He won the Moscow chess championship in 1938 and frequently thereafter defended his title successfully. In international chess tournaments, he was invariably a member of the U.S.S.R. chess team. His crowning glory came in 1957 when he became the World Champion Chessplayer by defeating Mikhail Botvinnik. However, in May, 1958, Botvinnik regained the world championship title by defeating Smyslov in a return match with a score of 12½-10½.

Vassily Smyslov developed what has become known as "a mystic or creative" approach to chess. It is Smyslov's contention that the challenge of chess lies in the ideas which two players develop as they express their opposing intentions on the chessboard. He maintains that chessplayers "should strive for paths that will move chess forward and release it from the elements of dogmatism alien to the Soviet chess school." He feels that the growing popularity of chessplay justifies an earnest interest in chess as a professional career.

As a chessplayer, Smyslov is a good strategist and a good tactician. He has the ability to attack his opponent with extreme precision. Dr. Euwe observes that Smyslov "has no aversion to playing long drawn out games; he never hurries." "And this factor," adds Dr. Euwe, "has enormous worth."

SOCIAL CHESS

A term coined by John Ruskin when he wrote a letter in 1884 to the *Daily Telegraph,* expressing his intention of publishing a series of articles designed to instruct a perverse generation on how chess *ought* to be played. In his later writings to the editors of the *Chess Monthly* magazine, he again used the expression "Social Chess." In 1900 James Mason published a book entitled *Social Chess.* See *Sociology, Chess.*

SOCIOLOGY, CHESS

Chess Sociology is the science dealing with those human relationships which are manifested in chess activities. A chess sociologist studies the existing behavior of individual chessplayers in order to find a representative pattern of behavior which might be said to be characteristic of a unified group of players, such as may be characteristic of a certain age, nationality or other groupings. For example, it is said that as a group, young chessplayers are more daring than older players, who are inclined to be more conservative. Du Mont is of the opinion that "the average Britisher may not take his chess as seriously as his continental rival. But I feel sure that nowhere is the game of chess played in a more pleasant and sporting spirit than in this land of ours." Fred Reinfeld commenting on du Mont's observation, says: "I have never known anyone to lose an important game with such dignity. You are a nation of gentlemen." Expressions concerning other groups of chessplayers can be found in books dealing with tournament games and in newspaper accounts written at the time of tournament play.

SOLITAIRE CHESS

A game of chess in which one person plays a game by himself and compares his playing skill with that of a master chessplayer. In a book entitled *Chess By Yourself,* by Fred Reinfeld, ten games are given with moves for both White and Black with several alternative moves and assigned values. By covering up the coming moves the reader is asked to make his best move and then compare it with that made by a master chessplayer by uncovering the following move. Self-evaluating schemes are given. See *Chess Review*— the picture magazine, which devotes a section in every issue to "Solitaire Chess." A method for self-evaluation is provided.

SOLKOFF

Ephraim Solkoff, originator of a tie-breaking method in chess tournaments, was born in Jersey City, New Jersey, on September 13, 1908. He is an alumnus of The Cooper Union in New York City. By profession he is a registered Civil Engineer in North Carolina. He is associated with a consulting firm, specializing in sanitary and structural design.

He learned chess at the age of twelve but did not pursue it. His interest in chess was rekindled while overseas in the Army. He is now a strong amateur chessplayer and a perennial runner-up for the City of Raleigh championship. He did considerable organizational work in chess. In 1947, he organized the Spartanburg (South Carolina) Chess Club. In 1948, he was Secretary of the South Carolina Chess Association. In 1949, he served as the Secretary of the North Carolina Chess Association, and the following year he was elected President of the North Carolina Chess Association. For the past number of years, he has also been the President of the Raleigh Chess Club. On several occasions, he served as a tournament director. He is a contributor to the *American Chess Bulletin* and *Chess Life.*

SOLKOFF TIE-BREAKING METHOD

A proposal for breaking ties in a Swiss-type of tournament. It is briefly referred to in chess literature as the "S-M." The Solkoff Method was used officially for the first time by the North Carolina Chess Association in its 1950 State Championship tournament. Essentially, this method consists of adding together the plus scores of each and every opponent faced by the players who finished in a tournament with a tie score. *Full* plus scores are added, independent of the game results whether won, drawn or lost.

According to Ephraim Solkoff, the proponent of this method, leadership in a chess tournament "is a battle of perfectionists" and an evaluation of their scores "can best be made by including the deviations from perfection." Hence, Mr. Solkoff believes that to provide a rateable comparison of the abilities of tied players, it is imperative that every win, every draw and every loss be given proper recognition. He propounds, for example, the idea that in every game each contestant is given one-half point which "he puts on the line." The player may then proceed to win his opponent's half point, lose his own half point, or retain his half point in case of a draw. This idea may be reduced into a formula as follows:

If a player wins, his score equals: his own ½ point plus opponent's ½ point.

If a player loses, his score equals: his own ½ point minus his own ½ point.

If a player draws, his score equals: the retention of his own ½ point.

For a brief discussion of how the Solkoff Method differs from the Sonneborn-Berger System, see "Solkoff versus Sonneborn-Berger," by Ephraim Solkoff, in the *American Chess Bulletin*, January-February, 1955, page 16.

SONNEBORN-BERGER SYSTEM

A proposal for breaking ties especially in a round-robin type of tournament. It is referred to in chess parlance as the "S-B System," or the "S-B principle." Essentially, this Sonneborn-Berger principle consists of adding to a player's score all the scores of all the players he has defeated plus one-half of the scores of all the players with whom he has drawn. Applying this principle to all the players who finished with a tie score, the one having obtained the higher resultant total is declared the winner.

The original idea underlying this S-B system was invented in 1873 by Oscar Gelbfuhs of Vienna. It was first employed in official chessplay at the British Chess Association Tournament held in London, in 1889. This system is now claimed to have been the joint product of two men who had published, unknown to each other, the same idea. William Sonneborn of London, had an article published in *The Chess Monthly,* February 1886, in which he proposed his system of resolving tie-scores in chess tournaments. In May, 1887, Johann Berger, of Graz, wrote an article in the same magazine, on the evaluation of tournament scores which was similar to Sonneborn's idea. In April, 1891, Sonneborn had another article published in the same periodical in which he presented a mathematical basis for his system of breaking tie-scores. Although chess writers have recognized the joint contribution of these men in developing this system, some writers prefer to reverse the names and call it the "B-S System," or the "Berger-Sonneborn System." For a fuller discussion, application and an evaluation of this Sonneborn-Berger system see *The Official Blue Book and Encyclopedia of Chess,* pages 153-157.

SPACE

The area in which to move. Space is one of the elements in chess and consists of the number of squares covered and controlled. It represents the terrain or "lebensraum" in which to operate. Since space on the chessboard is limited it is obvious that the more space a player controls, the less space is available for the opponent. Hence, everything else being equal, more space gives greater mobility and conversely less space makes for a congested situation or cramped positions.

SPANISH GAME

see *Lopez Opening*

SPIELMANN

Rudolph Spielmann, a famous chessmaster and author, was born in Vienna, on May 5, 1883. He learned to play chess in his boyhood days and was exhibited in public chess performances as a prodigy. As a chessplayer, he displayed a great imagination and an extraordinary talent for meeting complicated situations. He demonstrated unusual abilities in offensive procedures. In international chess competition he encountered the world's greatest chessmasters. Among other things, Spielmann believed that chess games can be won by giving up material. This thesis he developed in his book entitled *The Art of Sacrifice* in which he explained, classified and illustrated the different types of sacrifices. Dr. Fine observes that although Spielmann "was always looking for brilliancies and sacrifices on the chessboard, in real life he was the meekest and the most retiring of men." Reinfeld refers to Spielmann as a "younger edition of Tchigorin" and as "a latterday Don Quixote."

SPRINGER

A German word meaning "jumper." The word Springer is used in place of the English word Knight.

SQUARE CONTROL

A square which is guarded or controlled by a chess unit which can capture any opponent's man that might be placed on it. As Brian Harley says; "In effect, the square is *en prise*."

STALEMATE

A situation in which the only possible move is for a King who is not in check to move to a square where he will be in check. The King is then said to be stalemated.

Chess historians point out that in earlier days there were various meanings attached to a game which ended in a stalemate. In Arabia and Spain, a stalemate was considered an inferior type of victory for the player of the white pieces; in Great Britain, it was an inferior type of victory for the player of the black pieces; in France, the black player merely forfeited a move; and in Italy, it was a drawn game. In 1808, J. Sarratt introduced in England the rule that a stalemate is a draw. By 1820 he influenced practically all leading chess clubs to adopt the same rule. It is now an established rule in international chess that a stalemate is a draw. See *Laws of Chess*, Article 12, section 1.

ST. AMANT

Pierre Charles Fournier St. Amant, the strongest French chessplayer of his time, was born in Montflanquin in 1800. He was a gentleman of noble birth, trained as a soldier but later devoted himself to journalism—editing *La Palamedé* from 1841 to 1847. By occupation, he was a wine merchant.

St. Amant was a powerful chessplayer not only in his native France but also in England. He was the leader of the victorious French team which played a correspondence match in 1834 with the famous Westminster Chess Club. While on a business trip to England in 1836, he played chess with the celebrated English chessmasters George Walker and Howard Staunton, both of whom he defeated. Later, Staunton went to Paris for a return match and recaptured his honor and glory by defeating St. Amant. This French-English rivalry was in no small part responsible for the formation of the first international chess tournament in London in 1851. St. Amant abandoned chessplay in 1861. He retired to Algeria where he died in 1873.

STAMMA

Philip Stamma, a distinguished eighteenth century chessplayer and the originator of a system of chess notation, was a native of Aleppo, Syria, but spent a large part of his life in Europe where in 1745, he published a book entitled *The Noble Game of Chess* which was translated into several languages. In this book he propounded his system of chess notation which became better known as the "algebraic system" of chess notation. As shown in the illustration, each file was lettered from *a* to *h*, beginning at White's left; and, the ranks were numbered from 1 to 8 beginning on White's side of the board. See *Algebraic Notation*.

STAMPING OUTFIT

Rubber stamps used by chessplayers to present a diagramatic position of a game or problem. A complete outfit consists of six rubber stamps which make a light imprint of the pieces and Pawns for the White player's positions and six rubber stamps which make a darker imprint of Black's pieces and Pawns. Generally, both sets of rubber stamps are constructed alike (♔ ♕ ♖ ♗ ♘ ♙). The Black player then uses a black ink pad and the player of the white pieces uses a red ink pad. Imprints are made on specially prepared diagram blanks.

Complete stamping outfits may be obtained from many chess emporiums or they may be purchased through the office of the Secretary of the Correspondence Chess League of America, 816 South Cecelia Avenue, Sioux City 6, Iowa, or from *Chess Review*, the picture chess magazine, 134 West 72nd Street, New York 23, New York. Usual price: $2.50 to $3.00.

STAUNTON

Howard Staunton, British chess champion, author and designer of chessmen, was born in 1810 and died in 1874. He was interested in the theater, became an actor and a Shakespearean scholar. He was a member of the St. George's Chess Club of London and in time was not only recognized as the best chessplayer in England but the best chessplayer of Europe. In fact, Tartakower lists Staunton as the World Champion Chessplayer from 1841 to 1851.

An international chess feud developed between Staunton and St. Amant of France which had significant consequences. In 1836, St. Amant came to England and defeated Staunton. A few months later, Staunton went to Paris for a return match. He did recapture his chess glory by winning the match with a score of 11 wins, 6 losses, and 4 drawn games. This encounter stimulated the English chessplayers to seek opportunities to meet the best available chessplayers in other European countries. As a result, on May 26, 1851, a Committee on Management, under the leadership of Howard Staunton, was organized to summon an assemblage of all leading chessplayers of various countries to take part in what became known as the First International Chess Tournament. This tournament was held at the time of the Crystal Fair in London in 1851. Adolf Anderssen of Germany won the first prize and was considered the World Champion chessplayer.

Staunton was an aggressive chessplayer. Although in following up the Dutch Defense, Staunton did develop a Pawn gambit which bears his name, nevertheless, Fletcher points out that "Staunton was not a typical gambit player." The Staunton Gambit consists of the following opening moves: 1. P-Q4, P-KB4; 2. P-K4, which Black usually accepts. Staunton also developed another opening which was named after him. (See *Staunton Opening*.)

Staunton's literary contributions consist of his writings in the magazine he established under the title of *British Miscellany and The Chess Player's Chronicle,* and a number of books, such as: *Chess-Player's Handbook,* which was a popular and scientific introduction to the game of chess as exemplified in games actually played by the great masters; *Chess Praxis,* which was a supplement to the *Chess-Player's Handbook;* and the *Chess-Player's Companion.*

STAUNTON CHESSMEN

In 1849, Howard Staunton designed a set of chessmen which is now in common usage in many countries. Some manufacturers of chess equipment have made slight modifications. For example,

Staunton placed an orb on the top of the King whereas now a cross appears on the King. The crown on the Queen had originally eight points, symbolic of the eight directions in which the Queen may move from a centrally located position on the board whereas now the Queen's diadem has any number of points. The other chess units have retained more uniformly Staunton's original designs. For an illustration of Staunton's designed chessmen, see *Chessmen.*

STAUNTON OPENING

1.	P-K4	P-K4
2.	N-KB3	N-QB3
3.	P-QB3	

This is the so-called Staunton Opening which some writers distinguish from the opening beginning with 1. P-QB4 commonly known as the English Opening. The move 3. P-QB3 can be traced to the Gottingen Manuscripts but Staunton revived it in his games. Modern chess theorists believe that 3. P-QB3 is a weak move because it takes possession of a square which could be utilized more forcefully by playing 3. N-QB3.

STEIN, ELIAS

Elias Stein, a professor of chess at The Hague and one of the strongest chessplayers of Europe, was born at Vorback, in Alsace, in 1748. As a chessplayer, he had excellent powers of concentration and was considered the peer of Philidor, Stamma and other masters of world-wide renown. Through Stein's influence, especially after he was appointed to be the instructor of the young Princess of Orange, chess became the favorite amusement not only in the royal household but also in all good social gatherings. Mauvillon, Stein's pupil, published in 1827, a book entitled *Anweizung zur Erlernung des Schachspiels,* in which he stated: "Whoever had not taken a lesson of him (Stein) was regarded as no authority. Everyone crowded to his teachings and he was scarcely able to accept all the invitations sent him from foreign ambassadors, persons of rank, and distinguished travelers, who wished either to see him play, to receive his instruction, or to oppose him to some celebrated player from abroad." Stein maintained that good chessplay rests on these three basic principles: first, a good opening and a favorable position of the pieces; second, a good plan of attack; and third, a rapid rushing of Pawns to queendom. It is reported that Stein played successfully two games of chess while engaged at billiards. He died at The Hague in 1812.

STEINER, HERMAN

Herman Steiner, United States Chess Champion 1948-1951 and chess promoter, was born in Dunajaska Ffreda, Hungary, now Czechoslovakia, on April 15, 1905. He came to the United States at an early age and developed his chessplaying ability in Astoria, Queens, New York. He won the New York state championship in 1929. He was a high ranking chessplayer in tournaments conducted in Berlin, Mexico City, Chicago, Dallas, St. Louis and Los Angeles. His chessplaying strength was further demonstrated in 1931 when he drew a game with José Capablanca in the International Masters' Tournament played in Los Angeles. In 1932, he settled in Los An-

geles. Here he organized a chess club that attracted many celebrated visitors from the nearby movie-film world, notably Humphrey Bogart and José Ferrer. In 1942, he shared the United States Open Championship with Yanofsky of Winnipeg, and in 1946, he won the Open United States Chess Federation Championship title. He was a member of the United States team playing at The Hague, Hamburg and Prague. At times, he served as the captain of United States chess teams which played in foreign countries.

After World War II, he played with distinction in important tournaments held in London, Dubrovnik in Yugoslavia, Rome, Madrid, Vienna, Saltsjobaden in Sweden, and throughout Argentina. He was a vice-president of the United States Chess Federation and at the time of his death he was manager of a chess club in Hollywood, California, and chess editor of the Los Angeles Times. He died on November 25, 1955, of a heart attack after a tournament game for the California State Championship. The tournament was immediately cancelled in honor of his memory.

Ten days after the death of Herman Steiner, the editor of *Chess Life,* Mr. Montgomery Major, wrote that "it is not as a player but as an organizer, teacher and promoter of chess that he should be remembered," and then Mr. Major adds, few could match Steiner's "exuberant optimism which by its breezy fervor often accomplished what originally had seemed impossible." To perpetuate the memory of Herman Steiner, his friends have organized "The Herman Steiner Chess Club" located at 108 North Formosa Avenue, Los Angeles, California. Likewise, closely associated with the club, the Herman Steiner Foundation has been established which will be supported by individual contributions. The activities of this foundation will include making available chess instructions and materials to schools and other institutions, promoting national and international play, and assisting other chess organizations.

STEINITZ

Wilhelm Steinitz, founder of modern chess and World Champion chessplayer from 1866 to 1894, was born at Prague, Bohemia, on May 18, 1836. He was a student of engineering at the Vienna Polytechnic Institute but after having encountered eye and lung difficulties, he made chess his livelihood. His chess life was dominated by the rule of reason. Any idea that fitted into his scheme of thinking was considered to be right. Even if he lost a certain position repeatedly, he would still insist that his idea was right and that something else had gone wrong. In 1866, he defeated the reigning World Champion Adolf Anderssen. Steinitz retained the honor of being the World Champion chessplayer until 1894 when he was defeated by Dr. Emanuel Lasker. Steinitz died in abject poverty in the East River Sanatorium on Ward's Island, New York, on August 12, 1900.

Steinitz's basic ideas of chess were set forth in his book, entitled: *The Modern Chess Instructor,* published in 1889. He proposed an objective, scientific approach to the game of chess which, as Dr. Emanuel Lasker stated, was based on "order, system, logic, balance and broad basic postulates." As a result, Steinitz became known as the father of modern chess with special emphasis on modern positional style of chessplay. As Nimzovitch indicated: "Steinitz was deep and great, but deepest and greatest in his conception of the center."

Although Steinitz is now regarded as the greatest representative of the scientific tendency in modern chess, nevertheless, "in his own lifetime,"

says Reinfeld, "he was reviled more often than revered for his stubborn insistence on two basic points. These were: (a) superior forces must win, and (b) gambit play not grounded in positional advantage must lose." It is worthy of note that although Steinitz was above all a doctrinaire, nevertheless, Dr. Lasker observed that Steinitz "seemed to have the mysterious capacity for divining combinations long before they were realizable on the board." See *Modern Chess.*

STEINITZ DEFENSE

1.	P-K4	P-K4
2.	N-KB3	N-QB3
3.	B-N5	P-Q3

Steinitz played 3 . . . P-Q3 as a defensive continuation of the Ruy Lopez opening. However, modern chessplayers do not consider this to be the strongest reply because it tends to produce a cramped game for Black. Consequently, it is not in common usage in modern chessplay. See *Steinitz Defense Deferred.*

STEINITZ DEFENSE DEFERRED

1.	P-K4	P-K4
2.	N-KB3	N-QB3
3.	B-N5	P-QR3
4.	B-R4	P-Q3

This defense is considered a refinement of the original Steinitz Defense. It defers the P-Q3 move to the fourth move and as Dr. Emanuel Lasker says: "it provides Black with a much better position." Du Mont also thinks it is "an improvement on the Steinitz De-

fense proper and one of the soundest replies to the Ruy Lopez." For a procedural development of this Steinitz Defense Deferred opening with several variations and accompanying notes, see *Modern Chess Opening,* Ninth Edition, by Walter Korn, or, *Practical Chess Openings,* by Reuben Fine.

STEINITZ GAMBIT

1.	P-K4	P-K4
2.	N-QB3	N-QB3
3.	P-B4	PxP

This gambit play was introduced by Steinitz at the Dundee tournament in 1867. Today, this gambit is better known as the Vienna Gambit because the Vienna chessplayers have popularized it in their official chessplay. For a brief discussion and procedural development of this gambit see *Gambits Accepted,* by L. Elliott Fletcher, page 130.

STONEWALL PATTERN

1.	P-Q4	P-Q4
2.	P-K3	N-KB3
3.	B-Q3	P-K3
4.	N-Q2	

An aggressive opening which gives White a strong Pawn center with his heavy pieces ready to shift to the King-

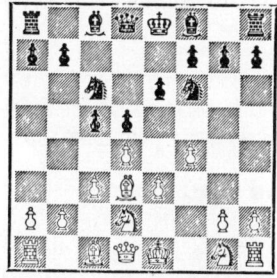

After White's sixth move.

side. This game usually proceeds with 4 . . . P-B4; 5. P-QB3, N-B3; 6. P-KB4, giving the pattern as shown in the diagram. The literature refers to this opening as a "murderous assault," or as one having menacing, formidable and smashing possibilities. "All this," observe Horowitz and Reinfeld, "is enough to give Black's King a persecution complex!"

STRATEGIC PROBLEM

A term loosely applied to problems which are more concerned with the manner in which a mating situation has been developed than in the actual mating position itself. See *The Enjoyment of Chess Problems,* by Kenneth S. Howard; and *Chess Strategy and Tactics,* by Fred Reinfeld and Irving Chernev.

STRATEGY

The science and art of designing and developing a master plan whereby a player's forces can exert their maximum power for offensive and defensive action. Strategy is concerned with the relative values of localities and the development of schemes for an effective mobilization, development and operation of one's forces. As the lines of battle change, it may be necessary to change one's strategy or at times it may be advisable to suspend temporarily the development of one's strategic plans. The wisdom of such procedures is explained in *Judgment and Planning in Chess*, by Dr. Max Euwe. For other references see *Strategy and Tactics in Chess*, also by Dr. Max Euwe; and *Modern Chess Strategy*, by Edward Lasker. See *Tactics*.

STRONG SQUARE

A square which is near the enemy's position, free from harmful attacks, and which can be firmly controlled. It is a square upon which a piece may be placed quickly and safely to serve a useful function, either offensively or defensively. As Dr. Euwe states, "it can be compared with a gun posted on a hill and on which the enemy cannot fire without himself running grave risks."

STUDIES IN CHESS

A term generally applied to those game positions or problem solving situations in which the number of moves are not stipulated as a requirement for finding the mating solution.

SUICIDE MOVE

An expression applied by Tarrasch to the move P-KN4 in the opening game. This move, says Dr. Tarrasch, "brings about a terrible loosening of the King's side, for which the only possible justification is the commencement of a strong attack or the securing of some immediate advantage."

SUI-MATE

Mating oneself. It is a term applied to a problem in which it is understood from the very beginning of play that White intends to commit suicide by forcing Black into a position from where he has no other available move except to mate the white King. Black's primary purpose of play in such a problem is to avoid giving mate to his opponent. Many players find this type of a problem more exciting and more difficult than the ordinary chess problem. See *Reflex Mate*.

SULTAN KHAN

Mir Malik Sultan Khan, the silent Oriental chessmaster, was born in the Punjab, Pakistan, India, in 1905. "Sultan" as used here was merely the first name of a serf of Sir Nawab Malik Mohammed Umar Hayat Kahn. Sultan Khan learned to play chess at the age of twelve. He became the Champion Chessplayer of India in 1928 and of the British Empire in 1929. Again in June of 1933, Sir Umar brought Sultan Khan to participate in an International Tournament at Folkestone, England. After the tournament the American team, of which Reuben Fine was a member, was invited to the London home of Sultan Khan's master. Dr. Fine observed that "we found ourselves in the peculiar position of being waited on at table by a chess grandmaster." For details of Sultan Khan's career see the September issue of the *British Chess Magazine*, vol. 49, 1929.

SUPPORT

To fortify a chessman's position in the face of threatening danger or opposition. This support is given by a fellow chessman who is in a position to capture any opponent's man who makes an attack.

SURPRISE MOVE

An unexpected move usually having forceful consequences. Sometimes such a move has the effect of a knockout blow in a seemingly harmless position.

In some of these moves, the most startling effect may consist in the exchange value which results when a player finds himself caught in a series of compulsory moves, which chessplayers refer to as *zugswang*. For a brief statement and thirty-six illustrations of different types of surprise moves, see *1001 Brilliant Chess Sacrifices and Combinations,* by Fred Reinfeld, Chapter 15, entitled "Surprise Moves." See *Zugswang.*

SWINDLE

A clever play whereby an apparently lost game is converted into a draw or on some occasions into a winning game. It is a deliberately planned trap whereby a losing player tries to ensnare his opponent and deprive him of winning the game. This may be accomplished by forcing complicated situations which will bewilder the opponent to the point where he is not sure of himself. For a full discussion of this topic with many illustrations, see *Chess Traps, Pitfalls and Swindles,* by I. A. Horowitz and Fred Reinfeld.

SWISS SYSTEM

A method of pairing a large number of contestants in tournament play. In utilizing this method, an unlimited number of participants can play in a limited number of rounds; for example, 150 contestants can play in twelve rounds. For the first round, pairings are made either by lot or by a ranking system. In subsequent rounds, players with equal scores or nearly equal scores are matched against each other, provided they have not played together in a previous round. No player is ever matched with the same opponent more than once in a Swiss tournament system. An odd contestant in any round who obviously cannot be paired, is given a "bye."

This Swiss system is said to have been invented by Dr. J. Muller of Brugg and was first utilized in official chess tournament play at Zurich in 1895. It was first utilized in the United States by George Koltanowski, who directed the Pennsylvania state championship chess tournament in 1943. Today, the Swiss system is used extensively throughout the United States, Canada, Great Britain and many other countries. For a detailed explanation of the history and operation of the Swiss system tournament see Chapter IV, in *The Official Blue Book and Encyclopedia of Chess.*

SWITCHBACK

A term frequently used by problemists when they refer to a situation in which a piece is moved back to the square from which it originally started.

SWORD PAWN

A fanciful term applied by chessplayers in Asia to an advanced Queen Pawn. See *History of Chess* by H. J. R. Murray, page 226.

SYMBOLICAL EXPLANATION OF CHESS

Using the game of chess as a visible means of explaining unseen people, places, things or events. In keeping with the spirit of the Middle Ages, attempts were made to find parallels between the game of chess and the social conditions of the times. It was maintained that the chessboard represents the battlefield of life itself. White and Black represent life and death; or the good and the evil. The chessmen represent the men of the world who before and after a game are kept in a box or bag to remind us whence we all came and where we must all return. When the chessmen come to life on the chessboard they take their positions as representatives of the various stations in life. The King symbolizes the entire kingdom; his life is the life of the nation. The Queen represents the influence of the woman. The Rooks are symbolic of itinerant justice. The Knights represent the worldly-minded aristocracy. The Bishops symbolize the ecclesiastical hierarchy. The Pawns are the common people. When all these people and officials intermingle the devil is always lurking to entice the player to make a weak, indifferent or poor move. If the player does make such a move, he commits a sin and must be punished by being captured, checked or checkmated. For an illuminating discussion of startling symbolical or allegorical explanations of the game of chess throughout the Middle Ages, see *A History of Chess,* by H. J. R. Murray, especially Part II, Chapter V, entitled, "The Moralists." See *Sign of the Cross Problem.*

SYMBOLS (Used In Chess Notation)

Signs, letters or abbreviations which by common usage convey a definite meaning. Symbols are used in chess writings as "short forms" are used in stenography. (See *Notation.*) The following are the more frequently used symbols.

- - means "move to" (as P-K3)
- x means capture.
- ! means (after a move) a very good move.
- !! means (after a move) an exceptionally good move.
- ? means (after a move) a questionable, weak or bad move.
- ?? means (after a move) a blunder; a very bad move.
- † means (after a move) check.
- + means (after a move) checkmate.
- e.p. means en passant.
- ch means check.

dbl ch means double check.

dis ch means discovered check.

0-0 means castling on King's side.
0-0-0 means castling on Queen's side.

SYMMETRICAL POSITION

Establishing a correspondingly similar position of Black's and White's forces. A perfect, symmetrical position exists on the chessboard at the opening of the game. A similarity of position may continue as long as Black makes the same identical moves as White. Petroff's Defense is a good example of a symmetrical position. However, it should be pointed out that sooner or later this continuation of making similar moves by both players must be abandoned. From the very beginning of the game each player strives to make the best responding move to that of his opponent. Eventually, one player will no longer be able to follow the tactics of his opponent. Horowitz pointed out very clearly that "symmetrical positions are tricky. They have the earmarks of a dead draw and yet often lead to losing games for the defender." See *Petroff's Defense,* and *Szen Problem.*

SYMMETRICAL PROBLEM

A problem in which the black and white pieces are placed to represent a harmonious pictorial design. Inasmuch as both players maintain similar positions in such a problem, there is "such little scope for the composer's skill," says Rayner, "that the solution is nearly always seen at a glance."

SYNTHETIC METHOD OF CHESSPLAY

A technique whereby all the elements of the science of warfare are combined and applied to chessplay. This method was developed by Franklin Knowles Young of the Boston Chess Club. It appeared on the American chess scene between 1894 and 1923. By this term "synthetic method of chessplay," Mr. Young means the scientific method of synthesis in contrast to the method of analysis. This synthetic method is based on the fact that, to quote Mr. Young, "scientific chessplay is the replica of scientific warfare and the process of Grand Strategy, High Tactics and Lesser Logistics, as established by the Great Captains, by the movements of their armies on the surface of the Earth, are identical with the processes established by the Great Chess Masters, by the movements of their Pieces on the surface of the Chessboard." By using this method, Mr. Young claims to have won games from Zukertort, Steinitz and others. For a fuller account see "The Synthetic Method of Chessplay," by Lawrence J. Fuller, in *Chess Review*, July, 1955, page 205. See *Young*.

SZEN PROBLEM

A theoretical problem proposed by Joseph Szen, a Hungarian chessplayer of the nineteenth century. This problem is also known as the "Three Pawns Game" or the "Little Game of Chess." As indicated in the accompanying illustration, symmetrical positions are established for both black and white players. This problem is admittedly pure theory and is not very likely to

occur in actual chessplay. It is used by problemists and theorists to illustrate several points which are peculiar to Pawn play; such as, the player whose King takes the file in front of the

Pawns has the advantage; and, the player having the first move should win.

T

TABULAR NOTATION

A method of recording the moves of White and Black in a game of chess. The moves are written in the form of a table. This arrangement was first utilized in a book published by John Allgaier in 1795. The following moves of the Allgaier's Gambit are recorded in tabular form.

	WHITE	BLACK
1.	P-K4	P-K4
2.	P-KB4	PxP
3.	N-KB3	P-KN4
4.	P-KR4	P-N5
5.	N-N5	

TACTICS

The science and art of executing various schemes which are deemed necessary for carrying out a strategical plan. Tactics is a concomitant notion of strategy. Dr. Fine pointedly observes that "strategy, the body of ideas, holds only as a framework. Tactics, the individual variations, is what goes into this framework." In other words, strategy is the over-all planning; tactics is the carrying out of the planning. Chess writers indicate that ninety per cent or more of a game of chess is concerned with tactical maneuvers. See *Strategy and Tactics in Chess*, by Dr. Max Euwe; and *Chess Strategy and Tactics*, by Fred Reinfeld and Irving Chernev. See *Strategy*.

TARRASCH

Dr. Siegbert Tarrasch, a noteworthy European chess theorist and chessplayer, was born in Breslau on March 5, 1862. He began to study medicine at the age of eighteen and later practiced medicine in Geroldsgrun, Nuremburg and Munich. He learned to play chess at an early age and made chess his hobby while engaged in his professional activities. Between 1889 and 1907, he managed to win seven international tournaments, two of which he won without the loss of a single game. In match games, he defeated such masters as Marshall, Mieses and others; he drew with Tchigorin and Schlechter. He nicknamed Karl Schlechter the "Master of the Vienna Remismonde," or the "Drawing Master." In 1908, Tarrasch tried to win the world championship title by playing a match with the World Champion, Dr. Emanuel Lasker. Lasker won.

In the last years of his life, Tarrasch devoted himself to literary works on the game of chess. He wrote nine books which, according to Cecil Purdy, taught Europe how to play chess, that is, "Europe but not England, and not other English speaking countries, for only one book was ever translated and that one after his death." The name of this book is *The Game of Chess,* by Dr. Tarrasch. Tarrasch died in Munich, February 17, 1934.

According to Reinfeld and Chernev, Tarrasch's "efforts have refined chess technique to an amazing extent; the Hypermoderns have not refuted or superseded Tarrasch—they have merely purified his theories by removing some of their weaknesses and exaggerations." For a statement of what Dr. Tarrasch thought of the game of chess, see *Importanc̨e of Chess.*

TARRASCH DEFENSE

1.	P-Q4	P-Q4
2.	P-QB4	P-K3
3.	N-QB3	P-QB4

The characteristic feature of this defense which was developed by Dr. Tarrasch is the advance of the Queen's Bishop Pawn on the third move before the development of the King's Knight.

The effect is that Black succeeds in opening his lines for a free develop-

ment of his pieces at the cost of a weakened Pawn structure, whereas White obtains a better grip on the center. For a presentation of the Tarrasch Defense procedural development and several variations see *Modern Chess Openings,* Ninth Edition, by Walter Korn.

TARTAKOWER

Dr. Savielly Grigorievitch Tartakower, who later in life preferred to gallicize his name into Xavier Tartakover, was a famous chessmaster and a prolific writer on the game of chess. He was born in Rostoff-on-Don, in southern Russia, on February 21, 1887. He was educated at the Geneva Gymnasium and at the University of Vienna, where, in 1909, he obtained the degree of Doctor of Laws. As time went on, Tartakower won a reputation in the literary world by writing books on chess such as *A Breviary of Chess* and numerous other non-chess literary works including translations of modern Russian poetry into both French and German. Dr. Fine referred to him as "a man of broad cultural attainments, a master linguist, a poet, a wit, a philosopher, and a most delightful conversationalist." He died in Paris, on February 5, 1956.

Tartakower learned to play chess from his father at the age of twelve. In 1909, he attained the rank of Master at the Nuremberg Hauptturnier, where, of fifty competitors, he attained the first place. In 1927, he shared first place honors with Nimzovitch at Niendorf and again at London. He won first prizes at Vienna in 1905 and 1923; at Ghent in 1926; at Paris in 1929; and at Hastings in 1926, 1927 and 1945. Nevertheless, he stated very humbly: "I have never achieved a complete triumph in any Master Tournament." This he explained was due to the fact that he was "always striving to avoid the well-known openings and taking delight in risky combinations." Tartakower was also an excellent blindfold chessplayer and a prolific contributor to periodical literature.

Tartakower was respected highly by his fellow chess colleagues. Golombek considered Tartakower "one of the world's leading end-game experts." He also claimed that Tartakower's "influence on the theory of the game was enormous." He pointed out that, with Réti, Nimzovitch and others, Tartakower "constituted the *avant-garde* of the hypermodern movement that so changed and enlivened the chess scene in the early 1920's." Réti indicated that the real foundation of Tartakower's success "is to be found in his admirable capacity for work, in an indefatigable search for truth with which to overcome an inborn scepticism that breaks out again and again." Fred Reinfeld stated that Tartakower was "famous for his venturesome, highly unorthodox style. His unconventional games and tricky surprise moves have often dismayed opponents and always delighted the chess public."

TCHIGORIN

Mikhail Tchigorin, an influential Russian chessplayer, was born in Russia in 1850. He was a petty governmental official in his native country. In 1880, he organized the first Russian chess

club at St. Petersburg. He edited a chess magazine and founded a school of chess which produced many famous master chessplayers. In match games, he encountered such notables as Steinitz, and other masters. In tournament play, he tied for first place honors at New York in 1889, and in 1895 he finished in second place at Hastings.

Tchigorin maintained that chess like life itself can be equally irrational, full of disorder, blunders, imperfections and unforeseen consequences. In his chessplay, he emphasized the subjective point of view in contrast to the objective point of view so strongly advocated by Steinitz. Hence, Tchigorin wanted in his games the elements of novelty, surprise, glitter and "the lightning stroke from a clear sky." His love for the attack was proverbial. He was convinced that a Knight is usually better than a Bishop. It is well known that Tchigorin developed a number of positional defenses of which the one bearing his name is best known. It is Dr. Emanuel Lasker's conviction that Tchigorin's "untiring efforts in promoting chess activities in Russia . . . gave the impetus for the tremendous development which attended Russian chess after his death" in 1908.

TCHIGORIN'S DEFENSE

1. P-Q4	N-KB3
2. P-QB4	P-Q3
3. N-QB3	QN-Q2
4. N-B3	P-K4

This defense leads to an immediate

counterattack in which Black usually fianchettoes his King's Bishop. Tartakower believes this defense "leads to a close but defendable game," and Marshall states that the Tchigorin Defense is "much better than the Dutch Defense." True to Tchigorin's belief, the Knights play an important part in this defense. For a presentation of procedural development of this defense and some of its variations, see *Modern Chess Openings,* Ninth Edition, by Walter Korn, or *Practical Chess Openings,* by Reuben Fine.

TEICHMANN

Richard Teichmann, a master chessplayer whose "sharp mind was a veritable treasure house of chess knowledge and skill," was born in Altenburg, on December 24, 1868. As a chessplayer, he emphasized the importance of making a move which would place a man in a favorable position and hasten the development of all pieces as fast as possible. In 1891, he won the championship of Berlin. In 1894, he made his debut in a masters' tournament at Leipzig where he finished in 3rd place. Because he finished in the third place in several tournaments, he used to be referred to as "Richard III of Chess." In match games, he defeated Mieses, Spielmann and many other masters. In 1892, he went to England where he resided for many years and at times played at Hastings as an English representative. He died in Berlin, on June 15, 1925.

TEMPO

A Latin word meaning time. The plural is tempi. In chess, a tempo is the unit of time expressed in terms of a move. A player who makes two moves to accomplish the same result he could with one move, is said to have lost a move, or "to have lost a tempo." Tarrasch calls it "the time value of a move." Generally, it is said that in exchange value, a gain of three tempi is the equivalent of gaining a Pawn.

THEME

Setting forth an idea. Chess problemists frequently use this term. By it they simply mean, as Harley says, "a composer's idea in setting up a chess problem." The term is also used in reference to opening themes. For example, the dominant theme of the Sicilian Defense is a struggle in the opening as well as in the middle game.

THEORY

A body of sound general principles offered to justify a specific procedure. Theory and practice are concomitant terms. Basically, theory is thinking; practice is doing. Theory helps to plan a course of action; practice tests out the theory in actual performance. Hence, theory is a guide to intelligent action. See *Principles.*

THERAPEUTIC USE OF CHESS

Utilizing the game of chess as a form of recreational therapy with some psychiatric patients. As early as the third century B.C., Hippocrates, a Greek physician and writer, seemed to have found chess to be a potent prescription for patients suffering from diarrhea and erysipelas. In our own century, Franklin K. Young reports that a great captain of industry, "on the advice of his physician, relinquished all business cares and for a limited period engaged Master chessplayers to teach him the game, and in its absorption, he regained his health and business control." In the January, 1949, issue of the *Journal of Mental Science,* it is reported that patients in a mental hospital were organized into teams to play chess with some city chess clubs. It was found that the game of chess was helpful in socializing some of the antisocial patients and in improving their general morale. See *Virtues (Inherent in Chessplay)*.

THOMAS

Sir George A. Thomas, a British Champion chessplayer, an international chessmaster, and a Life Member as well as a Vice-President of the British Chess Federation, was born in London, in 1881. In addition to being a noteworthy chessplayer, he was also, for several years, the British Badminton Champion and a first-class tennis player. He won repeatedly the City of London chess championship. He won the British chess championship at Southsea in 1923 and again in 1945 at Chester. He participated in many tournaments where his chess opponents were such eminent chessplayers as Euwe, Flohr, Capablanca and Botvinnik. Sir George Thomas has served as Games Editor of the *British Chess Magazine* and has become a highly respected chess annotator.

As a chessplayer, C. H. O'D. Alexander points out that at one time or another, Sir George Thomas "has beaten most of the leading masters of the time." Fred Reinfeld stated that the British style of chessplay is "best illustrated by the almost superhuman sportsmanship of Sir George Thomas."

THREAT

A move designed to inflict some injury upon the opponent. Since the days of Nimzovitch, it has become proverbial that "the threat is stronger than its execution." A threat may be very obvious or very subtle; very brutal and crude or very refined; sound or foolish; disastrous or avoidable. A threat is effective and meaningful in so far as it succeeds in gaining manpower or exchanging material of lower for higher value. A threat may be met by rallying a strong defense, interposing an obstruction, creating a counterthreat, causing a counterattack, capturing the threatening piece or Pawn, or moving away from the source of danger. The best solution for a threat depends upon the best judgment of the individual player. See *Nimzovitch*.

THREE DIMENSIONAL CHESS

A style of chessplay which utilizes the elements of length, breadth and depth (or height). Various kinds of 3-dimensional chess games have been proposed over the years with more or less success.

1. In 1954, a novelty game called "Space Chess" appeared on the market. This game consisted of the use of several clear plastic boards elevated over the ground board with the use of a player's own chess pieces from a conventional set. An accompanying pamphlet explained the rules and notation system.

2. Earlier, it was announced that a group of chessplayers of the Princeton University teaching staff had developed a new game known as "Three-Dimensional Chess."

3. In 1946, Charles Beatty reported in the *British Chess Magazine* a game entitled: "Total Chess," as another variety of 3-dimensional chess. This game was played on four superimposed boards of which the three upper ones were transparent. Special instructions explained the placing and moving of the various chessmen on different tiers.

4. In 1931, the *British Chess Magazine* reported a 3-dimensional game which had been developed in South America. This game was designed "to facilitate the teaching of air maneuvers." This game was played on an upper and lower board. The elevated upper board which consisted of transparent glass was marked off in conventional squares which matched those on the ordinary chessboard beneath. On the upper board, chess pieces were carried by aerial planes representing

the various types of aviation: Bombarding, Attacking, and Local and Distant Observation Planes. On the lower level, ground forces guarded against capture not only from the enemy's ground forces but also from aerial attack.

THREE KNIGHTS' OPENING

1. P-K4   P-K4
2. N-KB3   N-QB3
3. N-B3   B-N5
   (or 3 . . . N-N5)

A tame opening which threatens nothing. According to Freeborough and Ranken, the "Three Knights' Game" has been selected by first rate players for some of their most important contests. Occasionally Alekhine is known to have made use of this opening. Dr. Fine is of the opinion that today, this opening "is theoretically unsatisfactory." For a presentation of the procedural development of this opening, see *Practical Chess Openings*, by Reuben Fine.

THREE PAWNS GAME

see *Szen Problem*

TIE-BREAKING SYSTEMS

Procedures for determining the leading winner from a group of tournament contestants who have attained the same score. There are four such systems in common usage today. They are: the Sonneborn-Berger System; the Solkoff System; the Coons System and the so-called Median System. They are computed as follows:

Sonneborn-Berger—Sum of the scores of defeated opponents PLUS 50% sum of scores of opponents who drew.

Solkoff—Sum of the FULL scores of ALL opponents.

Coons—Sum of the scores of the defeated opponents PLUS 50% sum of scores of opponents who drew PLUS 20% sum of scores of opponents who won.

Median—Sum of the scores of all opponents except those of the highest and lowest.

TIGER

A figurine of a "tiger" is used by the Tibetan chessplayers as the equivalent of our Queen. See *Animals*.

TIME

In chess language, "time" means either time by the clock or it may denote the time taken in terms of the number of moves used to reach an objective. (*See Tempo*.) In chess, time is of the essence. The player who reaches his objective first, has gained an advantage. When a player wastes time, he gives additional time to his opponent.

Time can be wasted in several ways; 1) by making two moves to accomplish something that could be done with one move; 2) by giving useless check; 3) by playing a piece which can be driven away by advancing a Pawn; 4) by attacking a man which will cause him to flee to a square which will prove beneficial to the opponent; or 5) by forcing an exchange which develops an opponent's piece or gives it greater mobility.

In important matches and tournaments, the time used by chessplayers is usually measured by two separate clocks, one for each player. (*See Clocks*)

TIME LIMITS OF PLAY

Before the game begins, it is understood that a certain specified number of moves must be made within a definite period of time. A player who fails to do so, forfeits the game. World Championship tournaments are played at the rate of making at least forty moves in two and a half hours. In American tournaments, the minimum rate of play is usually twenty moves per hour. In match games, each player is usually allowed a minimum of fifteen moves per hour. In friendly games played for pure enjoyment, the average player takes about thirty to fifty minutes per game. Rapid Transit chess is played at the rate of about ten seconds per move. Blitz or Lightning Chess is played with "the speed of lightning," or approximately three seconds per move. (See *Blitz*.) In Postal Chess, it is common practice that the maximum time per move is three days or seventy-two hours from the time of having received an opponent's move to the time of getting a reply into the mail.

TIMING

The art of knowing when to play the right chessman in the right place. Correct timing is a matter of good judgment. The position of the chessmen and the space in which they may move is visible to the players but determining when the chessmen should be moved to the place where they will be most effective is not so obvious. Timing the movements of the chessmen can change the development and prosecution of the game. Good timing is the very life of the game.

TORRENT PAWN

A fanciful term applied to an advanced King's Bishop Pawn by chessplayers in some parts of Asia. See *History of Chess*, by H. J. R. Murray, page 226.

TOUCHED MAN

A chessman that has been touched. The Laws of Chess are very explicit in requiring that the first man touched must be either moved or captured, unless the opponent has first been notified that the player intends to adjust one or more men. See *Laws of Chess*, Article 8.

TOURNAMENT

A contest in which a number of individuals compete with one another. Tournaments are organized to encourage competition, to develop greater interest and publicity for chess, to stimulate new ideas for the promotion of better chess techniques, and just for the mere enjoyment of participating in organized chessplay. Tournaments may be "open" to all players without regard to class standing or they may be restricted to some class of players, such as a Masters' tournament, amateur tournament, intercollegiate tournament, and ladies' tournament. Tournaments are also named according to the manner in which they are conducted, such as, the Round Robin, Knockout, or Swiss type of tournament. (These terms are defined in their alphabetical order.) For an account of "How to Run a Chess Tournament" see *The Macmillan Handbook of Chess*, by I. A. Horowitz and Fred Reinfeld, pages 218-226.

TOWER

The word "tower" is in common usage, in place of the Rook, among many European chessplayers. This piece is designed as a tower or fortress in which the King could find refuge and safety. This seems to be the underlying explanation of the origin of the process of "castling." See *Castling*.

TRAP

A device or method of posting one's forces who lie in wait for the purpose of attacking the opponent's forces by surprise. Hence a trap may be said to be a tactical surprise party. It occurs in a situation in which an unwary chessplayer, without any encouragement or provocation from his opponent, makes a move which involves him in difficulties from which he can not escape. He is retained there at the mercy of his opponent. "Usually," says Kreymborg, "the trap is baited with a sacrificial Pawn no potzer can resist smelling and seizing." He adds that if the Pawn were "a consequential piece, the fellow would hesitate and look around." Georges Renaud of France is of the opinion that the setting of traps, except in sheer desperation, is not good chess. He indicated his resentment of having traps set for him by saying: "My personal feelings, when an opponent sets a purely tactical trap for me, are of an internal affront, of an insult to my self-respect. It seems to me that my opponent in underestimating my analytical capacity, is guilty of bad taste, of impoliteness. I am vexed." (From *The Art of the Checkmate* by Georges Renaud and Victor Kahn, New York: Simon and Schuster.)

Gambits are traps of one sort or another. The "Fool's Mate" is a good example of how the player of the white pieces gets himself caught in a trap. See *Traps, Pitfalls and Swindles*, by I. A. Horowitz and Fred Reinfeld; and *Winning Chess Traps*, by Irving Chernev. See *Fool's Mate*, and *Gambit*.

TREBLED PAWNS

A Pawn situation in which three white Pawns or three black Pawns are standing in the same file. This is a distinct disadvantage. The three Pawns can be held up by a single opposing Pawn or piece causing them to be immobilized as well as targets for attack.

TRY

A term used by the late problemist Brian Harley when he referred to "a plausible first move that nearly, but not quite, solves the problem." See *Mate in Two Moves*, by Brian Harley, page 11.

"TURK"

The name given to a mechanical chessplayer which was invented in 1769 by Baron Wolfgang von Kempelen of Austria. This mechanical robot appeared as a life-sized "Turk" seated behind a large box, the top of which served as a chessboard. The inside of the box, which was shown to the audience at the beginning of every exhibition, appeared as an intricate piece of machinery. In making a move, the machinery was heard to be in motion. The Turk's mechanical left hand would reach for the chessman to be moved, pick it up with its fingers, and place it on its new square.

After the death of the inventor, the Turk was sold to Johann Nepomuk Maelzel, a Bavarian musician who had it installed in a room in Schoenbrunn Castle. Later, it was resold and after being exhibited in various European countries and American cities, it was placed in the Chinese Museum in Philadelphia. After eighty-five years of utmost secrecy as to the nature of its real mechanical contrivance, it was destroyed in a fire.

Edgar Allen Poe, who scrutinized the Turk very carefully during its operations, believed that this automaton was a hoax. He was convinced that a small man, named Schlumberger, was concealed within the Turk and could see the chessboard through a small hole in the Turk's chest and then execute the robot's reply with relative ease. For a detailed account of how the Turk was exhibited and operated, see *Maelzel's Chess Player*, by Edgar Allen Poe. This account is also reproduced in *The Art of Chess-Playing*, by Edwin Valentine Mitchell. See *Kempelen*. For other mechanical chessplayers see *Ajeeb* and *Mephisto*.

"TWIN CHESS"

An unorthodox type of chess which utilizes two Kings and two Queens. Mr. V. R. Parton, the proponent of this type of chessplay, claims that logic, symmetry and balance demand an initial arrangement of pieces as shown

in the accompanying illustration. In this so-called "logical form of chessplay" the game is won when one of the opponent's King is checkmated. This idea has been bitterly criticized by Mr. S. Webb in the June 1955 issue of the *British Chess Magazine*. He stated that this self-styled logical game suffers from illogicality. "For instance," says Webb, "it is not logical to have two Kings and Queens each, but is merely uniform. Why should two of everything be thought logical? Is it that odd numbers are repellent in some way? Without odd numbers, even numbers could not be even." See *British Chess Magazine*, May, 1955, page 157.

TWO KNIGHTS' DEFENSE

1.	P-K4	P-K4
2.	N-KB3	N-QB3
3.	B-B4	N-B3

This opening also known in German as the Preussische Opening, is said to have been developed by Gianutio, a sixteenth century chess writer. It is essentially a gambit opening involving a Pawn sacrifice in return for a more

rapid development. Tartakower points out that "by resolutely giving up a Pawn, Black succeeds in turning the tables and in seizing the initiative." Gossip states that "Herr Steinitz and Herr Zukertort consider it (this Two Knights' Defense) inferior, while Herr Lowenthal, on the contrary, thinks it may be played with perfect safety." Dr. Fine observes that "since the well-known Fine-Reshevsky game in New York, in 1940, where White established a winning superiority very quickly with one of the main variations, it has come in for a good deal of analysis, especially by American masters." For a presentation of the Two Knights' Defense procedures with several variations and accompanying notes, see *Practical Chess Openings*, by Reuben Fine, or *Modern Chess Openings*, Ninth Edition, by Walter Korn.

TYRO

An inexperienced and audacious chessplayer who by his crudeness and eagerness to seize any proffered opportunity to make a capture is quickly trapped and mated. "To be a tyro is a universal lot," says Dr. Emanuel Lasker. "One may bear it in good humor, since the adventures of a tyro are richer, more emotional, more varied than those of the master. How glad is the tyro of a lucky chance!"

U

UEDEMANN

Louis Uedemann, the inventor of the "Uedemann Code" for telegraphing chess moves, was born in Saerbeck, Westphalia, Germany, on January 10, 1854. He came to the United States when he was twelve years of age. He made Chicago his home for the rest of his life. In 1900, Uedemann won at Excelsior, Minnesota, the championship title of the first chess tournament held under the auspices of the Western Chess Association. He was chess editor for the *Chicago Tribune*. He died in Chicago on November 22, 1912.

Uedemann is best remembered in the chess world for having developed a code for telegraphing chess moves. This telecommunication code, which bears his name, is based on a system whereby each square on the chessboard is designated by two letters as shown in the accompanying diagram. Accordingly, a move or capture is indicated by a four letter word. The first two letters indicate the square *from which* a piece moves and the last two letters reveal the square *to which* it moves. For example, White's move P-K4 would be recorded as GEGO. If Black would reply with P-K4, he would record SASO. Castling is expressed simply as a King's move; thus, White's move 0-0, would be transmitted as GAKA.

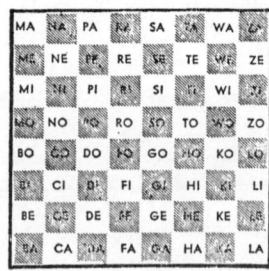

ULTRAMODERN CHESSPLAY

A style of chessplay which has developed since the nineteen twenties. It is based more on individualistic tastes and procedures than on a strict adherence to established and standardized patterns of play. Accordingly, the activities of chessplayers are viewed as being not only purposive, but purposeful in light of the individual player. Consequently, strategical planning is less obvious at the opening of the game and a reappraisal of a player's position becomes a constant and continuous process. This style of play is a direct reflection of the social, educational and psychological trend of the time. See *Victorian Era* and *Modern Chess*.

UNDERPROMOTION

Promoting a Pawn that has reached the eighth rank to a piece of lesser value than that of a Queen. At times, chessplayers may deem it more advantageous or preferable to promote the Pawn to a Rook, Bishop or Knight. This is underpromotion.

UNGUARDED PIECE

A piece which is placed in an exposed position where it can be captured without recompense. When an unguarded piece has been captured after having been exposed for some time it is usually considered a blunder.

UNIQUE MOVES OF CHESSMEN

Characteristic moves which are peculiar to a particular chessman or class of chessmen. Among the more unique features of the various chessmen, the most noteworthy are: first, that a Pawn is the only chessman which can be promoted; second, a Knight is the only piece which can jump over (or move between) other chessmen; and third, the King is the only one on the chessboard that, technically, can not be captured or exchanged—he may be mated but not captured.

UNIT

A chess "unit" is any one of the thirty-two chessmen in a game of chess.

UNITED PAWNS

Pawns of the same color stationed in adjacent files and in contact with one another so that they are able to support one another. Pawns that are not united are referred to as isolated Pawns.

UNITED STATES CHAMPION
CHESSPLAYERS

In the twentieth century, the United States Chess Champions are:

1897-1906 Harry Pillsbury
1906-1909 Jackson Showalter
1909-1936 Frank Marshall
1936-1944 Samuel Reshevsky
(In 1942, Reshevsky was co-champion with Kashden.)
1944-1946 Arnold Denker
1946-1948 Samuel Reshevsky
1948-1950 Herman Steiner
1951-1953 Larry Evans
1954-1957 Arthur Bisguier
1958-   Bobby Fischer

UNITED STATES CHESS FEDERATION

The official representative organization and voice of chessplayers in the United States. It is a non-profit, democratic organization of chessplayers who, by working together, further their own interests and make it possible for the USCF to perform its duties as the governing body of chess in the United States. The USCF is an affiliated member of the International Federation of Chess.

The United States Chess Federation had its beginnings in several earlier organizations, namely the Western Chess Association, the American Chess Federation and the National Chess Federation. These three organizations united in 1939 and formed the present United States Chess Federation. Its presidents were: George Sturgis (1939-1944); 2. Elbert A. Wagner, Jr., (1945-1949) 3. Paul G. Giers (1949-1950); 4. Harold M. Phillips (1951-1954; 5. Frank R. Graves (1954-1957); 6. Jerry Spann (1957-   ).

The activities of the United States Chess Federation consist of 1) promoting the science and art of chess; 2) cultivating an interest in chess in schools and colleges; 3) stimulating the development of chess talent throughout the nation; 4) bringing aid and comfort to hospitalized veterans by sponsoring chess activities; 5) conducting tournaments for the United States Championship and other national and regional titles and honors; 6) arranging zonal contests which will qualify American players to compete for the World Championship; 7) sponsoring United States participation in World Team Tournaments, and 8) establishing and retaining American leadership in international chess.

The business office of the United States Chess Federation supplies chess books and chess equipment to its members at substantial savings. Every member receives twice a month a copy of the official United States Chess Federation publication, entitled *Chess Life,* which is America's only chess newspaper. Membership in the United States Chess Federation, including a subscription to *Chess Life* costs $5.00 a year; $9.50 for two years; and $13.50 for three years. Applications should be sent to the Membership Secretary, United States Chess Federation, 80 East 11th Street, New York 3, New York. For rules and regulations sponsored by the United States Chess Federation see *The Official Blue Book and Encyclopedia of Chess,* by Kenneth Harkness; published for the Federation by David McKay Company, New York, 1956.

UNIVERSALITY OF CHESS

The unlimited and unrestricted use made of the game of chess. A. D. Gardner in "The Praise of Chess" states that chess "is a game for all ages, all seasons, all sexes, all climates, for summer evenings or winter nights, for land or for sea. It is the very water of Lethe for sorrow or disappointment, for there is no oblivion more profound than that which it offers for your solace."

UNORTHODOX CHESS

Games of chess which in one way or another deviate from the generally accepted and standardized rules of chess sanctioned by the International Federation of Chess. Some of these games propose a modification of the chessboard and/or chessmen, while others propose novel moves or procedures. Sometimes "unorthodox chess" is also referred to as "crazy chess" or "fairy chess." For further information write for a copy of *Jeux D'Echecs Non Orthodoxes* published in French by Professor Joseph Boyer, 3 Rue Leconte de Lisle, Paris 16, France. In the United States, Fred Galvin, 840 Algonquin Avenue, St. Paul 6, Minnesota, conducts correspondence games in unorthodox chess. For a few illustrations, such as Rotation Chess, Sixteen-Pawn Chess, Bughouse Chess, and others, see *The Official Blue Book and Encyclopedia of Chess, pp.* 247-251. See *Fairy Chess.*

V

VALUE OF CHESSMEN

The worth of the various chessmen in a game of chess. The value of any chessman can be determined by the extent of its utility in the hands of the chessplayer. In general, the average utility of a chessman to a player is proportionate to its average mobility.

(See *Mobility* and *Cruising Range.*) Values are always relative. They are never static. Chess pieces change their value with every move, with every position.

The utility of the relative values of chessmen is concerned with the mechanics of their exchange. When all other things are the same, chessmen have a market price, except of course the King, who is priceless in any game. Practical experience has reinforced the generally accepted market price of each of the following chessmen. The Pawn is the basic unit for establishing the market price of all other chess pieces. Hence, the relative scale of values follows:

Pawn............has the value of 1 point.
Knight.........has the value of 3 points.
Bishop..........has the value of 3 points.
Rook............has the value of 5 points.
Queen..........has the value of 9 points.

These relative values change throughout the progress of the game. It is an established principle that the less radiation a piece possesses, the smaller is its power and value. By virtue of the power of movement, a Knight is more valuable than a Bishop in cramped positions, but in an end game, a Bishop is generally more powerful and hence more valuable. Again, the power and value of a Knight decreases as the number of pieces on the chessboard diminishes, whereas that of the Rook, on the contrary, increases.

VARIATIONS

One or more playable moves which change, deviate or depart from an established order of procedure without destroying the essential features of the original theme. Variations suggest originality. It is practically a hopeless task to try to memorize the variations arising in games of chess. Horowitz and Reinfeld point out that "every year new variations are introduced, old variations are refurbished, popular lines are demolished, while hitherto discredited variations are rehabilitated." The English chessmaster James Mason asserted that the number of possible variations in the first four moves is 318,979,584,000. Tartakower offers a practical suggestion by saying: "Do not overload your memory with a large number of variations, but try rather to *comprehend* the strategy, the basic ideas underlying the various openings." See *Mathematical Calculations in Chess.*

VICTORIAN ERA OF CHESSPLAY

The Victorian era of chessplay was a period of time when a formal style of play was developed. This occured during the days when Queen Victoria ruled England (1837-1901). Chessplay reflected the then prevailing Victorian attitude in social life, which was one of a stilted desire to be always "edifying" and "respectable." Hence, rules of chess etiquette were formulated and strictly observed. Chess openings of master chessplayers were respected highly and attacks on the enemy King or pieces were made in heroic manner. Actual physical occupation of important squares, especially the center squares, was the dominant precept to be observed in gaining strategical advantages. This form of chessplay was in common practice up to the beginning of the World War in 1914. Its effects are still with us today. See *Etiquette, Chess, Modern Chess* and *Ultramodern Chessplay.*

VIDMAR

Dr. Milan Vidmar, an influential Yugoslavian chessmaster, was born in Ljubljana, on June 22, 1885. He learned the principles of chess when he was fifteen years of age. When he was seventeen, he was enrolled as a student in the Polytechnic Institute at Vienna and it was then, while a student, that he began playing in chess tournaments. His first international tournament in

which he participated was that of the German Chess Association at Nuremberg, in 1906, where he won a game against Dr. Tarrasch. In the great tournament at San Sebastian, in 1911, Capablanca won first honors and Vidmar shared second place honors with Rubinstein. By profession, Dr. Vidmar was a manager of an engineering works and Professor of Technical Electrical Science in the University of Ljubljana. After the first world war, he was appointed Rector of the University. Reinfeld states that Dr. Vidmar was a good all-around chessplayer with an even temperament and a genial attitude and that his tournament appearances were always subordinated to his career as a university professor. Dr. Fine observes that Dr. Vidmar "is one of the few chessmasters who has found a successor in his own family, his son Milan, Jr., who is a chessmaster and one of the top ten Yugoslav players."

VIENNA OPENING

1. P-K4   P-K4
2. N-QB3

This opening was originally known as the Queen's Knight Opening. It is also known as the Hamppe Opening, so-named after Herr Hamppe, a Viennese chessmaster who adopted and analyzed it. It was first brought into official tournament play at the Vienna Chess Congress in 1873. Many Vienna chessmasters popularized this as well as other openings with the result that this opening now bears the name of the Austrian city from where many noteworthy chessmasters originated. "These Vienna masters," says Reinfeld and Chernev, "have always been noted for their enormous theoretical knowledge, their analytical capabilities, their drawish inclinations, and their flair for defending difficult positions, no matter how laborious and complex the task may be."

The Vienna opening, according to James Mason, "may be solid or brilliant, a Gambit or not," depending upon how it is continued. Reinfeld believes it to be "theoretically inferior to 2. N-KB3 as it does not attack Black's King Pawn and therefore gives Black time to develop and to try to seize the initiative."

VIOLENT MOVE

A very forceful move that exerts extreme pressure upon the security of the opponent's position or the safety of his men. A violent move requires the immediate attention of the opponent. For example, a check always compels the opponent to focus his attention immediately on how to get his King out of check.

VIRTUES (Inherent in Chessplay)

Virtues in chessplay are the excellences of personal qualities which are sanctioned by the members of the chess fraternity. Good sound moral virtues find their expression in chessplay as well as in every other phase of human activity. Years ago, a Hindu pointed out that the virtues in chess "are as innumerable as the sands of the African Sahara." He pointed out that chess "heals the mind in sickness and exercises it in health. It is rest to the overworked intellect and relaxation to the fatigued body. It lessens the grief of the mourner and heightens the enjoyment of the happy. It teaches the angry man to restrain his passions, the light-

minded to become grave, the cautious to be bold, and the venturesome to be prudent." Experts seem to be agreed that the cardinal virtues inherent in chessplay are unconditional loyalty, cooperation and obedience. No chessman on the chessboard ever rebels, deserts or becomes a traitor. All chessmen are faithful unto death. An enthusiastic Persian once exclaimed that by orderly and correct chessplay, "all the faults which form the ailments of the soul are converted into their corresponding virtues." See *Importance of Chess.*

VISUALIZATION OF CHESSBOARD

Seeing the chessboard. Psychology indicates that it is not the eye but the mind that sees. When a chessboard is actually present before the chessplayer, it is the eye that transmits the position of the board and chessmen to the mind where the player gives meaning to the visual impressions. Hence, the chessboard may be seen as an actual object immediately present or it may be seen as an idea in one's mind without the physical presence of a chessboard. A blindfolded chessplayer develops a keen sense of keeping a picture of a chessboard before his consciousness. See *Mental Chess* and *Blindfold Chess.*

VOTARY, CHESS

A chess votary (plural: votaries) is one whose interest, devotion and enthusiasm are primarily concerned with one or more of the various phases of the game of chess. A chess votary may be a chessplayer, sponsor, organizer, patron, promoter, journalist or an otherwise chess enthusiast.

W

WAITING MOVE

A move which basically has no immediate significance except that of delaying action until the opponent has given an indication of his plan of action. A waiting move threatens nothing and produces no dangerous situation in the immediate position of the chessmen. For an illustration of a waiting move see *Barcza System*.

WAITING-MOVE PROBLEM

A term applied by the English problemist James Rayner to a problem in which White's first move does not produce any apparently important mating function. It is serviceable only because there is no other move available without interfering with the mate already planned for Black's immediate reply.

WEAK MOVE

A move which plays no important function in a player's tactical maneuvers or strategical development. Hence, it is an ineffectual move. In the opening phase of the game, a weak move is generally one which fails to increase the mobility of the player's pieces. It is also a weak move if a piece is moved twice to reach a square which could be reached in one move. The loss of a tempo (see *Tempo*) is considered an ineffectual or weak move. A move which gives or enhances the initiative of the opponent is a weak move.

WEAK POSITION

The position of any piece, especially that of the King, where a player's opponent encounters little, if any, opposition in making menacing contacts. Dr. Euwe explained a weak position as one "which is in a state of balance, that is, one which is threatened as often as it is defended, but to which extra pressure can easily be applied." A positional weakness is a focal point of attack. Znosko-Borovsky counsels: "We must always recognize the weaknesses as well as the strong points in our position; how they are brought about and how they can be reinforced." He further admonishes that "we must strive to the utmost to transform the position, so that its weakness may become its strength." He maintains that "precisely in this consists the real struggle in chess."

WEAK SQUARE

Any significant square which is not adequately protected. Dr. Euwe thinks of a weak square as one which "is threatened as often as it is defended." During the course of a game, a strong square may become weak, and a weak square may become strong depending upon how quickly a weakness is discovered and exploited or reinforced.

WEE WIZARD CHESSPLAYERS

A colloquial expression applied to children who are skillful in the art of chessplay. In 1954, Mrs. Margaret McLeod, Vice-President of the North Vancouver Chess Club, organized a Wee Wizard Chess Club. Its first year membership ranged in age from three to thirteen. These members meet every Friday afternoon in the home of Mrs. McLeod where they are taught the game and are given practical play opportunities. To maintain the interest of the club members, an annual Christmas party and in the summer garden picnic parties are given. Periodic chess matches and tournaments are conducted. Prizes and trophies are awarded to tournament winners. For books written especially for small children interested in chess, see *The Royal Game, Chess for Young People,* by Edith L. Weart; *The First Book of Chess,* by Joseph Leeming; and *John and the Chessmen,* by H. Weissenstein.

WESTERN CHESS ASSOCIATION

A chess organization founded in 1900. It held its first chess tournament at Excelsior, Minnesota, in 1900, at which Louis Uedemann of Chicago and the inventor of the Uedemann code for telegraphing chess moves, won the top honors and was declared the first champion. This Association held an annual tournament every year from 1900 through 1933. Among its champions were Jackson W. Showalter, Edward Lasker, S. D. Factor, Carlos Torre, Samuel Reshevsky and Reuben Fine. In 1934, this Western Chess Association broadened its scope and became the American Chess Federation. Five years later, the American Chess Federation united with the National Chess Federation and formed the present United States Chess Federation.

WESTPHALIA DEFENSE

1. P-Q4	N-KB3
2. P-QB4	P-K3
3. N-KB3	P-Q4
4. N-QB3	QN-Q2
5. B-N5	B-N5
6. PxP	PxP
7. P-K3	P-B4

A defense variation named after the transoceanic steamship "Westphalia" which in 1927, carried to a New York chess tournament a number of European masters who analyzed in detail this style of chessplay. It is essentially a counterattack in which Black plays 5 . . . B-N5 combined with 7 . . . P-B4. According to Réti this is an aggressive procedure which is "more correct than the Cambridge Springs Defense." See *Cambridge Springs Defense.*

WHITE

A term applied to the chessplayer who uses the light colored chessmen. His opponent plays with the darker colored chessmen and is always referred to as Black. Likewise, the light-colored chessmen are always called the white pieces and white Pawns in opposition to the dark-colored chessmen who are referred to as the black pieces and black Pawns. It has been indicated that "White has an advantage in every opening except Colle's." Between players of equal playing strength, White will, on an average, score in about fifty-five per cent of the games played. See "The Relative Strengths of the Openings," by C. H. O'D. Alexander and E. T. O. Slater, in the *British Chess Magazine,* June, 1955. For a practical book on how to play the white pieces, how to develop an aggressive game and winning combinations, see *How to Play the White Pieces,* by Fred Reinfeld.

WHITE, ALAIN C.,

see *Christmas Series*

WHITE BISHOP

The Bishop who moves along the light colored squares. See *Bishop.*

WINAWER COUNTER GAMBIT ACCEPTED

1. P-Q4	P-Q4
2. P-QB4	P-QB3
3. N-QB3	P-K4
4. PxKP	P-Q5

This developmental procedure was popular for a short time after it was introduced into official tournament play by Simon Winawer, in Paris, in 1900. After it was demonstrated that White could obtain an exceptionally strong position, this style of gambit play disappeared from master play. Fletcher states that "nowadays it is used to catch the unwary and is correctly dismissed in textbooks as unsound." See *Gambits Accepted* by L. Elliott Fletcher, page 180. See also *Practical Chess Openings,* by Reuben Fine, page 218.

WINAWER VARIATION

1.	P-K4	P-K3
2.	P-Q4	P-Q4
3.	N-QB3	B-N5
4.	P-K5	P-QB4
5.	P-QR3	BxN ch
6.	PxB	N-K2

A continuation or variation of the French Defense opening which was frequently played by Simon Winawer. World Champion Botvinnik played this opening on several occasions and consequently this developmental procedure was revitalized in current chessplay. For a presentation of this form of play see *Modern Chess Openings,* Ninth Edition, by Walter Korn.

WINDMILL MOVES

see *Seesaw Moves*

WING

The right or left side of the central position of the chessboard. See *King's Side.*

WING GAMBIT

1.	P-K4	P-QB4
2.	P-QN4	

One of the versions of a White gambit reply to the Sicilian opening. Fletcher, who has traced this gambit to an old Italian manuscript, dated 1623, states that "the title Wing Gambit was originally applied to the variation of the King's Bishop's Opening when White played 3. P-QN4, after the usual moves 1. P-K4, P-K4; 2. B-B4, B-B4." See *Gambits Accepted,* by L. Elliott Fletcher, page 133.

WINNING THE EXCHANGE

An expression used when an exchange of chessmen results in material profit or a more advantageous position which is considered of greater worth than the value of the sacrificed chess unit. A player is said to have won the exchange when he can exchange a man of less value for one of higher value, such as, exchanging a Knight for a Rook or Queen. "Winning the exchange" is the opposite of "losing the Exchange." See *Value of Chessmen* and *Losing the Exchange.*

WINNING MATERIAL

The gaining of an opponent's Pawn or piece. This may be accomplished by capturing an opposing unit without losing one's own men; or, by capturing an opposing unit of greater value in exchange of one's own men of lesser value. See *Winning the Exchange.*

WINNING SITUATION

A situation in which a player has superior manpower or a superior position. It is axiomatic that a superior force wins. Likewise, the superior position wins. However, there is an exception; the player with a weaker force may work for a draw, and thereby deprive the player with a winning situation, or a won game, from being victorious. Of course, these generalizations are based on the understanding that everything else is the same for both players.

WOMEN'S CHESS LIFE

Chess life which is concerned with the demonstrative and enthusiastic interest of women in the game of chess. All barriers for women to participate in chess activities have now been completely obliterated. A few of the more noteworthy events indicate the modern trend in "Women's Chess Life." Mr. D. J. Morgan states that "the first chess corner conducted by a woman was that by Miss F. F. Beechey (later Mrs. F. F. Rowland) in the *Matlock Register.* It first appears on December 8th, 1882." In more recent years, women have become very active as chessplayers in important matches and tournaments, in writing chess books and in chess journalism, and in chess organizational activities. In 1954, Mrs. Willa White Owens, the Ohio Women's Chess Champion and Secretary of the Ohio Chess Association, was elected to the post of Vice-President of the United States Chess Federation. This marks the first time in the history of the United States Chess Federation that a woman has been named to this post. As a further mark of recognition of the increasing activity of women in American chess, a feature

column entitled: "Women's Chess Life," devoted to the exploits, plans and activities of women in chess was inaugurated with the February 20, 1955 issue of *Chess Life*—America's Chess Newspaper.

Many chess organizations sponsor tournaments which are restricted to women chessplayers. However, with the 1955 annual United States Chess Federation's Open Tournament, women were given an opportunity to take their first step into officially organized chess competition open to men and women. This gave women an opportunity to try their playing strength against the strongest men or women chessplayers.

WON GAME

According to the Laws of Chess, a game is won by the player whose opponent resigns the game.

The expression of "a won game" is also used at times by a player when he has gained a sizable material advantage or a demonstrable mate. Accordingly, Dr. Emanuel Lasker once said that "the hardest game to win is a won game." Such a won game may be lost 1) by underestimating the opponent's ability to spring a surprise attack; 2) by striving for a brilliant execution while the opponent is accumulating small but decisive advantages; 3) by drifting aimlessly; 4) by faulty execution of a winning attack; or 5) by an oversight or an attack of chess blindness.

WOODPUSHER

A descriptive colloquialism sometimes applied to a novice chessplayer who merely knows the most elementary moves of the chessmen and proceeds to move them or "pushes them" from square to square without rhyme or reason. The term originated in the days when most of the chessmen were usually made of wood and anyone who pushed these wooden chessmen without logical development became known as a "woodpusher." Today, a woodpusher is generally regarded as one who is in the "kindergarten" grade in the school of chessplay. As the woodpusher shifts more and more from mere hand-play to brain-play, he is regarded to be on the road to chess mastery.

WORLD CHAMPION CHESSPLAYERS
The recognized best and most successful chessplayers in the world. In earlier days, there were many well-known chessplayers but no one had the title of World Champion bestowed upon him. In fact, such a supreme honor and title were unknown. Unofficially, Ruy Lopez, Greco, Philidor, Deschapelles, and de La Bourdonnais have been referred to as world champions. In 1843, the famous French player Saint-Amant of Paris, in his capacity as a wine merchant, visited London and played a series of games with Howard Staunton at the St. George's Chess Club. (See *St. Amant.*) A few months later, a return match between these two chess notables was played in Paris. (See *Staunton*) These Anglo-French encounters stimulated Staunton, who was regarded as "the best chessplayer in the world," to issue a challenge to St. Amant *"or any other player in the field"* to play 21 or 41 games. It was not until the Great Exhibition of London, in 1851, that master chessplayers assembled there and participated in this first International Masters' Tournament. Adolf Anderssen from Breslau won the first prize and thus emerged as Europe's Master of Chess.

Wilhelm Steinitz is given credit for having coined the title "World Champion," when on one occasion he is alleged to have said, "Here am I, Wilhelm Steinitz, the youngest child of a poor rabbi; and I am Steinitz, the Chess Champion of the World." Today, arrangements for a candidate to qualify and enter the tournament which will determine the right to challenge the reigning world champion, is within the jurisdiction of the Fédération Internationale des Echecs.

Tartakower in his *Breviary of Chess,* lists the world champions up to 1935. The others have been added in the following table to bring the list up-to-date.

Ruy Lopez	1570-1575
Leonardo	1575-1587
Greco	1622-1634
Philidor	1745-1795
de La Bourdonnais	1834-1840
Staunton	1841-1851
Anderssen	1851-1858
Morphy	1858-1863
Steinitz	1866-1894
Lasker	1894-1921
Capablanca	1921-1927
Alekhine	1927-1935
Euwe	1935-1937
Alekhine	1937-1946
Botvinnik	1948-1957
Smyslov	1957-1958
Botvinnik	1958-

For an account of the first tournament ever held to determine the chess championship of the world, see *World Chessmasters in Battle Royal,* by I. A. Horowitz and Hans Kmoch. See also *Championship Chess,* by Philip W. Sergeant, and *The Official Blue Book and Encyclopedia of Chess,* pp. 275-79.

WORLD CHESS FEDERATION
A title in common usage for the official title of Fédération International des Echecs. See *Fédération Internationale Des Echecs.*

WURZBURGER PROBLEM
A chess problem named in honor of the famous chess composer Otto Wurzburger (born in 1875) who, in 1937, entered this problem in the Third Cheney Miniature Tournament and for which he was awarded the first prize. Kenneth S. Howard, who

was the judge at this tourney, observed that although the mating positions in this problem are not new, nevertheless, he has never seen them presented as chameleon echoes. He considered this a constructive masterpiece. In solving the problem, the Rook and each Bishop in turn can execute the mate in any one of the following procedures.

I. Key: B-KB5   K-B8
   2. B-N4   K-B7
   3. B-Q2   K-N6
   4. B-K1 mate.
        or
   3. .... K-B8
   4. R-KB4 mate.

II. Key: B-KB5   K-B6
    2. K-N1   K-K7
    3. B-QB2   K-B6
    4. B-Q1 mate.
        or
    3. .... K-K8
    4. R-K4 mate.

III. Key: B-KB5 K-K7
     2. K-N2   K-K8
     3. B-Q3   K-Q8
     4. R-R1 mate

IV. Key: B-KB5   K-K8
    2. B-N4   K-B8
    3. B-K3   K-K8
    4. R-R1 mate.

White mates Black in four
moves.
Key: B-KB5

X

x

A chess symbol which indicates a capture. It is used when recording moves in a game of chess, as PxB, meaning that a Pawn captures a Bishop.

XADRES

Portuguese name for chess.

X-RAY ATTACK

An expression used in place of a "skewer attack." Fred Reinfeld and some other chess writers have used this term. See *Skewer.*

Y

YANOFSKY

D. A. Yanofsky, a chessplaying child prodigy, an international chessmaster and champion chessplayer of Canada as well as the British Chess Champion of 1953, was born at Brody in Poland on March 26, 1925. When he was eight months of age, he and his Russian parents came to Canada and settled in Manitoba. He was educated at Manitoba University where, in May, 1944, he was graduated and received the Bachelor of Science degree. Four years later, he became a student-at-law at the Manitoba Law School. After his graduation from this law school, he went in September, 1951, to the University College at Oxford, England, for a postgraduate course in law.

His chess career began at the age of eight when his father taught him the elements of the game. Further chessplaying experience was gained at the Winnipeg Jewish Chess Club. Due to the inspiration and encouragement received from his father and Bernard Freedman, who was a major influence in the Canadian Chess Federation, Yanofsky developed an unquenchable resolve to do all those things in the chess world that were expected of him. In 1937, he won the Manitoba chess championship which he retained and defended so successfully that further local competitive chessplay became nugatory. His chessplaying ability then took on meteoric proportions. He played successfully with the best and most powerful players in North and South America, Europe and Iceland. The biggest moment in Yanofsky's chess career came in 1946, when he defeated Botvinnik in the fifteenth round in an international chess tournament played at Groningen, Netherlands. To enumerate all of Yanofsky's chess opponents would be like a listing of Who's Who in Chess.

Dr. Tartakower wrote that Yanofsky created a sensation in Buenos Aires in 1937 and predicted at that time that Yanofsky's "elegant style will lead him to become a great star in chess." The former world champion, Dr. M. Euwe, stated: "I have no doubt that Abe Yanofsky will one day belong to the strongest of the strong ones, and many of my colleagues share this opinion."

Abe Yanofsky is a chess columnist for *The Free Press* newspaper of Winnipeg, Manitoba. In 1956, he succeeded Daniel A. MacAdam to the editorship of the *Canadian Chess Chat* — the official organ of the Chess Federation of Canada. For an interesting account of Yanofsky's chess career and some of the games he played with chess notables, see his book entitled: *Chess The Hard Way!*

YATES

Frederick Dewhurst Yates, six times Chess Champion of Great Britain, was born at Birstall, Yorkshire, England, on January 16, 1884. By training he was an accountant but in 1909, he went to London and entered the field of journalism for a few years. After World War I, he became a professional chessplayer.

He learned chess from his cousin. While at school, he played the game with his schoolmaster and a strong Yorkshire chessplayer named Illingworth, who introduced Yates to the chessplayers at the County Arcade Cafe in Leeds. In time, he became a first class chessplayer, entered several tournaments and eventually won the title of Champion Chessplayer of Yorkshire. After being admitted to the British championship class, he actively encountered many of the great masters. He played with Alekhine, from whom he won two games and drew four. He also won four games from Réti; three from Bogoljubow and three from Tartakower.

In his early chess career, Yates was noted for his brilliancy as a chessplayer. Later in life, he was noted particularly for his good judgment in developing sound positional procedures and for having developed an excellent technique in the end-game. He demonstrated his skillfulness in several Anglo-American cable matches as well as in simultaneous chessplay. His literary contributions to the game of chess demonstrated his ability as a splendid chess analyst. He wrote a book entitled *Modern Master Play*, and two analytical books of games: *Capablanca v. Alekhine,* and *Alekhine v. Bogoljubow.* He died in Bloomsbury on November 9, 1932.

Frank J. Marshall paid him the following compliment: "Yates always appeared to me as one who seemed to look upon life as a great mystery. He played fine, deep combinative chess, always striving for the beautiful." His biographer, W. Winters, stated: "Above all else he (Yates) hated to be in the limelight and no doubt suffered in his chess career through his reluctance to push himself forward."

YOUNG

Franklin Knowles Young, originator

of the "Synthetic Method of Chessplay" and chess writer, was born in 1857. He was an active member of the Boston Chess Club and had chess game encounters with such famous masters as Steinitz, Zukertort and others. He published: *The Minor Tactics of Chess,* 1894; *The Major Tactics of Chess,* 1898; *The Grand Tactics of Chess,* 1896; *Chess Strategetics,* 1900; *Chess Generalship — Grand Reconaissance,* 1910; *Chess Generalship—Grand Manoevers,* 1913; *and Field Book of Chess Generalship—Grand Operations,* 1923.

His writings were designed to present a complete system of chessplay. It was based on the theory that "scientific chessplay is the replica of scientific warfare, and that the processes of Grand Strategy, High Tactics and Greater Logistics, as established by the Great Captains, by the movements of their armies on the surface of the Earth, are identical with the processes established by the Great Chess Masters, by the movements of their Pieces on the surface of the Chessboard."

Young developed an elaborate terminology which was interspersed with such characteristic expressions as: "the left and right oblique." The following statement is a further illustration of his style of writing: "A Grand Strategic Front is formed by the extension of salient two points along the diagonal upon which the minor strategic front already is established. It may properly be aligned and reinforced by the minor crochet, the major crochet, the crochet aligned, or supplemented by the formations, echelons, enceinte and en potence." In the July, 1955 issue of *Chess Review,* it is stated that "at best, . . . the Young system requires a professional course in military science —to prepare to learn chess."

YUGOSLAV VARIATION

1. P-Q4   N-KB3
2. P-QB4   P-KN3

3. P-KN3   B-N2
4. B-N2   0-0
5. N-QB3   P-Q3
6. N-B3   P-B4

A so-called variation or continuation of the King's Indian Defense which has been popularized by Yugoslavian chessplayers. Larry Evans, the United States Chess Champion 1951-53, considers this variation "sound, safe and reliable." It is his opinion that this variation "offers Black promising chances and thus far White has not demonstrated any method for preventing him from obtaining strict equality or better." See *King's Indian Defense.*

Z

ZNOSKO-BOROVSKY

Eugene Alexandrovitch Znosko-Borovsky, a respected chessmaster, teacher and writer, was born in St. Petersburg on August 16, 1884. He was educated at the Lyceum of Emperor Alexander I, and served in the Russo-Japanese War and World War I.

He began his acquaintance with the game of chess when he was a schoolboy and soon became a prize winning chessplayer in local and regional tournaments in Russia. He sprang into fame in August, 1906, when he participated in the International Masters' Tournament which was sponsored by the German Chess Association at Nuremberg and was attended by such powerful masters as Dr. Tarrasch, Dr. Vidmar, Frank Marshall, Karl Schlechter and Tchigorin. In 1911, he won the St. Petersburg city championship and in 1913, he defeated Capablanca in a series of two games. During the Russian Revolution in 1918, Znosko-Borovsky went to Turkey and in 1920, he emigrated to France. Here he contributed to French and Russian papers writing about literature, drama and the game of chess. He was considered an authority on the Russian theatre. In his earlier years, he had written several plays which were produced in Russian theaters. He continued his chess interest in official chess tournaments in which he was very successful, especially those at Broadstairs, England, in 1922, and in Edinburgh in 1926. He won the Paris championship in 1931 and won the first prize in the Rumanian national championship in 1935. He was also considered an excellent simultaneous chessplayer.

His contributions to chess literature, apart from many articles in magazines all over the world, consisted of such books as, *How to Play Chess; How Not to Play Chess; How to Play Chess Openings; How to Play Chess Endings; The Middle Game; The Art of Chess Combinations;* and *Traps on The Chessboard.* Znosko-Borovsky died on December 31, 1954.

Shortly after his death, it was stated in the *Chess Review* magazine that "Znosko's prolific publications helped start the trend to education of the chess masses." His friend, Philip W. Sergeant, observed that "as a lecturer he (Znosko-Borovsky) has the gift of interesting and holding his audiences, and in consequence he has always been a success in this role. In the teaching of chess he may claim to have no superior." In the *British Chess Magazine* it is stated that "his great lucidity

as lecturer and writer had made him one of the greatest teachers the game has known."

ZONAL TOURNAMENTS
Tournaments conducted under the auspices of the Fédération Internationale des Echecs once in every four years. They are preliminary qualifying tournaments to find the strongest chessplayer in each organized chess zone. Winners are eligible to participate in the interzonal tournaments held the following year. See *Fédération Internationale des Echecs.*

ZUGSWANG
A German word meaning: a compulsion to move, or making a move under duress. Dr. Tarrasch and Znosko-Borovsky defined it as "a disagreeable obligation to move." In chess, a player has the right and obligation to move whether he likes it or finds it most irksome. Accordingly, Fred Reinfeld explains that the underlying idea of Zugswang is the making of a forced move which "is supposed to be an asset and a blessing," but actually, it "becomes a liability and a curse." For a brief statement of Zugswang and twelve illustrations, see *1001 Brilliant Chess Sacrifices and Combinations,* by Fred Reinfeld, Chapter 18, entitled, "Zugswang."

ZUKERTORT
Dr. Johannes Hermann Zukertort, a highly respected chessmaster, was born in the little town of Lublin in Russian Poland in 1842. He was graduated from the University of Breslau's School of Medicine. He was also a noted musician, a linguist, a foreign correspondent and a military officer.

He learned to play chess at the age of nineteen and developed into one of the strongest chessplayers in Germany. He defeated Anderssen in a set of two match games, and in 1871, he went to London where he challenged the great Steinitz. Chess now became his dominant interest in life. He was not only an excellent chessplayer but was also a forthright chess journalist and a fearless controversialist. In 1879, with the aid of Leopold Hoffer, he founded in London a chess magazine in which he carried on a series of bitter controversial articles with the great Steinitz. Dr. Zukertort had several successful chessplaying encounters with Steinitz. In 1883, Zukertort won the first prize over Steinitz. Again, in 1885, Zukertort defeated Steinitz in a series of games played at the Manhattan Chess Club in New York City; the result of which was 4 to 1 in favor of Zukertort. After experiencing years of poverty, Dr. Zukertort died in London, on June 20, 1888. Although Steinitz and Zukertort were critical of each other, nevertheless, Steinitz did recognize Zukertort as an excellent chess-player and as having produced "one of the most brilliant games on record!"

ZUKERTORT OPENING
1. N-KB3

This is an irregular opening. It is called the Zukertort opening because the great chessmaster whose name it bears, made frequent use of it. Mr. du Mont says that this opening "was popular for many years but it nearly always led to some form of the Queen Pawn opening or the Queen's Gambit."

ZWISCHENZUG

A German word which found its way into chess literature. It means an "in-between move" or an intermediary move. The term is applied to a move which places a chess unit in a position where it will interrupt a line of attack, or block the opponent's scope of controlling a large area of the chessboard, or serve as a stumbling block which will weaken a strong combination on the part of the opponent.